WORLD ECONOMIC OUTLOOK

and

INTERNATIONAL CAPITAL MARKETS

Interim Assessment

December 1998

**A Survey by the Staff of the
International Monetary Fund**

INTERNATIONAL MONETARY FUND
Washington, DC

World economic outlook (International Monetary Fund)
  World economic outlook: a survey by the staff of the International
Monetary Fund.—1980– —Washington, D.C.: The Fund, 1980–

  v.; 28 cm.—(1981–84: Occasional paper/International Monetary Fund
ISSN 0251-6365)
  Annual.
  Has occasional updates, 1984–
  ISSN 0258-7440 = World economic and financial surveys
  ISSN 0256-6877 = World economic outlook (Washington)
  1. Economic history—1971– —Periodicals. I. International
Monetary Fund. II. Series: Occasional paper (International Monetary
Fund)

  HC10.W7979   84-640155
                                      338.5'443'09048—dc19
                                             AACR 2 MARC-S

Library of Congress   8507

  Published biannually.
ISBN 1-55775-793-3

*The cover, charts, and interior of this publication
were designed and produced by the IMF Graphics Section*

Price: US$36.00
(US$25.00 to full-time faculty members and
students at universities and colleges)

Please send orders to:
International Monetary Fund, Publication Services
700 19th Street, N.W., Washington, D.C. 20431, U.S.A.
Tel.: (202) 623-7430   Telefax: (202) 623-7201
E-mail: publications@imf.org
Internet: http://www.imf.org

Contents

	Page

Assumptions and Conventions

A number of assumptions have been adopted for the projections presented in the *World Economic Outlook*. It has been assumed that real effective exchange rates will remain constant at their average levels during October 19–November 4, 1998 except for the bilateral rates among the European exchange rate mechanism (ERM) currencies, which are assumed to remain constant in nominal terms; that established policies of national authorities will be maintained; that the average price of oil will be $13.39 a barrel in 1998 and $14.51 a barrel in 1999, and remain unchanged in real terms over the medium term; and that the six-month London interbank offered rate (LIBOR) on U.S. dollar deposits will average 5.5 percent in 1998 and 5 percent in 1999. These are, of course, working hypotheses rather than forecasts, and the uncertainties surrounding them add to the margin of error that would in any event be involved in the projections. The estimates and projections are based on statistical information available in mid-December 1998.

The following conventions have been used throughout the *World Economic Outlook*:

. . .   to indicate that data are not available or not applicable;

—   to indicate that the figure is zero or negligible;

–   between years or months (for example, 1997–98 or January–June) to indicate the years or months covered, including the beginning and ending years or months;

/   between years or months (for example, 1997/98) to indicate a fiscal or financial year.

"Billion" means a thousand million; "trillion" means a thousand billion.

"Basis points" refer to hundredths of 1 percentage point (for example, 25 basis points are equivalent to ¼ of 1 percentage point).

In figures and tables, shaded areas indicate IMF staff projections.

Minor discrepancies between sums of constituent figures and totals shown are due to rounding.

As used in this report, the term "country" does not in all cases refer to a territorial entity that is a state as understood by international law and practice. As used here, the term also covers some territorial entities that are not states but for which statistical data are maintained on a separate and independent basis.

* * *

Inquiries about the content of the *World Economic Outlook*, including questions relating to the World Economic Outlook database and requests for additional data, should be sent by mail, electronic mail, or telefax (telephone inquiries cannot be accepted) to:

World Economic Studies Division
Research Department
International Monetary Fund
700 19th Street, N.W., Washington, D.C. 20431, U.S.A.
E-mail: weo@imf.org   Telefax: (202) 623-6343

Preface

This interim update of the IMF's latest regular reports on the *World Economic Outlook* (published in October 1998) and *International Capital Markets* (September 1998) provides a preliminary assessment of the unusual turbulence in international financial markets during much of the period August–November 1998, and its implications for the global economic outlook and for policy.

The analysis and projections contained in this report are integral elements of the IMF's surveillance of economic developments and policies in its member countries, developments in international financial markets, and the global economic system. The survey of prospects and policies is the product of a comprehensive interdepartmental review of world economic developments, which draws primarily on information the IMF staff gathers through its consultations with member countries. These consultations are carried out in particular by the IMF's area departments together with the Policy Development and Review Department and the Fiscal Affairs Department. For its evaluation of developments in financial markets, the report also draws, in part, on informal discussions with commercial and investment banks, securities firms, stock and futures exchanges, and regulatory and monetary authorities.

The analysis in this report has been coordinated in the Research Department under the general direction of Michael Mussa, Economic Counsellor and Director of Research. The project has been directed by Flemming Larsen, Deputy Director of the Research Department, together with Charles Adams, Assistant Director for Capital Market Studies, Graham Hacche, Assistant Director for the World Economic Studies Division, Donald J. Mathieson, Chief of the Emerging Market Studies Division, and Garry J. Schinasi, Chief of the Capital Markets and Financial Studies Division.

Primary contributors to this report also include John H. Green, Andrew Tweedie, Mark De Broeck, Charles Kramer, Jorge Roldos, Ranil Salgado, and Harm Zebregs. Other contributors include Peter Breuer, Burkhard Drees, Subir Lall, Douglas Laxton, Joaquim Levy, Sandy MacKenzie, Alessandro Prati, Anthony Richards, and Cathy Wright. The Fiscal Analysis Division of the Fiscal Affairs Department computed the structural budget and fiscal impulse measures. Gretchen Gallik, Mandy Hemmati, Yutong Li, Advin Pagtakhan, Subramanian Sriram, Peter Tran, and Kenneth Wood provided research assistance. Allen Cobler, Nicholas Dopuch, Isabella Dymarskaia, Yasoma Liyanarachchi, Olga Plagie, and Irim Siddiqui processed the data and managed the computer systems. Susan Duff, Caroline Bagworth, Sheila Kinsella, Rosalind Oliver, Lisa Marie Scott-Hill, Ramanjeet Singh, and Adriana Vohden were responsible for word processing. James McEuen of the External Relations Department edited the manuscript and coordinated production of the publication.

The analysis has benefited from comments and suggestions by staff from other IMF departments, as well as by Executive Directors following their discussion of the report on December 16, 1998. However, both projections and policy considerations are those of the IMF staff and should not be attributed to Executive Directors or to their national authorities.

I

Containing the Risks to the World Economy

Turbulence in world financial markets in recent months has raised questions about certain features of financial systems in the mature economies and has heightened uncertainty about global economic prospects. The crisis in Russia in mid-August, coming in the wake of the Asian crisis, led to a drying up of private financial flows to emerging markets, a broader increase in risk aversion among financial investors, and concerns about a global credit crunch. As a result, through early October fears escalated that the current economic slowdown might continue to widen and deepen in 1999. Partly in response, monetary policies have been eased throughout the industrial countries and in some emerging market economies. Together with several other positive developments, the easing of monetary conditions has helped to restore calm in financial markets. But while the danger of a global recession does seem to have diminished, the supply of funds to most emerging market economies is still sharply reduced, and conditions in financial markets remain fragile in several respects. It would therefore be premature to consider the difficulties to be over. The IMF staff's projections for world growth in 1999 have been revised further downward—but not substantially, and by much less than in the two preceding issues of the *World Economic Outlook*. The risks appear to remain predominantly on the downside, however.

* * *

The purpose of this Interim Assessment is threefold. First, given recent concerns about the risks to the global economy, the report reassesses world economic prospects and the policies needed to contain the global financial crisis and to foster recovery, taking into account new information available since the October 1998 *World Economic Outlook* was finalized. Second, the report attempts to shed light on the apparent disproportionality between the extraordinarily high degree of turbulence seen recently in both emerging and mature financial markets and the seemingly more limited scale of the "triggering events," the most important of which were probably the Russian crisis and, subsequently, the near collapse of a highly leveraged hedge fund, Long-Term Capital Management (LTCM). Third, the report seeks to identify some of the most critical shortcomings in private and public risk management systems that need to be addressed to

strengthen the resilience of capital markets in the face of future shocks.

The Crisis Intensifies up to Early October and Then Eases

Through the late spring and summer of 1998, developments indicated a further deepening and broadening of the global economic slowdown that was in train following the financial crisis that had erupted in southeast and east Asia in the second half of 1997. Among the countries at the center of the Asian crisis, the contractions in demand and output proved much more severe than generally expected in the early stages of the crisis. In Japan, a key export market for Asian crisis countries, recession deepened considerably, adding to concerns about the health of its banking system. During this period, pressures mounted on the Chinese renminbi and the Hong Kong dollar. Russia's and Ukraine's continued failures to tackle budgetary imbalances were other factors unsettling financial markets, and a number of emerging market countries in other regions experienced recurrent exchange market pressures amid concerns about the sustainability of fiscal or external imbalances. In North America and western Europe, growth appeared to be generally well sustained, indeed to be strengthening in some cases, but the impact of the Asian crisis was beginning to be felt, particularly in the industrial sector (Figure 1.1), and there were concerns that buoyant stock markets might undergo sharp corrections if the growth of activity and corporate profits began to slow. These problems and risks were highlighted in a draft of the October 1998 *World Economic Outlook,* prepared in early August 1998. That document revised down sharply projected world growth in 1998 from 3 to 2½ percent, and in 1999 from 3¾ to 3¼ percent, and cautioned that a significantly worse outcome was clearly possible. The potential for a broader and deeper economic downturn stemmed from a multitude of interrelated risks that made the economic situation unusually fragile. Viewed in isolation, any one of the risks, though serious, might not be sufficient to raise concerns about a sharper global slowdown. But the interrelated nature of these risks, with the scope for contagion and chain reactions this implied, warranted the attention of policymakers around the world.

Figure 1.1. World Industrial Production[1]
(Percent change from a year earlier; three-month centered moving average; manufacturing)

The slowdown in world industrial activity since mid-1997 has been most pronounced in Asia but has also been apparent in North America and Europe. There have been signs of recovery in some Asian countries in recent months.

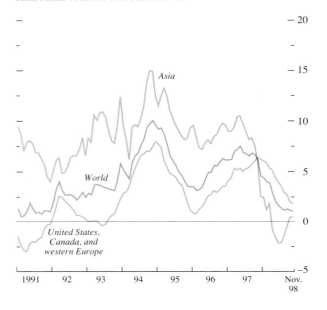

Sources: WEFA, Inc.; OECD; and IMF, *International Financial Statistics.*

[1]Based on data for 32 advanced and emerging market economies representing about 75 percent of world output. The world total includes five emerging market countries (Argentina, Brazil, Chile, Hungary, and Mexico) that are not included in either of the two subtotals. Data through 1994 exclude Indonesia.

In the event, the effective devaluation and unilateral debt restructuring announced by Russia in mid-August triggered a series of sharp market corrections indicating a generalized increase in perceived risk or risk aversion. Yield premia for emerging market bonds rose sharply, almost across the board, to an average of 1,700 basis points in early September from below 600 basis points in most of 1997 and early 1998; equity prices fell sharply in both emerging and mature markets; and exchange market pressures intensified in many emerging market countries. As a by-product of these developments, many international investors and banks suffered substantial losses, especially on highly leveraged investment positions, which in turn gave rise to margin calls and a rush to raise liquidity that exacerbated the decline in the prices of many financial assets. The widespread flight to quality and liquidity gave rise to a severe tightening of credit conditions, not only for emerging market borrowers but also for non-prime corporate borrowers in some mature markets, especially the United States. These developments led the staff to revise down further their projections for world growth in 1998 and 1999 to 2 percent and 2½ percent, respectively, in the *World Economic Outlook* published in October 1998, in which staff warned (page 1) that:

> Chances of any significant improvement [in world growth] in 1999 have also diminished, and the risks of a deeper, wider, and more prolonged downturn have escalated.

Developments since early October have been more reassuring, helping to restore a measure of calm to financial markets. This can be attributed in large part to a number of policy actions, including:

- Easing of interest rates by central banks in most industrial countries, including the United States, Canada, the United Kingdom, and the member countries of the prospective euro area.
- In Japan, new policy measures to address banking sector problems and announcements of further fiscal actions to stimulate demand. A significant strengthening of the yen, especially vis-à-vis the dollar—attributable partly to these policy actions by Japan, but also to the easing of interest rates in the United States and, perhaps most important, to technical factors related to the unwinding of short yen positions (as discussed in Chapter III)—has helped to improve financial market confidence in the rest of Asia, although it is likely to have a negative short-term impact on Japan's own economy.
- Commitments and actions by Brazil to address its chronic fiscal imbalances, and the large-scale support of the international community, agreed in mid-November, for a strong program to forestall a financial crisis that would potentially have severe contagion effects on other emerging market countries.

• Continued progress with stabilization and reform in the Asian crisis countries implementing policy programs supported by the IMF. With current account balances having moved into surplus and financial market confidence having begun to recover, the strengthening of exchange rates has allowed monetary policy to be eased, which in turn has helped to boost equity markets. With fiscal policies also having become expansionary, the easing of macroeconomic policies has significantly improved the prospects for recovery to begin in the course of 1999. This is not to deny that slow progress with reform in some areas—such as corporate debt workouts—threatens to retard growth in east Asia for some time.

• Progress toward implementation of the IMF quota increase and the New Arrangements to Borrow (NAB), which have improved the international community's ability to assist countries in the resolution of financial crises;[1] the Miyazawa initiative to provide assistance to the Asian crisis countries; and the proposal by Group of Seven (G-7) Finance Ministers and Central Bank Governors, in their end-October statement, to enhance financing facilities in the IMF and World Bank to help ward off destabilizing financial market contagion, along with their reaffirmed commitment to move forward with the agenda to strengthen the architecture of the international financial system.[2]

Also helpful has been the avoidance of protectionist and other market-closing measures in the large majority of countries, including those that have suffered competitiveness pressures and financial strains.

The positive impact of these policy actions on financial markets is particularly evident in the strong rebounds in global equity prices. With respect to emerging market countries, secondary market bond yield spreads have declined significantly, although they generally remain well above levels observed prior to the Russian crisis in August (Figure 1.2). Access for emerging market countries to external borrowing has also begun to ease, and there have been a number of new debt issues. There have as well been signs of greater

Figure 1.2. Financing Conditions for Emerging Markets

Bond yield spreads for emerging market countries have declined since mid-September, but gross capital flows have remained depressed.

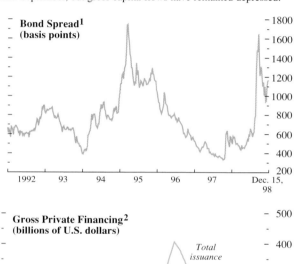

Source: Bloomberg Financial Markets, LP.
[1]J.P. Morgan Emerging Market Bond Index (EMBI, Brady narrow) sovereign spread over the theoretical U.S. zero-coupon curve.
[2]Three-month moving averages; annualized.

---

[1]The increase in IMF quotas of 45 percent, from SDR 146 billion (about $206 billion) to SDR 212 billion (about $300 billion), will take effect when member countries having not less than 85 percent of the total of present quotas have consented to their quota increases. The timing of ratification is still difficult to predict because parliamentary approval is needed in many countries. The New Arrangements to Borrow (NAB), which took effect on November 17, 1998, doubles the amount previously available under the General Arrangements to Borrow to up to SDR 34 billion (about $48 billion). The NAB is a set of credit arrangements between the IMF and 25 members and institutions to provide supplementary resources to the IMF to forestall or cope with an impairment of the international monetary system or to deal with an exceptional situation that poses a threat to the stability of that system.
[2]See the October 1998 *World Economic Outlook*, Box 1.2.

differentiation in favor of countries with strong funda-mentals and credible reform strategies. Nevertheless, gross new private financing flows have only recovered slightly so far, and considerable uncertainty persists about the willingness of international banks to maintain or extend credit lines to emerging markets. In mature markets, reduced supply of credit has been felt mainly by lower-rated borrowers in the United States, but the decline in new debt issues has been alleviated by the ability of such borrowers to draw on bank credit lines.

Overall, therefore, there is some evidence that con-ditions in capital markets have eased since early October. But there are still signs that perceived risks, or risk aversion, are considerably greater not only than during those periods of 1996–97 when spreads de-clined to unusually low levels, but also than has been normal in recent years.

Implications for the World Economic Outlook and Remaining Risks

The latest revisions to the staff's projections, incor-porating information through November 1998, reflect the restoration of relative calm in international capital markets. In particular, the global growth projection for 1999 has been lowered only slightly further—to 2¼ percent—a much smaller revision than those seen in the last two issues of the *World Economic Outlook* (Table 1.1). For some countries, including Japan, Brazil, and Russia, the outlook has deteriorated more significantly. The growth projections for some of the Asian emerging market economies in crisis have also been lowered somewhat further, reflecting the judgment that the im-proved prospects for recovery may not materialize until well into 1999. An exception is Thailand, where GDP is now projected to rise steadily, though slowly, through-out 1999. Among the most encouraging aspects of the baseline scenario are the continued solid growth perfor-mance, despite modest downward revisions, of the United States and the future euro area, although, as noted below, there are downside risks in both cases. In addition, projected growth in China has been revised up, reflecting stronger-than-expected performance in the second half of 1998, partly in response to policy stimulus. Australia's economic performance has also exceeded expectations, notwithstanding its close trade ties with the crisis-afflicted countries.

The modest scale of the further downward revision to the world growth projections for 1999 may reason-ably be viewed as indicating that the global economic situation and near-term prospects have begun to stabi-lize. At the same time, however, the balance of risks remains on the downside. Five such risks are of par-ticular concern.

- Some emerging market countries will have diffi-culties remaining current on their external obliga-

Table 1.1. Revisions to World Growth Projections
(Percent change in world real GDP)

World Economic Outlook Issued	1997	1998	1999	2000
October 1997	4.2	4.3	4.4	4.6
December 1997	4.1	3.5	4.1	4.4
May 1998	4.1	3.1	3.7	3.8
October 1998	4.1	2.0	2.5	3.7
December 1998	4.2	2.2	2.2	3.5

tions if private financing does not recover from the very low levels of capital inflows observed since August. Indeed, private financial flows to emerging market countries in all regions may well fall short of the levels assumed in the projections. This would necessitate greater trade adjustments by emerging market countries through weaker do-mestic demand growth, currency depreciations, or both.

- Japan's economic outlook remains particularly un-certain, and questions remain about the adequacy and implementation of recent initiatives to turn the economy around. The Bank of Japan has stepped up efforts to boost credit and liquidity, and further expansionary tax measures are being considered. A clear risk is that confidence and demand would remain depressed if the restructuring and recapi-talization of Japan's banking sector were either de-layed or pushed through without the fundamental changes needed to convince markets that banking weakness was finally being dealt with.

- The uneven pattern of trade adjustments among the industrial countries could lead to destabilizing movements in exchange rates among the major currencies. While some further appreciation of the yen and the euro against the U.S. dollar seems necessary over the medium term to restore a more sustainable pattern of current account balances, rapid and large realignments could be problem-atic. Further appreciation of the yen in the short term would be particularly unhelpful from the viewpoint of relative cyclical conditions.

- The large trade adjustments resulting from the Asian crisis could also lead to a resurgence of pro-tectionist pressures, with negative repercussions for world growth.

- The strong recovery of stock markets in some countries, especially the United States, following the recent period of market turmoil has again brought equity prices into a range that may not be sustainable, especially if future corporate earnings were to disappoint financial investors or if infla-tion and interest rates were to turn upward. The sharp deterioration in the private sector's saving-investment balance in the United States in recent years, and its current, unusually large, deficit position, may be attributed in part to positive wealth effects on consumer spending from the stock market boom. It underscores the potential for a stock market correction to lead to a rise in saving that, although desirable and necessary from a medium-term perspective, could in the short term markedly weaken demand, activity, and confidence.

In addition, the baseline scenario does not incorporate the further decline of oil prices in recent weeks. If the continued weakness of oil and other commodity prices is sustained, financing constraints for many emerging market countries will tighten further.

As discussed in Chapter IV, the materialization of the above risks, even on a relatively moderate scale, could easily cut world growth by a further percentage point in 1999—and extend what would then effectively become a global recession at least into 2000. The outcome will depend crucially on policies.

Policy Requirements

Recent developments have raised a number of questions about policies relating to the prudential regulation and supervision of financial systems, and these are considered in the next section. This section focuses on policies in the macroeconomic and other structural areas.[3]

Although macroeconomic policy requirements vary among countries, depending on priorities and economic circumstances, there has appropriately been a widespread easing of monetary policies in recent months. In the Asian emerging market economies in crisis, this has been allowed by a strengthening of exchange rates in a context of severe economic weakness. In Japan, interest rates had already been lowered close to zero, but the yen's recent appreciation has provided room for more aggressive injections of liquidity. In North America and western Europe, monetary easing has been a response to the weakening of growth prospects, continuing subdued inflation, and concerns in the United States about strains in credit markets, as well as the need for convergence of short-term interest rates in the prospective euro area, which is now almost completed following the concerted reductions in early December. Discretionary fiscal easing also is appropriately being used in the Asian crisis economies and Japan to support demand. In the case of Japan, the

---

[3]Reflecting the concerns motivating this report and its interim nature, the policy challenges facing the emerging market countries most affected by international financial market developments, and the major industrial countries, are given most emphasis. In contrast, policy issues facing the smaller industrial countries and the developing and transition countries less closely connected to global financial markets are generally not revisited on this occasion. They will be considered in the next *World Economic Outlook,* which will appear in May 1999.

need for medium-term fiscal consolidation, although an important concern, is outweighed by the need to counter the economy's extreme cyclical weakness. Thus, in a large part of the world economy, macroeconomic policies, or at least monetary policy, are usefully helping to support or stimulate aggregate demand and activity. There are two main exceptions to the scope for expansionary policies. First, in North America and western Europe, the need for medium-term budgetary consolidation—to reduce debt burdens and to allow for future demographic pressures—continues in most cases to make discretionary fiscal expansion inadvisable, as opposed to letting the automatic stabilizers operate. Second, some emerging market economies need relatively tight macroeconomic policies to address unsustainable fiscal or external imbalances, to adjust to adverse developments in financial and commodity markets, and to regain investors' confidence.

In the *Asian crisis countries,* following the large contractions of output in 1998, the main priorities are to end the decline of economic activity, limit the impact of the crisis on the welfare of the most vulnerable, and promote the resumption of sustainable growth, including by accelerating the restructuring of financial and corporate sectors—a key element of IMF-supported programs. In Korea, Thailand, and more recently Indonesia, the tightening of monetary policies that occurred in the wake of the crises has achieved considerable success in reestablishing financial stability, and the strengthening of exchange rates has allowed interest rates to be lowered significantly. In both Korea and Thailand, short-term market rates have fallen below precrisis levels of 5–8 percent, and although lending rates have been slower to decline owing to the burden of problem loans in the financial system, monetary conditions are now more supportive of recovery. In Indonesia, also, interest rates have begun to be lowered following the strengthening of the rupiah and the improvement of inflation prospects; assuming that program implementation remains on track, further gradual easing should be possible without undermining confidence. In each of these countries, the primary focus of monetary policy will need to continue to be the assurance of financial and exchange rate stability, with the authorities having to be prepared to resist significant downward currency pressure.

Fiscal policy, however, is available in each case to support domestic demand and promote recovery. In fact, in all three countries there is scope for fiscal policy to provide continuing support for activity, and this should help to secure a turnaround of activity in the course of 1999. The public finances in all three countries are sufficiently healthy to make significant fiscal stimulus feasible without adverse financial market repercussions, but medium-term sustainability must be safeguarded—for example, by concentrating on nonrecurrent spending, including infrastructure investment.

Macroeconomic policy requirements in Malaysia are similar to those in the three crisis countries worst hit. A stimulative budget was introduced in October, and there have been a number of efforts to promote private sector credit growth. Interest rates have fallen to levels similar to those in Korea and Thailand, but in the context of exchange and capital controls, introduced in September, that have damaged investor confidence. The Malaysian authorities have recently put together a more comprehensive strategy to restructure the banking sector, but the credibility of the reform efforts has been undermined by the weakening of loan classification and provisioning guidelines and by the imposition of minimum lending targets (see Annex). The Philippines is more constrained in its fiscal policy than the other four crisis countries, owing to its larger public debt, and the authorities in any event do not have to deal with such a large output decline as in the other four cases; but there too the government is contemplating a cautious easing of fiscal policy to support recovery. Market interest rates in the Philippines have come down substantially from their peaks of late 1997.

In China and Hong Kong SAR, the successful maintenance of the exchange rate regimes has helped to restore stability in Asian financial markets. In fact, currency pressures have eased considerably in recent months in both cases, partly owing to the weakening of the U.S. dollar relative to other major currencies. This has facilitated a lowering of interest rates in both economies. Fiscal policy is also providing helpful support to demand in both cases. In China, increased public investment has provided substantial support for activity in 1998, but nonstate investment and exports remain weak. It is unclear how slow or negative growth in other indicators of activity, such as electricity production and freight traffic, relate to the more buoyant data for GDP, especially given the limited information on the components of aggregate expenditure, including the absence of information on inventory accumulation. In fact, some observers consider that GDP growth in China has been overestimated by 1–2 percentage points a year for several years, and that the discrepancy may have increased somewhat in 1998 (see Chapter IV, Box 4.1). While fiscal stimulus is appropriate, its composition should be carefully tailored to ensure that unproductive spending is minimized and the quality of growth is not compromised. Interest rate policy will need to remain cautious in light of continuing outflows on the capital account of the balance of payments. In this context, it will be important for the recent intensification of capital controls to be implemented without adversely affecting legitimate trade and investment activities. The recent problems in the trust and investment corporations underscore the need for continued financial sector reform.

In Hong Kong SAR, the fiscal position has deteriorated significantly owing to the weakening of economic activity, with a deficit of about 3 percent of GDP projected for the current fiscal year. Although the flexibility of prices and wages is promoting rapid adjustment, the short-term prospect is one of continued economic weakness. It would therefore not be desirable to tighten fiscal policy in 1999, but it will be important to set the current and prospective fiscal shortfalls in the context of a medium-term framework to restore budget balance. The authorities' announced expansion of retraining and job placement schemes, and acceleration of labor-intensive projects, will help to contain the rise in unemployment, which has risen above 5 percent to its highest level in more than 17 years and seems likely to rise further until recovery is under way.

In *other emerging market countries,* the main priorities are orderly adjustment to adverse external developments, including weaker exports to Asia and lower commodity prices, as well as reduced capital flows; the reestablishment of investor confidence and, in several cases, financial stability; and the reduction of vulnerability to adverse shifts in investor confidence. In most cases, financial imbalances and external financing constraints require tight macroeconomic policies. Although these may increase the likelihood that activity will weaken in the short run, forceful measures to reduce financial imbalances are needed to reduce the risk of contagion, alleviate the need for monetary policy to defend exchange rates, and strengthen medium-term growth prospects.

In recent months, the main focus has been on Brazil, whose currency came under sustained pressure between July and October because of concerns about the fiscal situation and external competitiveness. Sharply higher domestic interest rates slowed the pace of capital outflows from mid-September, but a sustainable resolution of the difficulties, given the government's debt-service obligations, required action to reduce the fiscal deficit. Anticipation of such action, the implementation of some early measures, and expectations of large-scale financial support by the IMF and other multilateral and bilateral creditors led to a further easing of pressures in October and early November. Agreement on the policy program and financing package was announced on November 13 (Box 1.1). The determined and sustained implementation by Brazil, at all levels of government, of this front-loaded fiscal adjustment effort (including passage of measures recently delayed in Congress), accompanied by appropriately tight monetary policies and wide-ranging structural reforms, will make an essential contribution to sustaining the improvement in global financial market sentiment that has occurred over the past two months.

Many other countries in Latin America have appropriately adjusted macroeconomic policies to promote adjustment to adverse external developments and to strengthen the confidence of investors. In Argentina, domestic demand growth has slowed considerably. Fiscal policy has been tightened significantly in the past year, but even though the fiscal deficit is now quite small, continued consolidation may be needed, especially given the widening of the external current account deficit over the past two years. There is also scope for accelerating structural reforms that would strengthen external competitiveness by improving productivity and reduce unemployment by enhancing labor market flexibility. Chile has suffered a particularly marked deterioration in its external accounts over the past year, and its current account deficit in 1998 now seems likely to be about 6¾ percent of GDP. Currency pressures have been met by cuts in public spending and a tightening of credit conditions, as well as by adjustments of both the width and the rate of crawl of the exchange rate band, and the suspension of restrictions on capital inflows. The current account deficit is now declining, but a stronger fiscal position may be required to sustain a smaller current account deficit and ease the burden on credit policy. In Mexico, the authorities have appropriately cut government spending in the face of lower oil prices, and as a result are expected to come close to achieving their fiscal objective for 1998 of a deficit equivalent to 1¼ percent of GDP. They have also tightened monetary policy significantly to contain inflation in the face of the depreciation of the peso. Gains in international competitiveness and the slowing of domestic demand growth are expected to reduce the current account deficit significantly next year. Nevertheless, recent adverse developments have reemphasized the need for a strong fiscal reform effort to increase non-oil revenues, reduce the vulnerability of the budget to fluctuations in petroleum prices, and contain the growth of current spending. Problems in the banking sector also remain to be resolved. Venezuela and Ecuador also have been suffering from the weakness of oil prices, and their fiscal deficits have widened despite substantial spending cuts; further measures seem likely to be needed to secure financial stability. Also in Latin America, significant macroeconomic policy adjustments have been announced in Colombia to address large imbalances that have emerged as a result of past policy slippages as well as adverse external developments. In central America, economic recovery from the devastation caused by Hurricane Mitch in late October is being supported by emergency financial assistance from the IMF, World Bank, and other multilateral and bilateral sources.

In Asia, India has been experiencing a slowing of growth in the industrial sector, accompanied by higher inflation that reflects agricultural supply difficulties, rapid monetary growth, and the depreciation of the rupee since late 1997. The current account position has weakened, but international reserves remain comfortable, boosted by capital inflows from nonresident Indians. The first priority for macroeconomic policy is to take decisive steps toward medium-term fiscal consolidation, in order to reduce the public sector deficit

substantially from its recent level of close to 10 percent of GDP. It will also be important to avoid a premature easing of monetary policy: in fact, further tightening may be warranted if inflation does not slow. Aside from these macroeconomic policy requirements, a wide range of structural reforms are needed to boost confidence and reinvigorate growth.

The external financial crisis in Pakistan, which has been reflected in a sharp decline in international reserves and the accumulation of large external payments arrears, is being addressed by a policy package entailing substantial fiscal adjustment as well as broadly based structural reforms and the gradual removal of the temporary exchange restrictions imposed at the onset of the crisis, and by debt relief from official and private creditors.

Among emerging market countries in the Middle East and Europe region, Turkey suffered the worst contagion from the Russian crisis in August, reflecting its close trade links with Russia and its difficult fiscal position. While the country's international reserves have stabilized since September, domestic interest rates have remained high, partly owing to Turkey's reduced access to international capital markets and domestic political uncertainties. The budgetary situation has remained on its adjustment track, but substantial further progress in fiscal consolidation and structural reforms will be important to achieve the targeted reduction of inflation and to maintain investor confidence in the face of the heavy debt-service obligations falling due in the period ahead. In Israel, monetary policy has been tightened sharply in recent months in the face of downward pressure on the shekel and a pickup in inflation following earlier depreciation.

Many other countries in the Middle East are having to adjust to the weakness of world oil prices, with declines in export revenues resulting in acute budgetary and external pressures in many of the region's oil producers, including some of the wealthiest countries such as Saudi Arabia. At the same time, current conditions in global financial markets provide limited scope to offset export shortfalls through expanded foreign borrowing. Consequently, gross official reserves have been drawn down in a number of countries—including Algeria, Iran, Oman, and Yemen—to finance sizable current account deficits. Given prospects for continued weakness in the oil market in the period ahead, an immediate policy challenge is the adoption of measures to restore macroeconomic equilibrium and promote growth of non-oil activities, particularly in the oil producers of the Gulf region. Efforts to restrain public spending, broaden the revenue base, and press ahead with structural reform will all be important. Progress to date in these areas has been limited, and further delays would risk financial instability, with potential spillover effects on the non-oil economies in the Middle East, some of which—in particular, Jordan, and, to a lesser extent, Egypt—are already experienc-

Box 1.1. Brazil's Financial Assistance Package and Adjustment Program

The terms of a $41 billion IMF-led financial assistance package for Brazil, in support of the program of adjustment and structural reform described below, were released on November 13, 1998. Of the total amount, $18.1 billion (SDR 13,025 million) would be provided by the IMF in the form of a three-year Stand-By Arrangement, about $4 billion each from the World Bank and the Inter-American Development Bank, and $14.5 billion from 20 governments channeled through, or provided in collaboration with, the Bank for International Settlements (BIS). The U.S. government is the largest bilateral contributor, with a credit line of $5 billion. There is no explicit contribution from the private sector, since the Brazilian authorities believed it would be most effective to seek the voluntary participation of international banks in a rollover of credit lines once the financial package had been arranged. Initial contacts by the authorities with private banks suggest that banks will hold open their trade and interbank credit lines. The bilateral financing is not guaranteed by any collateral—something that distinguishes the package from the one arranged for Mexico in 1995, where U.S. repayment was guaranteed by oil revenues.

The financial package is significantly front-loaded, with about $37 billion available, if needed, in the first 13 months, and carries relatively high interest rates and short repayment schedules. In the case of IMF funds, 30 percent will be available under the credit tranches, at a floating interest rate, currently 4.25 percent, and a repayment period of five years. The remainder, 70 percent, will be available under the Supplemental Reserve Facility (first used in the case of assistance to Korea at end-December 1997), with a repayment period of two and a half years and an interest rate of 300 basic points above that applying to the credit tranches. In the case of the funds channeled through the BIS, a repayment period of two years will apply upon drawdown, with a 470 basis point spread over the London interbank offered rate (LIBOR). The first tranche of $5.3 billion from the IMF became available after the approval of the package by the IMF's Executive Board on December 2. The second tranche will become available from February 1999, or even earlier depending on circumstances.

* * *

Background

In the four years between the introduction of the *Real Plan* and September 1998, Brazil managed to wrench inflation down from rates in excess of 2,700 percent a year to under 3 percent. It was also able to advance the im-

plementation of its structural reform agenda, and to achieve annual growth of GDP of about 4 percent. In the structural area, its privatization program was particularly successful, but it also made progress in resolving the problems of the state banks and in other aspects of financial reform, deregulation, and the opening up of the economy.

Notwithstanding the *Real Plan*'s great success in reducing inflation, it has not been successful in reducing the public sector deficit. After a strong initial fiscal adjustment when the *Plan* was introduced, the fiscal stance was loosened. The public sector borrowing requirement (PSBR) reached 6.3 percent in 1997 and is projected to approach 8 percent in 1998. In addition to the impact of declining inflation on real expenditure, which had been held down by the lack of rapid and full indexation of nominal expenditure, the weakness of the public finances reflected some basic structural problems: an excessively generous pension system, inflexibility of civil service employment rules, the lack of a hard budget constraint on subnational governments, and a distorted system of indirect taxation. The increase in the PSBR was reflected in the deterioration in the external current account, which is projected to reach a deficit of 4 percent of GDP in 1998.

The fiscal and external deficits made Brazil vulnerable to changes in investor sentiment and the attendant capital outflows. It successfully responded to a bout of capital outflows in the wake of the Asian crisis in the fall of 1997, mainly because of the timely response of monetary policy and the announcement of a strong fiscal policy package. However, disappointment with slippages in fiscal adjustment in 1998 and the continued growth of the public debt contributed to the sentiment that Brazil remained vulnerable. The crisis in Russia led quickly to pressures on emerging markets, and particularly Brazil's external capital account, as described in the text. Liquidation of Brazilian Brady bonds to cover losses on Russian securities and, more generally, the buildup of short positions in Brazilian offshore debt instruments resulted in arbitrage by resident investors seeking the higher return on "Brazil risk" offered by Brady bonds. Nonresident holdings of Brazilian debt and equity instruments were also significantly reduced, and capital outflows by residents took place in other forms. Overall, most of the outflows were by nonresidents.

The government reacted initially by announcing a number of measures to increase the attractiveness of capital inflows; it then announced measures to tighten the

ing a drag from weaker export growth and workers' remittances.

Among developing countries in Africa, financial markets in South Africa have stabilized in recent months following the period of severe downward pressure on the rand in midyear, but activity has slowed sharply. The authorities' tight monetary policy appears

to have been the main factor contributing to a partial recovery of the exchange rate, which has led to rebounds in bond and equity markets. Financial market stabilization has allowed monetary policy to be eased somewhat since October. A durable strengthening of economic growth continues to require structural reform in a number of areas.

fiscal stance, as well as an increase in interest rates. With the outflow of capital continuing unabated, it hiked interest rates by 20 percentage points, raising the overnight rate to over 40 percent. This stemmed but did not stop net capital outflows, and the government began to prepare the policy package described below and to intensify its dialogue with the IMF and other members of the international community to seek their support.

Policy Program

On the macroeconomic front, the program is focused on a set of fiscal measures announced by the Brazilian government in late October, aimed at increasing primary surpluses of the public sector sufficiently (given the assumption that interest rates will decline gradually, from 40 percent in early November to 20 percent by mid-1999 in terms of the overnight rate) to arrest in 2000 the rise in the ratio of public debt to GDP. Thus the program sets a target surplus of 2.6 percent of GDP for the primary balance of the consolidated public sector in 1999, followed by surpluses of 2.8 percent of GDP in 2000 and 3.0 percent in 2001. Contributions to the fiscal adjustment effort are expected from all levels of government, and a series of expenditure-saving and revenue-raising measures have been announced, some of which have already been enacted (see below). In terms of domestic public debt management, the government will aim at securing a progressive lengthening of the maturity of the debt and, as interest rates decline, at increasing the share of fixed-rate securities in total debt. Monetary policy will continue to be conducted to support the exchange rate regime, a crawling peg whereby the *real* depreciates against the U.S. dollar at a rate of about 7½ percent a year. Reliance on the *real* as the nominal anchor is seen as the key to low inflation. The improvement in the fiscal position is to take place despite a projected decline in real GDP of 1 percent in 1999, reflecting the high interest rates expected to prevail through early 1999, the fiscal contraction itself, and slower export market growth. Economic recovery is projected to begin in the latter part of 1999, with growth of 3 percent projected for 2000, helped by improvements in international competitiveness implied by the crawling exchange rate peg and the projected low rate of inflation and continued robust productivity gains. In addition to the structural reforms of the public sector described below, the government also intends to advance financial sector and labor market reforms and to avoid reversals of the trade liberalization program.

Fiscal Policy

Most of the program's fiscal adjustment is to occur at the federal government level, with about two-thirds resulting from revenue measures. In addition to an increase in the tax on financial transactions, these include increases in the payroll taxes paid by civil servants to finance their pension plan, which is unusually generous.[1] The program's expenditure cuts are intended to spare sensitive social expenditure programs. Adjustment at the state and municipal levels is based on the increased control the government has over the states' financing sources, on the discipline imposed by the fiscal adjustment agreements most states have signed with the federal government, and on the impact of a law imposing a ceiling on the civil service wage bill in relation to revenue. Tariff increases will raise the operating surpluses of those enterprises remaining in the public sector, and privatization-related investment will fall.

Public sector structural reforms will make a growing contribution to the fiscal adjustment over time. The recently passed constitutional amendment to social security will achieve expenditure economies by increasing the effective retirement age of participants in the private sector pension scheme. The administrative reform, whose implementing legislation is now being passed, will reduce excess staffing in the civil service at all levels of government.

The social security reform that congress recently approved will be bolstered by a more fundamental reform that the government is now preparing, based on the principle that what a participant, or his or her employer, contributes must bear a reasonable relationship to the pension he or she can expect to receive. Administrative reforms of public sector pension plans at the state and local levels are also planned. The government has also been working for some time on a reform of the country's indirect tax system, under which the value-added taxes administered by the states, whose bases have been eroded and whose rate structure has been affected by excessive tax competition, will be replaced by a VAT with a common base and rate structure. Its revenues will be shared between the different levels of government, and it will probably be administered by the states.

---

[1]This payroll tax increase was voted down by the congress in early December. It is to be resubmitted to the new congress in February 1999, and the government has announced that measures will be taken to compensate for any revenue loss resulting from the delay.

Among the countries in transition, Russia continues to lack macroeconomic policies that would help to restore the confidence of investors and establish the preconditions for sustainable growth. The central areas of concern remain the large underlying fiscal imbalance, which has widened further since the August crisis, and the distortions arising from the associated arrears and broader culture of nonpayment in the economy. Russia urgently needs a fiscal policy by which the bulk of expenditures would be financed by tax revenues, without resort to arrears, and whose financing would allow inflation to be reasonably well contained, without price controls. To reduce the deficit to the levels required, measures need to be taken as early as possible to enhance government revenues—particularly through improvements in tax administration and an end to ad hoc negotiated tax deductions—and to cut government spending. The authorities' current budget plans fail to meet these requirements. Macroeconomic stabilization will also require a monetary policy that avoids substantial central bank financing of the banking system as well as the government. The reestablishment of stability-oriented macroeconomic policies will have to be accompanied by actions to address severe difficulties in the banking system (discussed in the Annex), the normalization of relations with creditors, and a return to the unfinished task of structural reform, which needs to be accelerated on many fronts. Strong spillovers from the Russian crisis have been felt in Ukraine, although continued lags in progress there with macroeconomic stabilization and structural reform have been a greater source of difficulty. Particularly important now is the satisfactory resolution of uncertainties regarding the implementation of the 1999 budget and the elimination of fiscal overruns.

In central and eastern Europe, Hungary and Poland have weathered the financial market turmoil of recent months reasonably well: the progress in recent years with fiscal consolidation has helped to maintain confidence in their foreign exchange markets. With inflation having been reduced significantly in both cases, the continued improvement of external financial market conditions should allow domestic interest rates to be lowered gradually further. In the Czech Republic, output is estimated to have fallen by 1½ percent in 1998 following a tightening of policies that was needed to reduce fiscal and external imbalances. Since July, the strength of the koruna has allowed reductions in interest rates amounting cumulatively to 4½ percentage points, which should help to ease banking sector difficulties and, along with a slightly expansionary budget, help to support the economy in 1999.

Among the industrial countries, *Japan* stands out as the economy with the weakest growth performance in the 1990s, and as the only economy in recession, having suffered four successive quarters of output decline since late 1997. The main objective for policy continues to be to end the recession and reignite growth. A key element among the policies needed to achieve this objective is the resolution of the problems in the banking system, and in this area significant steps have recently been taken (Box 1.2). The critical challenge for the authorities is still to catalyze a quick and forceful recapitalization and restructuring that will restore the financial health and profitability of the banking system, including a full and transparent accounting of banks' financial positions to restore investor confidence. But macroeconomic policies also have a major role to play in stimulating domestic demand—a role that is facilitated by the absence of inflation and the large external current account surplus. In addition, further progress with deregulation and broader structural

reform is essential for the economy to regain its dynamism and meet the needs of its aging population.

The scope to reduce interest rates further has been very limited since the Bank of Japan lowered its operating target for the overnight call rate to around 0.25 percent in early September. But the marked appreciation of the yen that occurred in early October effectively tightened monetary conditions and, at the same time, provided additional room for monetary easing since it substantially reduced the risk that faster monetary expansion would add to destabilizing exchange rate pressures in the region. Thus the Bank of Japan has recently broadened the scope of its operations in the private debt market to boost liquidity growth and support private sector credit creation. These operations can continue to play a useful role in helping to moderate deflationary pressures.

With regard to fiscal policy, increases in public works contracts since September indicate that the April stimulus package has begun to take effect. The further package of measures introduced in mid-November—the third supplementary budget to be introduced since the beginning of the current fiscal year, on April 1—promises significant additional stimulus in 1999. As a result, the fiscal tightening of 1997 will have been more than fully reversed. The "headline figures" referring to the size of the package—including estimates that it is equivalent to 5 percent of GDP—overstate its additional stimulative effect, partly because some of the measures replace temporary ones implemented earlier. The stimulus to be provided by fiscal policy in the next fiscal year (beginning April 1999)—measured as the change in the structural general government deficit from the current fiscal year—is tentatively estimated by IMF staff at about 1 percent of GDP; this estimate will need to be reviewed in the light of the budget and tax policy decisions to be made in coming weeks. The general government deficit (excluding social security) would then rise to almost 10 percent of GDP. While Japan clearly faces a difficult challenge of fiscal consolidation in the medium term, in the short term the paramount need is to ensure a resumption of growth. The expansionary fiscal stance need have only modest effects on debt-servicing costs in view of the continuing very low level of interest rates; although the recent downgrading of Japan's sovereign debt by a credit-rating agency has contributed to a recent upturn in government bond yields, they remain only a little over 1 percent.[4]

For the *other industrial countries*, although there have been widespread downward revisions to growth projections for 1999, the outlook in most cases is still fairly good. Continuing low inflation—close to zero in

---

[4]For analysis of Japan's economic crisis and policy options, see the October 1998 *World Economic Outlook*, Chapter IV; and IMF, *Japan—Selected Issues*, IMF Staff Country Reports, No. 98/113 (Washington: October 1998).

Box 1.2. Recent Developments in the Japanese Financial System

This box describes Japan's new bank laws, the nationalization of Long-Term Credit Bank (LTCB)—a first test case for those laws—and the measures taken by the Bank of Japan (BOJ) in response to the breakdown of the bank credit channel in Japan.[1] It also briefly discusses the withdrawal of Japanese banks from several foreign markets, and the implementation of Big Bang financial reforms in the current environment.

The Legislative Package

The key provisions in the bank laws approved by the Japanese parliament in October are the following:
- The funds available to the banking sector were raised to ¥60 trillion, with ¥25 trillion targeted to the recapitalization of "viable banks,"[2] and ¥18 trillion mainly targeted to failure resolution schemes including public bridge banks and the nationalization of failed banks; ¥17 trillion continued to be reserved for guaranteeing deposits at failed banks.
- The creation of a new high-level body (the Financial Revitalization Commission, FRC) within the Prime Minister's Office. This body will be responsible for drafting and implementing the regulations necessary for bridge banks and carrying out the nationalization of failed banks. It will also oversee the recapitalization of banks, and centralize all financial supervisory activities (the Financial Supervisory Agency will be put under the FRC).
- Existing agencies (the Resolution and Collection Bank, RCB, and the Resolution and Collection Organization) will be consolidated into an asset management corporation shaped along the lines of the former Resolution Trust Corporation (RTC) in the United States. That agency will be in charge of receiving and disposing of bad assets from banks.

By early December there were indications that most of the major banks would apply for relatively small injections, in the range of ¥100–700 billion, with the bulk of the resources being used for accelerating the provisioning of bad loans, in face of (among other factors) the worsening of the economy (debts of firms filing for bankruptcy grew by 53 percent year-on-year in October, totaling more than $100 billion in the first ten months of 1998).

The passage of the new laws reduced the risk of a collapse of the Japanese banking system and provided some institutional and financial mechanisms that could help to accelerate the restructuring and consolidation of the banking system. They could lead to a quid-pro-quo between banks and the government, in which heavy provisioning by banks would be cushioned by injections of public funds and buttressed by major changes in management structures. Steps in that direction could also be supported by the provisions in the new laws that allow banks to receive funds in order to facilitate "realignments" (consolidation) in the sector. Prospects for success are still far from certain, however. The Japanese framework does not yet have explicit mechanisms that would force weak but viable financial institutions to access available public monies and undergo a fundamental restructuring.[3] Thus, a more effective balance still needs to emerge within this evolving framework between establishing clear incentives for the largest banks to accept recapitalization funds, and conditions that would help to facilitate the badly needed restructuring and consolidation that is required in the Japanese financial system.

Nationalization of LTCB

LTCB filed for temporary nationalization on October 23, about four months after its market valuation had dropped markedly, on rumors that the bank was facing difficulties in raising funds.[4] The original plan of merging LTCB with the smaller Sumitomo Trust Bank was ultimately abandoned, in part because of the reticence of the latter in taking over LTCB substandard loans. In September, after one of the main affiliates of LTCB with more than ¥1.5 trillion in debts (including ¥256 billion to LTCB itself and ¥150 billion to Sumitomo Trust) failed, little doubt about the bank's insolvency remained. At the time of the filing for nationalization, the bank declared a negative net worth of ¥350 billion (1.5 percent of total liabilities), including unrealized losses on securities holdings. An audit by supervisors indicated that LTCB's prob-

(Box continues on next page.)

---

[1]The challenges facing the Japanese banking system were extensively analyzed in the September 1998 *International Capital Markets* report; this box updates that analysis for the period since July 1998.

[2]The new legislation allows "well-capitalized" banks (that is, banks with a BIS capital ratio above 8 percent) to apply for public funds if they are participating in a bank consolidation (including by absorbing a failed bank) or if the capital injection can help to alleviate the credit crunch. More generally, funds to banks deemed solvent are to be injected through the purchase of debt instruments and stocks (typically preferred stock, or common stock in the case of severely undercapitalized banks).

---

[3]As part of their applications for public funds, well-capitalized banks are required only to announce plans that include cuts in the number of employees, compensation, and the number of directors; the sale of unessential facilities; and reduction of dividends.

[4]Until 1996 the price of LTCB's stock hovered around ¥900. By April 1998, it had fallen to ¥300, dropping to ¥37 in June and ¥3 at the time of the nationalization of the bank.

---

some cases, after allowing for measurement biases—provides scope for further monetary easing if warranted to support demand and output growth, and also to help stabilize financial markets. But the current economic conjuncture does not call for fiscal policies to be diverted from the important medium-term objective of reducing imbalances and debt burdens. Fiscal policies can, nevertheless, help to moderate the slowing of growth, and counter downside risks, through the operation of the automatic stabilizers.

Box 1.2 *(concluded)*

Japan: Derivatives Positions of Selected Japanese Banks
(Fiscal year 1997, March 1998)

	Notional		Credit Equivalent[1]	
	Trillions of yen	Billions of U.S. dollars[2]	Trillions of yen	Billions of U.S. dollars[2]
LTCB	51	425	. . .	. . .
IBJ	220	1,833	3.4	28.3
BTM[3]	250	2,083	. . .	. . .
DKB	166	1,383	1.7	14.2
Sumitomo	182	1,517	3.8	31.7
Sanwa	165	1,375	2.3	19.2
Fuji	337	2,808	2.2	18.3
Sakura	107	892	1.8	15.0
Total	1,418	12,317	15.2	126.7

Source: Banks' annual reports.
[1]Using BIS weights.
[2]Using the ¥120/US$ exchange rate.
[3]End of FY1996.

lem assets accounted, net of provisions, for ¥4.6 trillion, or 19 percent of the bank's total assets.

The new management appointed by the government has indicated that the bank should be privatized within a year but has not announced any major plan to break up the bank to facilitate its sale. Since the takeover, the BOJ has provided LTCB with ¥5 trillion to keep credit flowing to bank clients and to smooth the unwinding of LTCB's off-balance-sheet positions (*see table*). The table indicates that Japanese banks in general have large positions in derivatives instruments; interest rate swaps account for most of their notional value.[5]

Reaction of the BOJ to the Breakdown of Monetary Transmission Channels

Since late 1997, the BOJ has followed an accommodative monetary policy stance. Throughout 1998 it has purchased commercial bills and high-quality commercial

---

[5]Disclosure rules in Japan require banks to state the notional and market value of their derivatives positions every half-year. Recently, Fuji Bank also retained a foreign auditing company to evaluate its portfolio and risk management practices, after rumors about large losses in that portfolio depressed the bank's market valuation. The audit indicated that those practices were in line with international standards, and that Fuji's derivatives portfolio had not sustained extraordinary losses. (To improve transparency, Fuji Bank has also disclosed the results of the self-assessment of its loans.)

paper on a repurchase basis in large volumes.[6] On September 9, the Bank lowered the target call interest rate to 0.25 percent. Despite these measures, and reflecting the breakdown of the monetary and credit transmission mechanisms, bank lending dropped by 3.3 percent in the 12 months to October 1998. The authorities anticipated severe liquidity problems ahead of the end of the calendar year, manifested in the growing funding difficulties of Japanese banks, especially abroad.[7] By late October, it became evident that the liquidity injected into the Japanese financial system was being used to finance Japanese banks' activities abroad—including through interest swaps of yen payments for dollar cash flows. Yen funds became so abundant that for a brief period in early November some foreign banks were ready to lend yen at negative interest rates, and the yield on treasury bills fell below zero (*see figure, upper panel*).

In those circumstances, the monetary authorities opted for opening new channels to finance the corporate sector. On November 13, 1998, the BOJ announced that it would enlarge the scope for repurchasing commercial paper and establish a new lending facility for refinancing half of the new bank lending in the fourth quarter of 1998. The bank also indicated that it would consider the purchase of bills issued by financial institutions and collateralized by corporate bonds and loans on deeds.

Withdrawal of Japanese Banks from International Markets

In October and November 1998, several Japanese banks indicated their intention to withdraw at least partially from overseas activities, which signaled a change in the pace and nature of a process of retrenching from international finance that had been apparent since the mid-1990s.[8] In particular, the announcement by some major

---

[6]The BOJ holds about one-third of the stock of commercial papers, which has grown by about 40 percent since mid-1997. After a big surge in late 1997, the issuance of corporate bonds by Japanese firms became increasingly difficult in the course of 1998 as the credit rating of Japan and Japanese companies worsened. Strong companies have issued securities backed by receivables and raised credit lines abroad, but the scope of these forms of financing is limited.

[7]Large Japanese banks were also facing funding problems domestically, with regional banks preferring to invest their cash surpluses in government paper rather than in the interbank market.

[8]The withdrawal of Japanese banks from international activities has in part been driven by the Japanese prudential regulations, which allow banks without overseas activities to maintain a ratio of capital to risk-weighted assets of just 4 percent (instead of the 8 percent BIS ratio). In early 1998, Fuji Bank sold part of

---

The United States and the United Kingdom are close to cyclical peaks, and in both cases signs of slowing growth have been evident, albeit less so in the United States. Although unemployment is low in both countries, wage growth has risen only moderately, and price

inflation has remained relatively subdued. In both cases, a slowdown of growth from the above-potential pace of recent years is desirable to avoid inflationary pressures and a hard landing later on. The authorities therefore need to steer a balanced course between avoiding over-

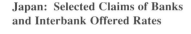

Japan: Selected Claims of Banks
and Interbank Offered Rates

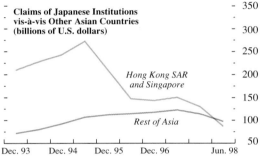

Sources: Bank for International Settlements; and
Bloomberg Financial Markets, LP.

from the head of the FRC, prodding banks to reduce their needs for foreign currencies. Because of the size of Japanese banks and the clustering in time of the decisions to review the scope of their foreign business, the strengthening of the yen in October could be linked to their retrenchment (see Chapter III, Box 3.1).

A temporary reduction in the flow of private capital from Japan to emerging markets might be expected from that withdrawal. Nevertheless, the impact even on Asia may be limited, because net flows from Japanese banks have already fallen substantially in recent years (see lower panel of figure), with official capital flows playing a greater role since the beginning of the Asian crisis. In view of the overcapacity of the Japanese banking system, the closure of foreign branches might represent a first step toward a "realignment" among top Japanese banks. On balance, the overall effect of the withdrawal (especially on mature capital markets) will depend largely on whether the Big Bang financial reform will provide room for foreign banks to intermediate a significantly larger share of Japanese saving and facilitate the recycling of these funds.

Preparations for Big Bang

Although still at an early stage, Japanese financial institutions are starting to respond to Big Bang.[9] Tie-ups of Japanese institutions with foreign partners have become an almost daily occurrence, and several alliances among major Japanese banks have been announced to develop specific businesses. Major banks are also positioning themselves to benefit from the switch to a real-time gross settlement payment system by the end of 2000, which will open new business opportunities to institutions with the capacity to act as clearing banks. Some alliances have involved the shift of profitable businesses (for example, asset management) from old de facto publicly insured institutions into newly created institutions. The issue of the distribution of risks in a changing environment is not, however, restricted to banks. For instance, the legislative requirement that the securities sector establish an industry-sponsored insurance scheme has resulted in the creation of two such schemes: one for domestic houses and one for foreign houses that were concerned about the potential liabilities of participating in a single industry-wide scheme.

banks of plans to close a large number of foreign branches and sharply contract their lending to non-Japanese borrowers was accompanied by statements

its holdings in the U.S. institution, Heller Financial, and Sumitomo sold its California bank, Zions Bancorp. Among the banks that have recently announced a major overseas retrenchment are the small city bank Daiwa (which had already been battered by its expulsion from the United States in 1995 and carries large unrealized losses in its securities holdings), Fuji Bank, and the relatively strong and large Sanwa and Sumitomo Banks. Some trust banks, including Mitsubishi Trust, followed suit. On its part, Nomura Securities is also retrenching, after suffering large losses in its U.S. unit.

[9]See the September 1998 *International Capital Markets* report for the implementation schedule of the reforms, which has so far been adhered to. In December 1998, the sale of mutual funds at commercial banks was further liberalized, as planned.

stimulating demand—which would exacerbate future risks to the economy—and preventing the likely near-term slowdowns from turning into recessions.

In the United States, a widening external deficit (partly reflecting the Asian recession), slowing private

investment growth, significant recent inventory accumulation, and the likelihood of an upturn in private saving from its exceptionally low recent levels point to overall growth falling somewhat below its potential rate next year. Activity will be supported in the period ahead by the cuts in interest rates by the Federal Reserve Board since end-September, amounting to 75 basis points, and by the depreciation of the dollar to which the cuts have contributed. With financial markets having stabilized and recovered in large measure since early October, it would now seem appropriate for the Federal Reserve to pause before taking further action, while being prepared both to ease again if U.S. growth prospects deteriorate significantly, and to tighten if inflationary pressures increase. The Federal Reserve's recent easing actions have been facilitated by the fiscal consolidation achieved in recent years, and the budget surpluses in prospect should be allowed to accumulate to help address the social security and health care financing shortfalls that are projected to arise in the next decade as a result of population aging. While it would be appropriate to let the automatic stabilizers operate, discretionary fiscal easing would not be warranted unless the slowdown were to become much more severe than seems likely at present.

Significantly slower growth is projected for the United Kingdom in 1999 than for the United States, reflecting the more severe tightening of monetary conditions that was needed in the economic upswing to hold prospective inflation to its target. With forecast inflation having fallen below the target amid the deterioration of global economic conditions, the Bank of England appropriately reversed the direction of monetary policy in early October, cutting its key interest rate between then and early December by a total of 1¼ percentage points. Monetary policy is still relatively tight, however, and there is significant scope for rates to be cut further as growth weakens and inflation concerns recede.

Growth in the Canadian economy has slowed significantly since early this year, largely reflecting the impact of the Asian crisis on commodity markets. A significant depreciation of the Canadian dollar has eased monetary conditions in spite of a hike in official interest rates in August that was mostly reversed in October and November. Particularly given the low rate of inflation—recently in the lower half of the 1–3 percent target range for core consumer price inflation, on a 12-month basis—further interest rate reductions will be warranted if the growth outlook worsens. The strong fiscal position, meanwhile, should be maintained to reduce the government's debt burden further.

In the euro area, the transition to a single common currency at the start of 1999 is proceeding smoothly. European Economic and Monetary Union (EMU) is a major achievement. The euro area will rival the United States in terms of trade and output, and the role of the euro in financial transactions eventually may match that of the U.S. dollar. The impact of euro area policies on the world economy will therefore be as important as that of U.S. policies in fostering an environment conducive to sustainable growth worldwide and in helping to restore global economic and financial stability in times of turbulence such as those experienced recently.[5]

The convergence over recent months of short-term interest rates in the euro area toward the level prevailing in Germany, France, and the other core countries, and the welcome reduction of interest rates in the core countries in early December from 3.3 percent to 3.0 percent (in terms of central banks' operating rates) has lowered average short-term rates in the area by about 50 basis points since midyear. This decline in short-term rates has been timely in view of the weakening of external conditions and the need to ensure that domestic demand growth remains sufficient to sustain slack-absorbing recoveries. Given the subdued prospects for inflation, the considerable amount of slack, and the more severe implications of downside—relative to upside—risks, scope remains for additional interest rate reductions should growth prospects weaken further.

As discussed in the October 1998 *World Economic Outlook,* structural fiscal positions in most euro-area countries still fall short of the medium-term requirements set out in the Stability and Growth Pact. In some cases, including Germany and the Netherlands, structural deficits widened in 1998. However, the medium-term shortfall for the area as a whole is not large (1 percent of GDP), and some of the needed improvement can be expected to come from declining debt-service payments. Nevertheless, any move to support demand in the euro area other than through allowing the automatic stabilizers to operate could weaken confidence in the policy framework for EMU and limit the European Central Bank's room for maneuver. In this context, increases in public investment—which would be welcome, not least because such spending has borne a disproportionate share of recent fiscal adjustment—would need to be compensated by other budgetary adjustments. Countries need to focus their fiscal efforts on structural reforms—aimed at lowering the growth rate of spending and creating room for tax cuts—as part of a broader strategy of reforms to reduce structural rigidities and strengthen employment performance. In particular, labor market reforms remain crucial to bring unemployment down on a sustainable basis.

Systemic Issues Arising from Recent Financial Market Turbulence

The recent turbulence in global financial markets was unusual for a period characterized by relatively strong macroeconomic policies and conditions in many of the advanced economies. The volatility re-

---

[5]For a detailed discussion of the external implications of EMU, as well as the policy challenges facing the euro area, see the October 1998 *World Economic Outlook,* Chapter V.

flected a sudden heightened perception of, and aversion to, risk following Russia's effective debt default in August and an associated flight to quality. Emerging markets were particularly seriously affected as interest rate spreads on their external debt increased significantly and new private external financing virtually ground to a halt. But the repercussions were not limited to these countries, as the global flight to quality led to sharp increases in spreads on financial assets in some of the deepest capital markets in the world, especially in the United States, and to sharp volatility in the dollar-yen exchange rate.

Subsequent actions by the Federal Reserve and other central banks to lower short-term interest rates have helped to alleviate fears of a deepening global credit crunch, as has the international support package for Brazil. However, the process of deleveraging and portfolio rebalancing in response to heightened risk aversion may not have run its course, and the situation remains fragile, especially in the emerging markets but also in some of the mature markets. Moreover, following their correction in the late summer, equity markets in a number of advanced economies have risen to levels close to previous peaks, even as the short-term macroeconomic outlook has weakened and uncertainty has further increased.

The global economy's close brush with a widespread credit crunch has raised a number of important questions about international capital market dynamics and the measures needed to improve financial sector resilience and reduce the risk of systemic problems, including:

- Why did Russia's effective debt default in August trigger a massive global reassessment and repricing of emerging market risk?
- Why did the accompanying turbulence generate severe strains, sharp increases in credit and liquidity spreads, and extreme price movements in some of the world's deepest financial markets, including the U.S. market for government securities and the dollar-yen foreign exchange market, especially in the wake of the near-collapse of LTCM?
- What measures can be taken to strengthen international capital markets and reduce the risk of systemic problems?

The recent turbulence in global financial markets followed several years of sharp spread compression across a wide range of debt instruments and record capital flows to the emerging markets. Even though the Asian crisis briefly punctuated this process, the effects were felt mainly in the region, and many of the mature markets benefited from a flight to quality from Asian markets. In the event, the Russian default in August served as a trigger for a very broad-based reassessment and repricing of risk. This not only severely curtailed emerging markets' access to external financing but also led to a sharp widening of interest rate spreads in key mature markets and severe short-term liquidity problems.

The severe reaction to the Russian default was partly due to the sizes of the losses on Russian exposures and positions, but these were not in aggregate large enough to account fully for the ensuing turbulence. More important was the role of Russia's default as a defining event that challenged widely held views about the default risks associated with *all* emerging market investments, and the willingness and ability of the international community to provide assistance to countries in difficulty. That Russia had been "permitted" to default was seen by some market participants as calling into question the readiness of the international community to provide support to other countries in difficulty. The general ensuing reevaluation of emerging market risk may subsequently have been compounded by Malaysia's decision to impose capital controls, which heightened the risk that countries in a similar economic predicament might also impose controls. This has so far not proved to be the case, and many emerging markets have reiterated their commitment to open capital markets.

A second issue concerns the sources of the vulnerabilities that led to the Russian default producing severe liquidity problems in some of the deepest capital markets in the world, and prompting action by a major central bank to facilitate the private rescue of a hedge fund (LTCM). The drying up of liquidity resulted mainly from many investors attempting at the same time to rapidly unwind highly leveraged positions, built up either to arbitrage mature market credit spreads or to exploit perceived differences in funding costs between major currencies, most notably the dollar-yen carry trade.[6] Modern risk management techniques and extensive marking to market encouraged a very rapid rebalancing and cutting of positions judged to have become more risky. The positions that were unwound had been part of a large number of "plays" encouraged by—and themselves contributing to—a sharp narrowing of spreads on many mature market fixed-income instruments in the period leading up to the Asian crisis in the second half of 1997.

In response to the global flight to quality, spreads between credits of "low" and "high" quality in several mature markets widened dramatically, especially in the United States, resulting in margin calls, reassessments of counterpart risk, and further deleveraging. Several hedge funds, including LTCM, that had large positions on yields spreads were reported to have had difficulty meeting margin calls in the period after the Russian default, and to be seeking additional liquidity. Hedge funds, however, were not the only participants

---

[6]For further discussion, see IMF, *International Capital Markets: Developments, Prospects, and Key Policy Issues* (Washington: September 1998).

in these trades and may not have been the most significant. While comprehensive data are not available, the proprietary trading desks of many of the large internationally active commercial and investment banks appear also to have taken highly leveraged positions on a variety of credit spreads. In these circumstances, the system was vulnerable to a sudden sharp increase in risk aversion, since it would trigger attempts by many financial institutions to close out their positions and reduce leverage. Against this background, the Federal Reserve made the decision in late September to facilitate a private rescue of the troubled LTCM hedge fund to avoid an even more disorderly unwinding of positions and further financial market turbulence.

Finally, the turbulence raises a number of important questions about financial market transparency, the internal risk management and control procedures of some of the largest internationally active financial institutions, and the adequacy of prudential supervision and systemic financial market surveillance. The key issue is how very large leveraged positions could be built up across a large number of financial institutions to the point where systemic risk was raised to extraordinary levels. Providing answers to these questions and limiting future vulnerabilities is critical.

- *Lack of Transparency.* The failure of market participants and financial supervisors to see warning signs of impending vulnerabilities appears to have been related to a general lack of transparency about the sizes of the positions built up. The lack of transparency reflected a number of factors including the opaque nature of the over-the-counter markets in which much of the off-balance-sheet trading takes place, the difficulties in assessing complex positions in layers of highly structured off-balance-sheet financial instruments, and the desire of the institutions involved to maintain secrecy to exploit profit opportunities. There are unlikely to be easy solutions to improving transparency in over-the-counter markets, but the recent turbulence suggests a need to strengthen position reporting to at least allow for the better monitoring by authorities of overall exposures.
- *Financial Firms' Risk Management Models Displayed Weaknesses.* Internal risk management models are intended to identify and limit the market risks assumed by financial institutions. At least in hindsight, the models used by some of the major financial institutions did not provide adequate safeguards. The recent episode of turbulence suggests at least three problems. First, insufficient attention was paid to low-probability events, perhaps as a result of inadequate stress testing and the belief that financial markets would continue their long rally. Second, the models typically assumed that market liquidity would be present to allow a rapid unwinding of positions without significantly affecting prices. This assumption was called into question where many institutions held similar positions. Finally, inadequate attention was paid to the interplay between credit and market risk, such as occurs in periods of extreme stress. Improvements in risk modeling are required but will need always to be complemented by sound judgment and strong overall risk management procedures—in order to limit excessive risk taking.
- *Inadequate Market Surveillance and Prudential Supervision by Authorities.* Although weaknesses in private risk management were evident in the period leading up to the turbulence, market surveillance and prudential supervision also paid insufficient attention to the buildup of highly leveraged positions across many institutions. Central banks and supervisory authorities therefore need to give consideration to ways by which they can monitor more adequately the degree of market-wide and cross-market leverage and deal with "excessive" leverage, through higher margin-type requirements, stricter capital requirements on the off-balance-sheet activities of financial institutions, or both. These efforts need to be accompanied by a reexamination of the adequacy of current controls on the largely unregulated hedge fund industry, including the scope either for more direct controls or for encouraging stronger bank oversight of their positions vis-à-vis the funds. Given that proprietary trading desks of the major banks are increasingly engaged in activities similar to those of many hedge funds, the focus will need to be on ensuring appropriate oversight and control of these highly leveraged activities so as to contain risks to individual institutions as well as systemic risk.

The issues raised by the most recent financial market turbulence are complex, including the adequacy of private and public risk management in some of the most sophisticated financial institutions in the world, the growing linkages between emerging and mature financial markets, and the role of leverage in magnifying the system's vulnerability to shocks. Against this background, current bilateral and multilateral initiatives to consider the adequacy of current prudential controls over financial institutions—especially the highly leveraged activities—and to revisit the treatment of credit and market risk under the Basle capital adequacy ratios are critically important. These will need also to be complemented by stepped-up efforts to improve the transparency of financial institutions' off-balance-sheet activities with a view to lessening the risks of the kind of large buildup of highly leveraged positions that contributed to the severity of the recent problems in mature financial markets.

II

The Crisis in Emerging Markets

The financial market turmoil first evident in Asia in the summer of 1997 intensified sharply following Russia's decision on August 17, 1998 to devalue the ruble and impose a forced restructuring of domestic government debt. This development and to a lesser extent Malaysia's decision to impose capital controls, which followed shortly thereafter, were defining events that led both to a dramatic reassessment of the credit, market, and transfer risks associated with holding emerging market financial instruments, and to a general decline in risk tolerance among mature market investors. In part, the dramatic response of investors to Russia's actions reflected a reassessment of their earlier view that Russia was "too big to fail." In addition, some highly leveraged institutions that have been important investors in emerging market securities suffered large losses as a result of the Russian debt restructuring and faced higher margin calls. A relatively indiscriminate sell-off in emerging market securities ensued, which led to a sharp widening of secondary market interest rate spreads and a virtual cessation of financial flows to many emerging markets. Investor concerns that a sustained period of illiquidity could adversely affect emerging market economies with large domestic and external refinancing needs led to substantial capital outflows and sustained pressures on foreign exchange and domestic money markets in a number of countries, particularly in Latin America.[1]

Following the extreme nature of the financial market turbulence and collapse of new issuance activity experienced during the August–October period, there was a rebound in secondary bond and equity markets. Private capital flows showed a tentative recovery in early November following an easing of monetary policies in several mature markets and the announcement of a support package for Brazil—policy actions that demonstrated the commitment of the international community to stop the contagion and liquidity-driven sell-off. However, as financial institutions have continued to consolidate their balance sheet positions, new international debt and equity issuances by emerging markets have remained low, and international bank lending has continued to decline. The shrinkage of the investor base with an appetite for emerging market

risk is likely to persist in the near term, and the willingness of commercial banks to maintain or extend their lines of credit is likely to be a key factor governing the scale of net capital flows to emerging markets.

The partial recovery of secondary bond and equity markets since early October means that some of the deals that were taken out of the market because issuers found the cost of funds to be too high may now be brought back in.[2] Moreover, multilateral and bilateral initiatives and some existing options could substitute for or support private financing. The new Miyazawa Initiative will make available $30 billion for loans and short-term financing, and also provide guarantees and interest subsidies, for the crisis-affected Asian countries. In Latin America, the Inter-American Development Bank has approved a borrowing program that is expected to expand borrowing from $4 billion in 1998 to $9 billion in 1999 and thereby to contribute to recovery programs in the region. The World Bank has also created an emergency financing facility to step up financial support to emerging markets and has recently provided guarantees for a Thai bond issue. Export credit agencies, the International Finance Corporation (IFC), and other agencies such as the Overseas Private Investment Corporation (OPIC) have reportedly also been called by banks to step up involvement in loan syndications to provide protection against transfer risk. Furthermore, while the downturn of the credit cycle has been quick and deep because of deleveraging and mark-to-market practices, the speed of the adjustment has the advantage that it will facilitate quick rebuilding once losses are realized. Moreover, the new issuances that are occurring, albeit still small, suggest that investors are discriminating in favor of those countries with strong fundamentals and sustainable reform programs—such as Argentina and Poland.

The downside risks are nevertheless still high. Most investors are consolidating their balance sheets and seem unlikely to increase significantly their exposures to emerging markets before year-end at the earliest. At the same time, external financing needs of emerging market economies are relatively heavy in the last quarter of 1998, as shown by the Eurobond maturity profile (Figure 2.1). Moreover, it is possible that the

---

[1]The Annex contains an analysis of the impact of recent financial market turbulence in selected emerging market banking systems.

[2]Also, in the last week of October 1998, international emerging market funds enjoyed their largest inflow since the beginning of April 1998.

**Figure 2.1. Emerging Markets:
Maturing Eurobonds[1]**
(Billions of U.S. dollars)

Maturing Eurobonds are relatively large in the last quarter of 1998.

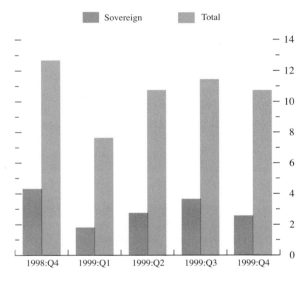

[1]Maturing Eurobonds for 1999 are IMF staff projections.

shrinkage of the investor base, including banks with an appetite for emerging market risk, has not yet run its full course. In particular, the ongoing retreat of the Japanese banks from overseas operations may have a strong impact on the Asian region, where they held an exposure of more than $100 billion in December 1997. Furthermore, a number of emerging market countries have had their credit ratings downgraded since June, and none had been upgraded in the period through October (Table 2.1). Market participants are also closely monitoring the implementation of the Brazilian package and will be waiting for clear signals of its full implementation. Finally, although a string of successful sovereign debt issues could restore capital market confidence by early next year, private sector issuance typically takes longer to return to normalcy.

Russia's Financial Crisis

The Russian financial crisis had its origins in the stubbornly large fiscal deficit and the associated increase in holdings of Russian government debt by domestic and foreign investors. The Russian government was relatively successful in selling GKOs/ OFZs[3] until late 1997, with nonresident investors holding about one-third of domestic treasury securities (with a value of about $20 billion at the prevailing exchange rate) by May 1998. However, a series of domestic political events and external shocks (including weak oil prices) in the first half of 1998 led to increased difficulties in selling ruble-denominated debt. As yields on ruble-denominated securities rose, the authorities increased their issuance of U.S. dollar-denominated Eurobonds—including two large issues in June—albeit at successively higher interest rates. By midyear it was clear that the government faced a marked bunching of amortizations in the treasury bill market during the second half of 1998, with GKO/ OFZ redemptions and coupon payments averaging somewhat over $1 billion a week through May 1999 (Figure 2.2). An attempt in July to stretch the maturity structure of the debt in the context of an IMF program and a voluntary domestic debt restructuring failed to restore market confidence, in part because only a relatively modest stock of debt was involved.[4] As investor confidence fell, selling pressures mounted in debt, equity, and foreign exchange markets, and liquidity dried up in the interbank market as fears of bank failures led to deposit withdrawals from banks. In addition, pressure on the ruble was aggravated

---

[3]GKOs are ruble-denominated discount instruments, and OFZs are ruble-denominated coupon bonds; both are issued by Russia's Ministry of Finance.

[4]As part of this debt exchange, the Russian government converted about $4.4 billion of GKOs into 7- and 20-year dollar-denominated Eurobonds. Market analysts have suggested that nonresidents accounted for about 45 percent of the transaction.

Table 2.1. Sovereign Credit Ratings of Emerging Market Borrowers

	Moody's		S&P		Fitch IBCA	
	June 1998	Oct. 1998	June 1998	Oct. 1998	June 1998	Oct. 1998
Africa						
Mauritius	Baa2	Baa2	NR	NR	NR	NR
Morocco	Ba1	Ba1	BB	BB	NR	NR
South Africa	Baa3	Baa3 ◆	BB+	BB+	BB	BB
Tunisia	Baa3	Baa3	BBB−	BBB−	BBB−	BBB−
Asia						
China	A3	A3	BBB+	BBB+	A−	A−
Hong Kong SAR	A3	A3	A+	A ▼	A+	A+
India	Ba2	Ba2	BB+	BB ▼	NR	NR
Indonesia	B3	B3	CCC+	CCC+	B−	B−
Korea	Ba1	Ba1	BB+	BB+ ◆	BB+	BB+
Malaysia	A2	Baa3 ▼	A−	BBB− ▼	NR	BB
Pakistan	B3	Caa1 ▼	B−	CCC− ▼	NR	NR
Philippines	Ba1	Ba1	BB+	BB+	NR	NR
Singapore	Aa1	Aa1	AAA	AAA	NR	NR
Taiwan Province of China	Aa3	Aa3	AA+	AA+	NR	NR
Thailand	Ba1	Ba1	BBB−	BBB−	BB+	BB+
Vietnam	B1	B1	NR	NR	NR	NR
Europe						
Bulgaria	B2	B2	NR	NR	NR	B+
Croatia	Baa3	Baa3	BBB−	BBB−	BBB−	BBB−
Cyprus	A2	A2	AA−	AA−	NR	NR
Czech Republic	Baa1	Baa1	A	A	BBB+	BBB+
Estonia	Baa1	Baa1	BBB+	BBB+ ◆	BBB	BBB
Hungary	Baa2	Baa2	BBB−	BBB− ◆	BBB	BBB
Kazakhstan	Ba3	Ba3	BB−	B+ ▼	BB	BB
Latvia	Baa2	Baa2	BBB	BBB ◆	BBB	BBB
Lithuania	Ba1	Ba1	BBB−	BBB− ◆	BB+	BB+
Malta	A3	A3	A+	A+	A	A
Moldova	Ba2	B2 ▼	NR	NR	NR	B
Poland	Baa3	Baa3	BBB−	BBB− ◆	BBB	BBB
Romania	Ba3	B1 ▼	B+	B− ▼	BB−	BB−
Russia	B1	B3 ▼	B+	CCC− ▼	BB	CCC ▼
Slovak Republic	Ba1	Ba1	BBB−	BB+ ▼	BBB−	BBB− ▼◆
Slovenia	A3	A3	A	A	A−	A− ◆
Turkey	B1	B1	B	B	B+	B+
Turkmenistan	B2	B2	NR	NR	B	B
Ukraine	B2	B3 ▼	NR	NR	NR	NR
Middle East						
Bahrain	Ba1	Ba1	NR	NR	NR	NR
Egypt	Ba1	Ba1	BBB−	BBB−	BBB−	BBB− ◆
Israel	A3	A3	A−	A−	A−	A−
Jordan	Ba3	Ba3	BB−	BB−	NR	NR
Kuwait	Baa1	Baa1	A	A	A	A
Lebanon	B1	B1	BB−	BB−	BB−	BB−
Oman	Baa2	Baa2	BBB−	BBB−	NR	NR
Qatar	Baa2	Baa2	BBB	BBB	NR	NR
Saudi Arabia	Baa3	Baa3	NR	NR	NR	NR
United Arab Emirates	A2	A2	NR	NR	NR	NR

(Table continues on next page.)

when Russian banks had to meet margin calls on their foreign currency debt-repurchase operations with foreign counterparts.[5]

On August 17, the Russian government announced a package of measures designed to deal with the currency, debt, and banking crises. The exchange rate band was devalued (and later abandoned),[6] a 90-day moratorium was placed on principal payments on private external obligations (including payments on forward contracts), and it was announced that a compulsory restructuring of the domestic government debt would

---

[5]Repurchase agreements are essentially a short-term loan to the seller, with securities used as collateral. As the value of a security falls, margin calls are triggered.

[6]The band was initially devalued from Rub 5.3–7.1 per dollar to Rub 6.0–9.5 per dollar on August 17. However, amid the economic and political turmoil and central bank credit expansion, the market exchange rate depreciated through the Rub 9.5 level on August 26.

Table 2.1 *(concluded)*

	Moody's		S&P		Fitch IBCA	
	June 1998	Oct. 1998	June 1998	Oct. 1998	June 1998	Oct. 1998
Western Hemisphere						
Argentina	Ba3	Ba3	BB	BB	BB	BB
Bahamas	A3	A3	NR	NR	NR	NR
Barbados	Ba1	Ba1	NR	NR	NR	NR
Bermuda	Aa1	Aa1	AA	AA	AA	AA
Brazil	B1	B2 ▼	BB−	BB−	B+	B+
Bolivia	B1	B1	BB−	BB−	NR	NR
Chile	Baa1	Baa1	A−	A− ◆	A−	A−
Colombia	Baa3	Baa3	BBB−	BBB−	NR	NR
Costa Rica	Ba1	Ba1	BB	BB	NR	NR
Dominican Republic	B1	B1	B+	B+ ▼◆	NR	NR
Ecuador	B1	B3 ▼	NR	NR	NR	NR
El Salvador	Baa3	Baa3	BB	BB	NR	NR
Guatemala	Ba2	Ba2	NR	NR	NR	NR
Honduras	NR	B2	NR	NR	NR	NR
Jamaica	Ba3	Ba3	NR	NR	NR	NR
Mexico	Ba2	Ba2	BB	BB ◆	BB	BB
Nicaragua	B2	B2	NR	NR	NR	NR
Panama	Baa1	Baa1	BB+	BB+	NR	NR
Paraguay	NR	NR	BB−	BB−	NR	NR
Peru	Ba3	Ba3	BB	BB	NR	NR
Trinidad and Tobago	Ba1	Ba1	BB+	BB+	NR	NR
Uruguay	Baa3	Baa3	BBB−	BBB− ◆	BBB−	BBB−
Venezuela	Ba2	B2 ▼	B+	B+	BB−	BB−

Sources: Fitch IBCA; Moody's; and Standard & Poor's.

	Moody's[1]	S&P and IBCA
Investment grade	Aaa, Aa, A, Baa	AAA, AA+, AA, AA−, A+, A, A−, BBB+, BBB, BBB−
Noninvestment grade	Ba, B	BB+, BB, BB−, B+, B, B−
Default grade	Caa, Ca, C, D	CCC+, CCC, CCC−, CC, C

[1]In addition, numbers from 1 (highest) to 3 are often attached to differentiate borrowers within a given grade.

▲ Upgrade.
▼ Downgrade.
▲● Under review for upgrade.
▼● Under review for downgrade.
◆ Confirmed.
▲◆ Positive outlook.
▼◆ Negative outlook.

take place. The details on the debt restructuring were announced the following week, and they provided domestic debt holders with two options—entailing 5 percent of the bond principal paid in cash, with the rest converted into either ruble-denominated bonds or U.S. dollar-denominated bonds, with coupons substantially lower than prevailing market rates. Trading of GKOs and OFZs has been suspended since the restructuring was announced, but some market analysts estimated the value of the restructuring package at around 20 cents per U.S. dollar of original debt, and have revised this valuation down as the ruble has depreciated further.

The freezing of the GKO/OFZ market and the ruble's subsequent depreciation (by more than 60 percent during the last two weeks of August) caused severe liquidity problems for the domestic banking system and paralyzed the payment system. Domestic banks held $27 billion of government securities (at face value) at the time of the moratorium, and many of them had borrowed abroad to finance the purchases.

Total on-balance-sheet external liabilities of commercial banks amounted to $19 billion (of which $16 billion had maturities of less than one year) and off-balance-sheet liabilities—mostly U.S. dollar forward and nondeliverable forward (NDF) contracts with non-residents—were estimated to be at least $10 billion.[7] By mid-September, the Central Bank of Russia took control of the two largest private banks—SBS Agro Bank and Inkombank—and ordered them and other banks to offer clients the option of moving their deposits to the state-controlled Sberbank.

An agreement between the Russian authorities and foreign creditors on the GKO/OFZ restructuring has not been reached yet, and discussions are ongoing. The authorities have nevertheless approved a plan to restructure the debt, but several issues remain outstand-

---

[7]See Fitch IBCA Sovereign Comment, "Russia and Its Creditors" (London: September 1998).

ing. According to the authorities' plan, debt holders would receive a new ruble-denominated liability with 10 percent paid in cash during the first year, 20 percent paid in the form of securities that could be tendered for equity in Russian banks or used to pay tax arrears, and the remaining 70 percent paid in OFZs with step-down coupons starting at 30 percent and declining to 10 percent. The provisions for converting rubles to dollars and other details of the plan remain unclear.

Russia faces heavy official external debt-service obligations, amounting to some $20 billion over the next 14 months (see Figure 2.2, lower panel), and the authorities have warned that the country might be unable to service its foreign debt in the near future. Russia's current external debt is estimated at around $160 billion, with about half of the total consisting of debt inherited from the Soviet Union that has already been restructured. Russian officials have suggested that priority might be given to maintaining payments on post-Soviet debt and have indicated to the Paris and London Clubs their intentions to request a rescheduling of Soviet-era debt service, which amounts to about $8.7 billion in 1999. The post-Soviet debt includes $26 billion owed to the IMF ($19 billion) and other international financial institutions, $9 billion owed to foreign governments, $16 billion in Eurobonds, and less than $0.5 billion to commercial creditors. Market analysts regard the Eurobonds as the least likely candidates for restructuring, since the interest payments due in 1998 on them are only about $1.6–1.7 billion (or 10 percent of debt service) and negotiating a restructuring of Eurobonds would be especially difficult. Nonetheless, current market valuations of the Eurobonds—which have yield spreads of 45–60 percent—imply that investors are still concerned with potential defaults.

Deleveraging and the Terms and Conditions of Market Access

The financial market turmoil that followed the Russian debt restructuring led to a sharp deterioration in the terms and conditions under which many emerging market economies could access global financial markets. As a result, issuance of new emerging market debt and equity instruments virtually collapsed in the period July–October 1998.

One key issue raised by the recent financial market turbulence is why the announcement of Russia's forced debt restructuring, and to a lesser extent Malaysia's imposition of capital controls (Box 2.1), had such a dramatic effect on emerging market economies' access to global financial markets. It is difficult to attribute the extent of the financial market turbulence either to the scale of Russia's activities in global financial markets or to the relative size of Russia's domestic financial markets. For example, Russia's external debt just before the forced debt restructuring amounted to about

Figure 2.2. Russia: Federal Government Domestic and External Debt

Russia faces a heavy debt-redemption schedule in 1998 and 1999.

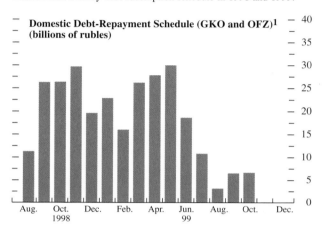

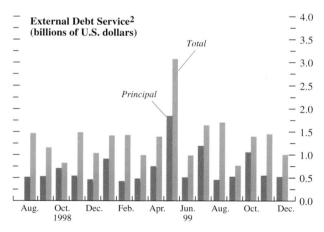

Source: Russia, Ministry of Finance.
[1]As of August 14, 1998.
[2]Includes IMF repurchases and the total of Minfin bonds and excludes payments to nonresidents on GKO-OFZs. GKOs are ruble-denominated discount instruments, and OFZs are ruble-denominated coupon bonds; both are issued by Russia's Ministry of Finance.

Box 2.1. Malaysia's Capital Controls

On September 1, 1998, Malaysia imposed capital controls to try to insulate the domestic economy from international financial volatility, to curb capital flight and speculation against the ringgit, and to eliminate offshore transactions in the domestic currency. Bank Negara Malaysia announced that proceeds from the sale or maturing of local currency securities must be placed in local currency deposits for one year from the date of the transaction and cannot be converted into foreign exchange. In addition, domestic credit to nonresident banks and brokers was prohibited, and general payments and transfers between external accounts now require official approval for any amount. Domestic residents cannot invest abroad more than M$10,000 without official approval. These measures do not contravene Malaysia's commitments under the IMF's Article VIII and they differentiate foreign direct investment from portfolio investment. Foreign direct investors are free to repatriate interest, dividends, capital gains, and capital at any time. On September 2, 1998, the Malaysian currency was also fixed to the U.S. dollar at a rate of M$3.8/US$1.

The forced liquidation of swap positions and repatriation of offshore ringgit accounts at below-market rates caused severe disruptions in offshore markets—especially in Singapore, where most offshore ringgit trading had taken place.[1] Market participants report that losses attributable to the forced liquidation of outstanding ringgit swaps varied depending on the nature of counterparties. Positions booked with onshore counterparties lost the most, since they were reportedly settled using a yield curve with implied ringgit interest rates similar to U.S. rates, whereas actual ringgit interest rates were at much higher levels before the imposition of controls. Positions booked with offshore counterparties suffered smaller losses, since international banks agreed to liquidate their exposures based on the forward exchange rates quoted just before the imposition of controls.

Despite explicit assurances from other countries that controls would not be imposed, Malaysia's actions prompted international banks and securities houses to re-examine their exposure throughout the region. International institutions focused specifically on swap exposures to onshore institutions in Indonesia, Thailand, Korea, and Hong Kong SAR. As a result of losses in Malaysia, derivatives exposures were separated into those held with offshore institutions and those held with onshore institutions, and international banks started unwinding the latter.

---

[1]The Labuan International Offshore Center was directly affected by the September measures because licensed offshore banks were no longer allowed to trade in ringgit instruments.

$160 billion. However, this was equivalent to only one-third of the combined external debts at the end of 1996 of the five Asian countries (Asian-5) most affected in the early stages of the current crisis, and just 8 percent of emerging markets' total external debts. Similarly, the exposure of BIS reporting-area banks to Russia at the end of 1997 was 28 percent of their exposure to the Asian-5 countries (Table 2.2). Moreover, Russia accounted for just over 3 percent of the total international loan commitments and issuance of international bonds and equities by emerging markets in the period from 1992 to end-June 1998.

A more important consideration is that the events in Russia and Malaysia highlighted the perceived vulnerability of even hedged local currency positions to counterparty default and convertibility risk and led to a fundamental reassessment by many investors of the attractiveness of holding emerging market instruments. Moreover, as discussed in Chapter III, a reassessment of the risks associated with holding "high-yield" instruments in mature markets was evident even prior to the Russian debt restructuring. This was reflected in both a decline in equity prices and a widening of the interest rate spreads between high-yield corporate bonds and U.S. treasury bonds. Nonetheless, this reassessment of risks and adjustment of portfolio positions accelerated in the second half of August as a result of both the losses incurred by some highly leveraged investors on their holdings of Russian securities and by the portfolio adjustments required by the risk management systems employed in many commercial and investment banks when asset price volatility increases sharply.

A number of hedge funds with large holdings of Russian securities suffered large losses as they were forced to mark down the value of these securities, and several of these funds were dissolved. The failures, as well as the higher asset price volatility that followed the Russian debt restructuring, led creditor banks to demand that hedge funds meet higher margin requirements on many of their transactions. This situation deteriorated even further once the difficulties confronting Long-Term Capital Management (LTCM) emerged (see Chapter III). At the same time, the internal risk management systems in place at the proprietary trading desks in large commercial and investment banks required that higher asset price volatility be accompanied by higher capital charges against trading activities, reductions in trading positions in assets whose perceived price volatility had increased, or both.[8] Market participants report that in most cases the

---

[8]See David Folkerts-Landau and Peter Garber, "Capital Flows from Emerging Markets in a Closing Environment" (London: Deutsche Bank Research, Global Emerging Markets, October 1998).

Table 2.2. Russia in International Capital Markets

(Billions of U.S. dollars)

	Total External Debt[1] (end-1996)	International Bank Lending[2] (end-1997)	Total Gross Financing[3] (1992–June 1998)	Stock Market Capitalization[4] (June 1998)
Emerging markets	2,095	897	1,037	1,922
Russia	125	72	33	53
Asian-5	459	259	251	175
Indonesia	129	58	51	13
Korea	158	94	92	44
Malaysia	40	28	33	67
Philippines	41	20	22	29
Thailand	91	59	53	22

[1]World Bank, *Global Development Finance* (Washington).

[2]Bank for International Settlements (BIS), *The Maturity, Sectoral and Nationality Distribution of International Bank Lending* (Basle).

[3]IMF staff calculations.

[4]International Finance Corporation (IFC), *Emerging Markets Database* (Washington). The figure for emerging markets includes only the group of countries covered by the IFC.

decision was made to reduce trading positions. This combination of higher internal and external margin calls sharply increased the liquidity needs of many institutional investors, which they attempted to meet, in part, through a broad sell-off of emerging market securities, thereby creating a major channel of contagion from Russia to other emerging markets, particularly Brazil.

The abrupt deleveraging of the financial positions and trading activities of hedge funds and the proprietary trading desks of commercial and investment banks had such a pronounced effect on the terms and conditions of market access because these institutions have increasingly taken on the role of "investors of last resort" in emerging markets instruments. As noted in recent *International Capital Markets* reports, a new set of institutional investors (for example, mutual funds, pension funds, and insurance companies) began to invest in emerging market securities in the mid-1990s as the credit ratings of a growing number of emerging markets reached "investment grade" levels (Baa for Moody's and BBB⁻ for Standard and Poor's). However, as the credit ratings of a number of emerging market economies declined below investment grade from July 1997, these new institutional investors either sharply reduced their purchases of emerging market securities or eliminated their holdings.[9] As a result, the proprietary trading desks of commercial and investment banks and hedge funds became the dominant institutional investors in emerging market securities. The reduction in new issuance activity and the large-scale price movements experienced by all classes of emerging market securities in the period fol-

lowing the Russian debt moratorium reflected, to an important degree, the efforts of even these "investors of last resort" to scale back their holdings of emerging market instruments.

The effects of the deleveraging of institutional investors' financial positions, as well as the ongoing withdrawal of commercial bank lending, were evident in all secondary and primary markets for emerging market instruments.

Emerging Bond Markets

Secondary Markets

In the secondary markets for emerging market bonds, interest rate spreads on J.P. Morgan's Emerging Market Bond Index (EMBI) rose as high as 1,705 basis points on September 10—a level not witnessed since the period surrounding the Mexican crisis of 1995—in response to concerns that the Russian crisis would spill over and affect Brazil and other emerging market countries (Figure 2.3). As a result of these concerns, the markets for Latin American Brady bonds were the most seriously affected; and market participants reported that, at some points in early September, the only significant buyers of Argentine, Brazilian, and Venezuelan Brady bonds were institutions residing in these countries.[10] In the Eurobond markets, spreads widened across the board (Figure 2.4). By the second week of November, however, the EMBI yield spread had declined to about 1,100 basis points, with a corresponding decline in Eurobond yield spreads.

---

[9]In the United States, for example, if securities are downgraded below investment grade, pension funds are obligated, by law, to remove these securities from their portfolios.

[10]Argentina bought back $700 million of par bonds in September, while Venezuela purchased an unspecified amount and Brazilian buyers were reportedly active during late August and early September.

Figure 2.3. Secondary Market Bond Spreads and Equity Market Returns

The sell-off in emerging market securities caused a sharp widening of bond interest and bid-ask spreads.

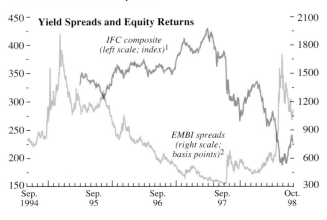

Yield Spreads and Equity Returns

IFC composite (left scale; index)[1]

EMBI spreads (right scale; basis points)[2]

■ Before Russian crisis *(May 1–August 14, 1998)* ■ After Russian crisis *(August 17–November 10, 1998)*

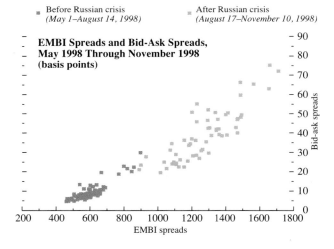

EMBI Spreads and Bid-Ask Spreads, May 1998 Through November 1998 (basis points)

EMBI spreads

Bid-ask spreads

Sources: Bloomberg Financial Markets, LP; and J.P. Morgan.
[1]International Finance Corporation's (IFC) Investable Total Return Composite Index.
[2]J.P. Morgan's Emerging Market Bond Index (EMBI) spread relative to the theoretical U.S. zero-coupon yield curve.

Nonetheless, these spreads remain well above those prior to the Russian debt-service moratorium. Market participants attribute this reduction in interest rate spreads to an easing of monetary policies in a number of mature markets, the completion of the portfolio adjustments of a number of highly leveraged institutional investors, a general recognition that market prices had overestimated default probabilities for many emerging markets in the immediate aftermath of the Russian debt restructuring, and the prospect of official support for Brazil.

The flight to quality also produced a dramatic reduction in liquidity in emerging bond markets, as reflected in much higher bid-ask spreads and reduced trading volumes. As spreads in the Brady bond markets rose to the 1,700 basis points, bid-ask spreads on the EMBI tripled to 60–80 basis points—compared with the 10 to 20 basis points evident in the period prior to the crisis (see Figure 2.3, lower panel). Preliminary data from the Emerging Markets Traders Association also show a 28 percent reduction in the value of emerging market debt traded during the third quarter of 1998, compared with the second quarter (Table 2.3). The reduction in trading volume was particularly large for Mexican, Philippine, and Korean securities. Market participants report that the reduction in volumes was even stronger in October, with, for instance, Brazilian C-Bonds recording trading volumes of $200–250 million a day, compared with $3 billion a day before the Russian crisis.

New Issues

As interest rate spreads confronting emerging market issuers widened sharply, international bond issuance by emerging markets plummeted in the third quarter of 1998—falling to $14 billion, half the volume reached in the second quarter, with July issuance accounting for almost the entire volume and only a single issue in September (Table 2.4). This negative trend was particularly pronounced for Asia, where issuance virtually dried up. During the third quarter, Latin American bond placements declined by slightly more than half over the previous quarter, to reach $5 billion, while European borrowers (excluding Russia) fared similarly. In the case of Russia, the high third-quarter issuance ($6.4 billion in par value terms, but less in market value terms) reflected the July exchange of domestic GKOs for 7- and 20-year Eurobonds, in an attempt to reduce the rollover risk on domestic debt.

In October, bond issuance picked up slightly from the year's low of $350 million in September to reach $1.2 billion. However, this is still far below the $9.4 billion monthly average for the period January through July 1998. Issuance remained subdued in the first ten days of November—with just four bonds sold, for a total amount of $935 million.

Emerging Equity Markets

Secondary Markets

The emergence of debt-servicing difficulties for Russia accelerated the decline in emerging markets equity prices that had been evident since the summer. As a result, the IFC Investable (IFCI) Composite declined 21.7 percent in the third quarter, reflecting a 7.6 percent loss in the Asia index and a 26.6 percent decline in the Latin America index (Figure 2.5). In Latin America, the Brazilian and Venezuelan bourses were among the hardest hit. The Argentine stock market was the best-performing market in the region. In Asia, the Philippines and Singapore stock indices fell most, while the Thai index posted the only positive return. In other markets, the Russian index closed 75 percent lower in U.S. dollar terms than at end-June, while the index for Turkey fell 45 percent. The IFCI index began to recover in September, posting gains of 4.7 and 11.5 percent, respectively, in September and October, and a further increase of 1.9 percent in the first two weeks of November. Asian shares rebounded by 17.9 percent in October, with market participants attributing the improvement to positive external developments (in particular, the recovery of the yen), improved market liquidity, and the likely bottom in the earnings cycle for corporates, as signs of an output recovery became apparent in some markets. The Hong Kong SAR market continued the strongest recovery in the region, supported in part by official intervention in August and subsequently by other domestic and external developments (Box 2.2, page 30).

New Issues

International equity issuance came to a virtual standstill after the Russian crisis, declining from $3.7 billion in the second quarter to $239 million in the third quarter—with no placements in the period from July through October. In the week of November 9, the Polish government completed the initial phase of what will be the largest share offering ever for a Polish company and sold $622 million of shares of the national telecom operator TPSA in international markets, which was seen as a signal that investors were reentering the central and eastern European markets and consolidating the separation of Russian and non-Russian risk in the region.

Syndicated Lending

The decline in international bank lending to emerging markets that has been evident since the second quarter of 1998 accelerated in the period surrounding the Russian crisis and has continued despite the modest recoveries evident in emerging bond and equity markets in October. Loan commitments to emerging

Figure 2.4. Secondary Market Yield Spreads on U.S. Dollar-Denominated Eurobonds by Selected Emerging Markets[1]
(Basis points)

The events in Russia led to an across-the-board widening of secondary market yield spreads.

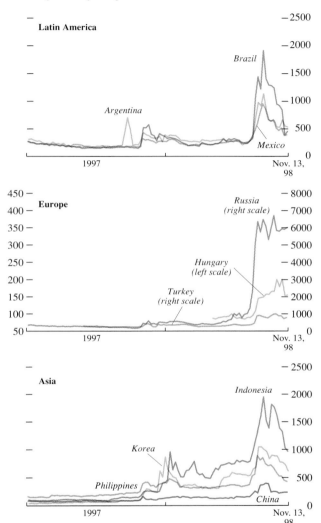

Source: Bloomberg Financial Markets, LP.

[1]Latin America: Republic of Argentina bond due December 2003, United Mexican States bond due September 2002, and Republic of Brazil bond due November 2001. Europe: National Bank of Hungary bond due April 2003, Republic of Turkey bond due May 2002, and Ministry of Finance of Russia bond due November 2001. Asia: People's Republic of China bond due November 2003, Republic of Indonesia bond due August 2006, Republic of Philippines bond due October 2016, and Korea Development Bank bond due November 2003.

Table 2.3. Emerging Markets' Debt Trading Volume[1]

(Billions of U.S. dollars)

	1998:Q3	1998:Q2	1997:Q3	Percent Change 1998:Q3 vs. 1998:Q2	Percent Change 1998:Q3 vs. 1997:Q3
Emerging markets	1,007.1	1,391.0	1,322.6	−27.6	−23.8
Latin America and Caribbean	669.7	933.2	1,014.9	−28.2	−34.0
Argentina	152.4	183.3	312.8	−16.9	−51.3
Brady bonds	66.4	69.3	135.6	−4.2	−51.0
Sovereign non-Brady bonds	48.6	51.6	80.9	−5.7	−39.9
Local instruments	23.0	36.8	57.3	−37.6	−59.9
Brazil	322.0	419.8	333.0	−23.3	−3.3
Brady bonds	237.6	286.7	204.3	−17.1	16.3
Sovereign non-Brady bonds	12.2	30.5	46.2	−59.9	−73.5
Local instruments	36.5	41.7	33.1	−12.4	10.2
Mexico	124.8	230.7	228.9	−45.9	−45.5
Brady bonds	16.7	29.4	42.0	−43.0	−60.2
Sovereign non-Brady bonds	36.4	42.7	65.7	−14.8	−44.7
Local instruments	57.8	136.8	77.0	−57.7	−24.9
Venezuela	47.5	53.1	78.3	−10.6	−39.4
Eastern Europe	245.5	292.8	218.6	−16.2	12.3
Bulgaria	7.9	10.5	25.4	−24.6	−68.9
Poland	23.4	31.3	14.7	−25.1	59.1
Russia	207.5	241.7	172.2	−14.1	20.5
Africa	27.6	69.1	52.0	−60.0	−46.9
Middle East	25.0	37.0	12.9	−32.3	94.1
Asia	39.0	56.0	23.7	−30.4	64.4
Hong Kong SAR	13.3	9.6	5.9	38.3	126.3
Philippines	2.6	6.3	5.9	−58.1	−55.3
Korea	16.5	26.9	2.9	−38.7	475.4
Multinational institutions	0.4	2.9	0.3	−87.7	5.9

Source: Emerging Markets Traders Association.
[1]Preliminary figures.

markets declined to $14.1 billion in the third quarter from $18.1 billion in the second quarter of 1998 (Table 2.4).[11] Asian borrowing declined only slightly to $4.5 billion, from $4.8 billion in the second quarter, but this level is still less than one-third of precrisis levels. Lending to entities in Europe and the Western Hemisphere declined more sharply (to $1.8 and $3.9 billion, from $3.4 and $8.5 billion in the second quarter, respectively), with an increase in lending to entities in the Middle East. The latter, however, was due to a $2.6 billion loan extended to the Saudi Arabian Oil Company. Activity in the syndicated loan market fell to around $2 billion in October. Market commentaries attribute this decline in syndicated lending to emerging markets to a number of factors, including the perception that the credit and transfer risks associated with such lending have increased, and the weak financial position of Japanese banks, which have reduced their lending capacity.

---

[11]Figures published by the BIS provide further evidence of the decline in syndicated lending, with the total syndicated loan volume dropping by 23 percent (to $204 billion) in the third quarter of 1998, relative to the second quarter.

Net Capital Flows to Emerging Markets

While data on the issuance of bonds and equities, as well as commitments on syndicated loans (Table 2.4), provide one indicator of the scale of emerging markets' access to global financial markets that is available with short reporting lags, there are other important capital flows that influence the overall net resources transferred to emerging markets. First, large amounts of maturing external debt can make the picture of net capital flows look much different from that implied by gross inflows. Moreover, issuance data exclude foreign direct investment flows, which accounted for 40 percent of net capital inflows to emerging markets in 1990–96, compared with 39 percent from portfolio investment and 21 percent from bank lending.[12] Foreign direct investment flows were quite resilient after the Mexican crisis of 1994–95. Finally, the data exclude official flows, which exceeded $40 billion in 1997 and are likely to do so again in 1998. Despite these limitations, however, there has been a high degree of correlation between the gross flows as-

---

[12]See 1997 *International Capital Markets* report.

Table 2.4. Emerging Market Bond Issues, Equity Issues, and Loan Commitments

(Millions of U.S. dollars)

	1994	1995	1996	1997	1997 Q1	Q2	Q3	Q4	1998 Q1	Q2	Q3	Sept.	Oct.	Nov. 1–15
Total issuance	**136,268**	**157,848**	**218,427**	**286,357**	**56,168**	**87,165**	**84,836**	**58,188**	**39,534**	**50,259**	**28,452**	**6,916**	**3,287**	**2,184**
							Issuance							
Bond issues[1]														
Emerging markets	**56,540**	**57,619**	**101,926**	**128,142**	**27,723**	**42,977**	**45,035**	**12,407**	**25,343**	**27,995**	**14,091**	**350**	**1,256**	**935**
Africa	2,116	1,947	1,648	9,358	0	1,022	6,898	1,438	1,381	0	0	0	0	0
Asia	29,897	25,307	43,144	45,532	12,748	15,892	14,176	2,716	2,743	6,653	318	0	372	0
Europe	3,543	6,583	7,408	16,217	2,824	6,538	3,726	3,129	5,437	8,084	7,954	0	153	561
Middle East	2,993	710	2,570	2,671	275	798	273	1,325	1,000	0	750	350	175	0
Western Hemisphere	17,990	23,071	47,157	54,365	11,876	18,727	19,962	3,800	14,738	13,259	5,069	0	556	374
Loan commitments[2]														
Emerging markets	**56,979**	**82,972**	**90,729**	**123,398**	**23,294**	**32,718**	**29,878**	**37,508**	**10,973**	**18,072**	**14,122**	**6,566**	**2,031**	**627**
Africa	672	6,783	3,183	4,557	1,007	427	717	2,406	170	351	0	0	440	0
Asia	38,118	46,707	56,200	58,933	14,940	15,614	16,231	12,148	2,521	4,848	4,508	2,523	710	157
Europe	7,004	9,644	12,576	18,300	1,139	5,989	3,777	7,395	1,361	3,440	1,803	573	276	345
Middle East	7,670	7,707	6,465	10,755	1,436	1,693	1,510	6,116	0	896	3,957	3,437	100	0
Western Hemisphere	3,516	12,131	12,304	30,853	4,772	8,994	7,644	9,443	6,922	8,536	3,854	33	505	125
Equity issues														
Emerging markets	**18,038**	**11,193**	**16,414**	**24,802**	**3,213**	**8,160**	**6,290**	**7,139**	**3,148**	**3,744**	**239**	**0**	**0**	**622**
Africa	574	542	781	1,118	0	330	788	0	534	352	11	0	0	0
Asia	12,130	8,864	9,789	13,240	2,873	3,526	2,181	4,660	1,730	1,923	0	0	0	0
Europe	641	570	1,289	2,945	166	1,180	400	1,199	713	982	82	0	0	622
Middle East	89	256	894	2,395	93	1,507	386	409	170	412	57	0	0	0
Western Hemisphere	4,604	962	3,661	5,102	80	1,617	2,534	871	0	74	90	0	0	0
							Facilities							
Fixed income[3]														
Emerging markets	**19,312**	**41,965**	**32,445**	**22,163**	**2,736**	**11,142**	**3,457**	**4,829**	**2,544**	**2,475**	**1,027**	**130**	**115**	**0**
Africa	1,600	400	500	0	0	0	0	0	0	1,000	0	0	0	0
Asia	4,951	23,270	19,137	15,036	651	8,740	3,217	2,429	44	440	993	130	115	0
Europe	1,003	5,668	680	1,812	85	527	0	1,200	0	35	34	0	0	0
Middle East	326	0	1,250	900	0	600	0	300	0	0	0	0	0	0
Western Hemisphere	11,432	12,627	10,878	4,415	2,000	1,275	240	900	2,500	1,000	0	0	0	0
Loan[4]														
Emerging markets	**22,621**	**33,966**	**44,153**	**71,575**	**14,360**	**21,013**	**17,814**	**18,388**	**3,984**	**12,760**	**7,164**	**3,161**	**475**	**0**
Africa	1,031	2,217	2,660	4,536	12	482	2,593	1,450	272	192	363	0	0	0
Asia	11,792	18,092	16,617	26,356	6,942	8,539	5,792	5,083	781	1,598	1,303	345	346	0
Europe	3,085	2,970	5,063	11,277	1,364	5,123	2,551	2,239	1,355	1,626	1,712	761	129	0
Middle East	319	2,977	1,140	3,204	416	1,147	1,208	432	61	2,766	1,230	500	0	0
Western Hemisphere	6,394	7,711	18,674	26,202	5,627	5,723	5,669	9,184	1,515	6,578	2,556	1,556	0	0

Source: IMF staff calculations; November 1998 figures are preliminary.

[1]Includes note issues under Euro medium-term note (EMTN) programs.

[2]Includes cofinancing and note issuance facilities, certificate of deposit programs, and commercial paper programs.

[3]Includes term, construction, mezzanine, and tax-spared loans.

[4]Includes revolving credits, bridge facilities, export/supplier/acceptance/buyer credits, and overdraft facilities.

27

Figure 2.5. Stock Market Total Return Indices

(IFC weekly investable indices, January 1997 = 100)

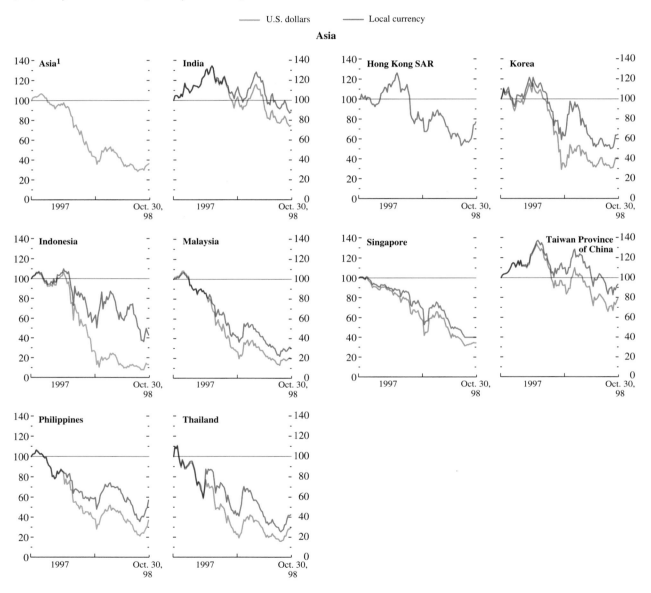

Figure 2.5 *(concluded)*

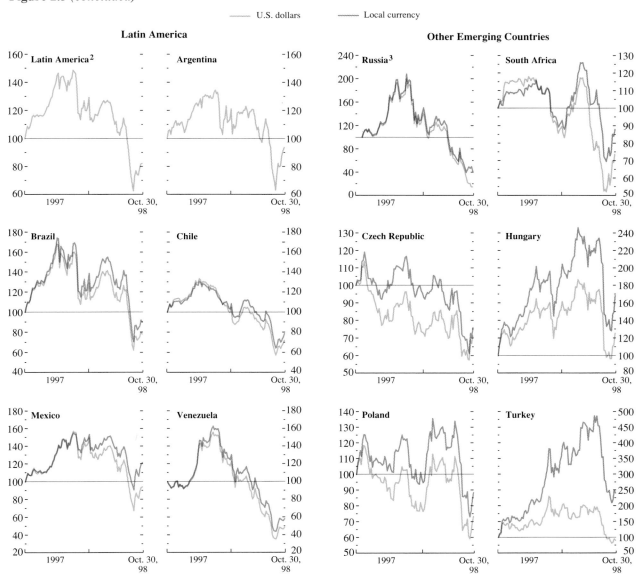

——— U.S. dollars ——— Local currency

Latin America

Other Emerging Countries

Sources: International Finance Corporation (IFC), Emerging Markets Database; Reuters; and WEFA, Inc.

[1]China, India, Indonesia, Korea, Malaysia, Pakistan, Philippines, Sri Lanka, Taiwan Province of China, and Thailand.

[2]Argentina, Brazil, Chile, Colombia, Mexico, Peru, and Venezuela.

[3]February 7, 1997 = 100.

Box 2.2. Hong Kong's Intervention in the Equity Spot and Futures Markets

In mid-August, 1998, the Hong Kong SAR dollar came under renewed speculative attack—the largest since October 1997—and the Hang Seng index was 56 percent lower than its peak in August 1997.[1] The authorities argued that the markets were being manipulated and that the stability and integrity of financial markets needed to be protected; therefore, they intervened in the equity spot and futures markets. Total intervention amounted to $15 billion, around 6 percent of stock market capitalization at end-August. Intervention in the equity spot and futures markets has since ceased, but the authorities have indicated that they do not rule out further action if manipulation reemerges.

Hedge funds and other speculators were reportedly following a "double play" strategy, which consisted of building up short positions on the equity spot and futures markets and then shorting the currency. Because of the currency board mechanism, the resulting pressure on the foreign exchange market would cause interest rates to rise. This would in turn reduce stock prices, allowing speculators to gain on their short positions on securities and futures markets. In contrast to events in October 1997, when speculators had to pay high interest rates to fund their short Hong Kong dollar positions, during the August 1998 attack the speculators had prefunded themselves at lower rates and apparently threatened to cause a serious market dislocation. The intervention succeeded in supporting the level of the Hong Kong stock market in August, and was followed by a sharp rebound in the market—aided by external developments, including the fall in U.S. interest rates.

In the first week of September, the authorities announced a series of measures aimed at improving liquidity management and strengthening market discipline in the equity spot and futures markets. Among the first set of measures, the Hong Kong Monetary Authority replaced the Liquidity Adjustment Facility with a discount window and removed restrictions on repeated repo transactions involving Exchange Fund Bills and Notes, to increase interbank liquidity and reduce interest rate volatility. The second set of measures included a number of regulatory changes aimed at increasing the cost of speculative activity and lessening the potential for market dislocation. The measures included an increase in margin requirements for investors holding large open positions in the futures markets, tighter enforcement of the T + 2 settlement rules, and increasing penalties for illegal short-selling. More recently, an independently managed company was established to manage the government's share holdings in a transparent and orderly manner.

[1]See the September 1998 *International Capital Markets* report for a description of the October 1997 turbulence in Hong Kong SAR.

sociated with new issuance of international bonds and equities and the syndicated loan commitments and the overall net flows (Figure 2.6).

Spillover Effects Among Emerging Markets: The Extent of Differentiation

The dramatic widening of interest rate spreads on emerging market bonds in September and October and reduced market access led investors and rating agencies to focus on the vulnerabilities facing emerging markets with large external refinancing needs or large stocks of short-term domestic debt. As a result, despite the sharp deterioration in the terms of market access confronting all emerging markets, there have been differences in the extent of the spillover from the Russian crisis among emerging market economies. Apart from the impact on neighboring countries, the spillovers from Russia were felt with most severity in those Latin American countries perceived as having the largest financing needs. Financial turbulence affected not only Brazil, but also Argentina, Chile, Colombia, Ecuador, Mexico, and Venezuela, where the pressures were felt, to varying degrees, in foreign exchange, bond, and equity markets. At the same time, market participants reported that bank credit lines were being cut to many countries in the region. In contrast, Asian emerging market economies were less affected, since their external financing needs were regarded as relatively small in view of the emergence of large current account surpluses in a number of the countries in the region. Similarly, most European emerging market economies were viewed as less vulnerable to an interruption of external finance than some of the Latin American countries, owing to smaller external financing needs, relatively low reliance on portfolio inflows, and the perception that the authorities in most countries have pursued sound macroeconomic policies.

In Latin America, the country most affected by events in Russia was Brazil, where pressures in domestic debt and foreign exchange markets began to build up during the second half of August. Despite the efforts of the Brazilian authorities and several market participants to differentiate Brazil's position from that of Russia, investor concerns focused on the large external financing requirements, the fiscal deficit of more than 7 percent of GDP, and the need to refinance domestic debt redemptions of more than $100 billion before the end of the year (Figure 2.7).[13] Nonetheless,

[13]In contrast to the situation in Russia, foreign residents held less than 7 percent of Brazil's official domestic debt, international reserves were above $70 billion in July, the banking system was relatively sound, and the country's economic team had earned a strong reputation among market participants in part because of their successful defense of the *real* after the October 1997 speculative attack (see September 1998 *International Capital Markets* report).

the sharp rise in emerging market interest rate spreads and the collapse of new issuance activity in the aftermath of the Russian crisis led many analysts to question whether Brazil could sustain both its existing fiscal position and its exchange rate arrangement. These concerns contributed to an acceleration of foreign exchange outflows (Figure 2.7, lower panel) in particular, through the floating foreign exchange market.[14]

To stem the loss of reserves, the Brazilian authorities adopted several measures to encourage capital inflows (including the elimination of the 15 percent income tax on foreign fixed-income investments), increased official interest rates to almost 50 percent, and subsequently announced several fiscal measures. These actions reduced but did not eliminate the pressures in domestic debt and foreign exchange markets. The treasury and the central bank canceled two domestic debt auctions in September. Auctions resumed later in the month and proceeded with reduced volumes. While the hike in interest rates led to a reduction in the daily average foreign exchange outflow to $500 million in the last three weeks of September, from levels of $1–2 billion in late August and early September (Figure 2.7, lower panel), the floating market continued to experience outflows significantly larger than the $50 million daily average over the previous two years. As a result, international reserves fell to $41.6 billion at the end of October, after having reached $70.9 billion in July.[15] By November, however, outflows through the floating-rate market fell to $90 million a day, and reserves stood at $41 billion at the end of the month.

To restore market confidence, the Brazilian authorities initiated a dialogue with the IMF, other multilaterals, and officials of the United States and other industrial country governments that resulted in an IMF-led financial package announced on November 13, 1998 (see Chapter I, Box 1.1). The announcement of the package was initially well received by financial markets, with a 14 percent increase in the stock market, a reduction of 100 basis points in Brazilian Brady bond yield spreads, and a further slowdown in foreign exchange outflows in the week immediately following. Market participants noted, however, that the key issues remained the implementation of the programmed fiscal measures and the rollover of the domestic debt and international claims, especially by banks. The implementation of fiscal

Figure 2.6. Private Capital Flows to Emerging Markets
(Billions of U.S. dollars)

There is a strong correlation between gross and net private capital flows since 1980.

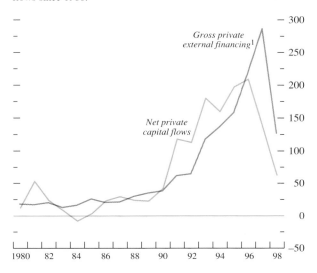

[1]Data for 1998 only up to November 13, 1998.

---

[14]Formally, Brazil has a dual exchange rate market that comprises a commercial and a tourist (or floating) exchange rate. Most current and capital account transactions are channeled through the commercial dollar market, and the floating foreign exchange market is the usual channel for domestic capital outflows. However, the floating rate is managed such that the spread between the two markets remains at around 0.5 percent.

[15]Notwithstanding the large loss in international reserves, Brazil had more than $6 billion in privatization-related capital inflows in October.

measures will influence, among other things, the speed at which domestic interest rates can be brought down and the impact of the program on economic activity. Other Latin American domestic currency markets also faced severe pressures in August and September, with interest rates soaring in some cases to extremely high levels (Figure 2.8). However, these pressures subsided in October and early November, in line with the reduced turbulence in global financial markets. In September, Argentina's short-term interest rates more than doubled from precrisis levels, although they still remained well below those in other Latin American countries, especially those that allowed for a greater degree of exchange rate flexibility. The Mexican peso depreciated by more than 12 percent between end-June and end-September, with short-term interest rates in Mexico doubling to 40 percent in September. The resulting higher refinancing costs prompted the Mexican authorities to cancel several government securities auctions and subsequently to concentrate on issuing short-term instruments. However, the pressures eased, and the Mexican peso appreciated more than 2 percent in October, while interest rates have fallen to around 30 percent.

In contrast to the situation in Latin America, Asian foreign exchange markets were relatively stable in the aftermath of Russia's crisis, supported in part by the strengthening of the yen and large current account surpluses. Moreover, interest rates in Korea, Malaysia, the Philippines, and Thailand generally declined to levels not seen since before the depreciation of the Thai baht in July 1997 (see Figure 2.8). The yen's recent strength, combined with interest rate cuts in the United States and other mature markets, have also contributed to a sharp reduction in interest rates in Hong Kong SAR. The Korean won appreciated in conjunction with interest rate declines into the summer, but later depreciated in September and early October and appreciated again to reach W 1,246 at end-November. The Thai baht and the Indonesian rupiah appreciated in September–October, and the latter was relatively resilient in early November amid political and social unrest.

While the Russian crisis brought central and eastern European and the Turkish currencies under pressure and regional stock markets tumbled, most countries in the region—with the exception perhaps of Turkey—are relatively insulated from the risk of portfolio capital outflows and their external financing needs are not viewed by market participants as that large.[16] Since trade and financial links to Russia are limited and the prospects of accession to the EU are widely seen as ensuring adequate policy responses to external pres-

Figure 2.7. Brazil: Domestic Debt and Foreign Exchange Flows

The need to roll over large amounts of domestic debt in September–November 1998 contributed to the pressures in foreign exchange and money markets.

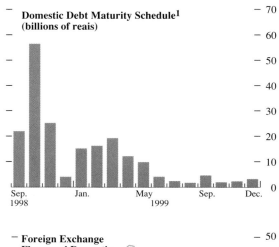

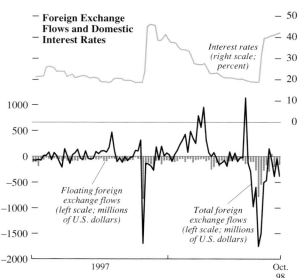

Sources: Brazil, Central Bank and Ministry of Finance.
[1]As of August 1998.

---

[16]Total portfolio funds invested in the Czech Republic and Hungary are estimated by market participants to be just over 50 percent of central bank reserves; in Poland they are around 15 percent.

Figure 2.8. Interest Rates, Exchange Rates, and Reserves

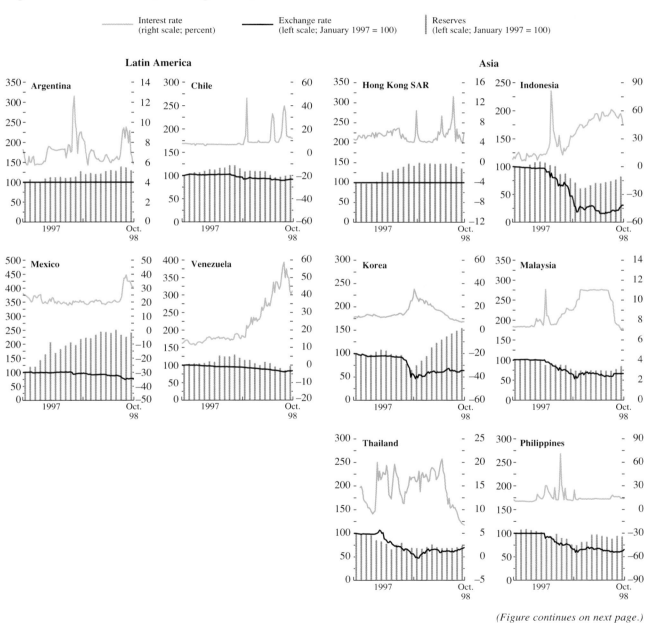

(Figure continues on next page.)

Figure 2.8 *(concluded)*

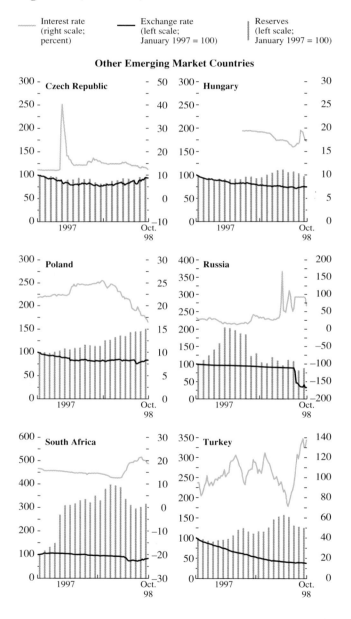

Interest rate	Exchange rate	Reserves
(right scale; percent)	(left scale; January 1997 = 100)	(left scale; January 1997 = 100)

Other Emerging Market Countries

Sources: Bloomberg Financial Markets, LP; IMF, *International Financial Statistics;* and IMF staff estimates.

sures, the capital account effects of emerging market turmoil in central and eastern Europe were much more muted than in other regions. Currencies in central Europe depreciated between 4 and 10 percent in the month after August 17, 1998, but have recovered since, albeit not to precrisis levels. Interest rates have also fallen (see Figure 2.8). Official reserves initially fell in Hungary, but the National Bank of Hungary responded by raising interest rates by 100 basis points, helping to calm the foreign exchange markets.

An exception to the modest spillover effects in Europe was Turkey, which experienced significant capital outflows in the aftermath of the Russian crisis as more than $4.5 billion of foreign funds invested in local fixed-income and equity markets left the country. The outflows caused domestic yields in Turkey to soar to 140 percent in late October, with large reserve losses being necessary to prevent the lira from falling below its devaluation path (see Figure 2.8). Treasury bill yields jumped above 150 percent after the political crisis in the second week of November, and reserves fell to some $20 billion, from $25 billion in mid-August 1998.

Between end-May and August, the South African *rand* depreciated by 20 percent against the U.S. dollar, but subsequently it has appreciated by nearly 13 percent (see Figure 2.8). Spot foreign exchange reserves and the South African Reserve Bank's forward foreign exchange positions have been fairly stable since end-July, after the monetary authority shifted toward a more flexible exchange rate policy.

III

Turbulence in Mature Financial Markets

Until July 1998, the mature financial markets in the United States and Europe remained buoyant, largely avoiding significant negative spillovers from the Asian crisis despite some episodes of increased volatility, most notably in October 1997.[1] Government bond yields continued to decline, while equity prices recorded further strong gains, especially in continental Europe, where markets surged in a number of countries by 45–65 percent over end-1997 levels. Favorable economic developments, including very subdued inflation, solid domestic demand growth in most countries, and increased confidence in a successful launch of EMU contributed to this market buoyancy.[2] In addition, the mature financial markets were boosted by a "flight to quality" as investors shifted funds away from Asia and other emerging markets. Despite these generally favorable developments, however, there were some signs of a weakening in sentiment in the months leading up to July 1998. Major stock market indices in the United States and the United Kingdom continued to advance, but the gains were increasingly narrowly based, and market indices for "small cap" stocks began to weaken. Also, yield spreads on below-investment-grade bonds in the United States widened by about 90 basis points from their historic lows reached in mid-1997 prior to the Asian crisis.[3] Elsewhere, equity markets and the exchange rate weakened further in Japan, where domestic economic conditions continued to worsen, and also came under downward pressure in countries with strong trade links to Asia or heavy reliance on commodity exports (notably, Canada, Australia, New Zealand, and Norway).

Equity markets in the United States and Europe generally peaked in mid-July. While it is difficult to identify a particular event that triggered the initial downturn, several factors may have led investors to reassess

---

[1]For details, see the September 1998 *International Capital Markets* report, Chapter IV.

[2]Initial positive effects of the Asian crisis on economic activity in the United States and Europe, including declines in inflation and interest rates and an associated boost to real incomes, may have contributed to a perception that negative spillovers from the crisis would be relatively limited. In addition, market participants generally viewed the prospect of a moderate slowdown in the United States as beneficial in terms of reducing overheating risks.

[3]This widening coincided with a general weakening in U.S. corporate earnings growth and an increase in the number of corporate credit rating downgrades relative to upgrades.

Figure 3.1. Major Industrial Countries: Stock Market Price Indices[1]
(National currency; week ending January 2, 1997 = 100)

Equity markets mostly peaked in mid-July before a sizable correction led by bank stocks; markets have since rebounded quite strongly, particularly in the United States.

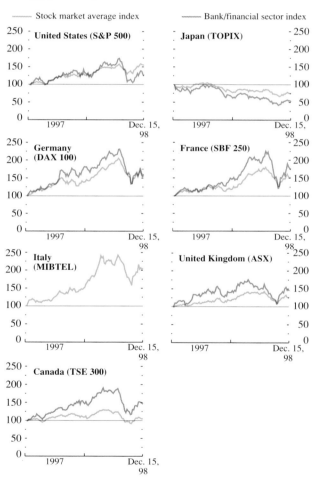

Source: Bloomberg Financial Markets, LP.

[1]For United States, Standard & Poor's 500 Index; for Japan, Price Index of Tokyo Stock Exchange; for Germany, DAX 100 Index; for France, Société des Bourses Françaises 250 Index; for Italy, Milan Stock Exchange MIB Telematico Index; for United Kingdom, Financial Times Stock Exchange All-Share Index; and for Canada, Toronto Stock Exchange 300 Composite Index.

Figure 3.2. Major Industrial Countries: Nominal Interest Rates
(Percent)

The downward trend in bond yields accelerated in the wake of the Russian crisis, while short-term rates have also declined, reflecting cuts in official interest rates.

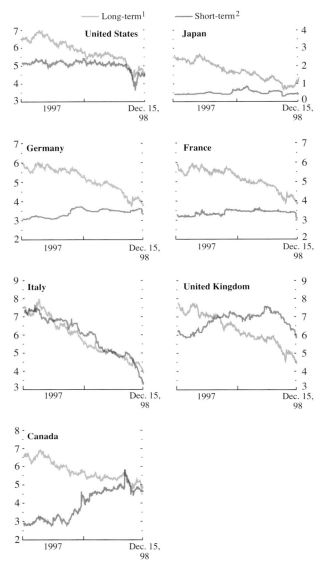

Sources: WEFA, Inc.; and Bloomberg Financial Markets, LP.
[1]Yields on government bonds with residual maturities of ten years or nearest.
[2]Three-month maturities: treasury bill rates for United States and United Kingdom; interbank rate for Germany, France, Italy, and Canada; and deposit rate for Japan.

the sustainability of historically high equity market valuations reached after a period of sustained and rapid price increases. First, the negative effects of the Asian crisis on output growth and corporate earnings were becoming more visible, particularly in the United States. In addition, it was increasingly apparent that the contraction in the Asian emerging market economies was much deeper than initially expected, and that prospects for early recovery in Japan had diminished. The deteriorating situation in Russia also contributed to concerns that the emerging market crisis might spread beyond Asia. Bank stocks were hit particularly hard, in part unwinding earlier sharp gains but also reflecting concerns about bank exposures to emerging markets (Figure 3.1, preceding page). In credit markets, spreads on lower-quality U.S. corporate bonds widened by a further 50 basis points in the first half of August, but there was only a modest widening in spreads on investment grade bonds.

Recent Developments

The situation deteriorated rapidly in the second half of August as the devaluation and unilateral debt restructuring by Russia sparked a period of turmoil in mature markets that is virtually without precedent in the absence of a major inflationary or economic shock. Neither Russia's relative importance in the world economy nor the size of bank exposures to Russia[4] can fully explain the magnitude of the market movements that followed, including a broad-based reassessment of the risks associated with emerging market investments and a large-scale—partly involuntary—portfolio rebalancing across a range of global financial markets. In subsequent weeks, conditions in the mature financial markets deteriorated sharply. The equity market sell-off intensified, largely wiping out the gains recorded earlier in the year. In the United States, equity markets bottomed out in late August, roughly 20 percent below their highs, while European markets continued to decline through the first half of October, falling on average by about 35 percent. At the same time, the decline in government bond yields accelerated, taking yields to their lowest levels since at least the mid-1960s and in some cases since World War II, as investors increasingly sought to shift funds into the safest and most liquid assets (Figure 3.2). In the six-week period between mid-August and early October, for example, government bond yields fell by about 70 basis points in Germany, 110 basis points in the United Kingdom, and 120 basis points in the United States, implying price gains in the range of 6–11 percent for the benchmark seven- to ten-year bonds. Elsewhere in

[4]In 1997, Russia accounted for roughly 1½ percent of world GDP and 1.2 percent of world trade; BIS bank claims on Russia accounted for less than 1 percent of BIS total claims.

Europe, yield spreads over German rates widened to their highest levels of the year within the euro area, and even more dramatically outside the euro area, with spreads for Denmark and Sweden widening by 30–40 basis points in less than a month.

Corporate bond spreads also widened sharply, both relative to government bond yields and in terms of the spreads between high- and low-quality corporate bonds. Comprehensive data are most readily available for the United States, where the corporate bond market is relatively large and well developed (Figure 3.3). Yield spreads over U.S. treasury bonds for below-investment-grade bonds widened from about 375 basis points immediately before the Russian debt restructuring to almost 600 basis points by mid-October, the highest level since the collapse of the U.S. junk bond market at the beginning of the 1990s. For an average high-yield bond, this spread widening was equivalent to a loss of about 8 percent on the value of the bond, more than half the average loss recorded over a longer 4½ month period at the height of the market turmoil in 1990–91. Spreads for the highest rated (Aaa) investment-grade bonds also widened from about 90 basis points in early August to about 150 basis points in mid-October, while spreads for lower-rated (Baa) bonds rose from about 150 to 230 basis points, in both cases reaching levels that typically have been observed only during periods of recession. For the most part, the rise in spreads on higher-grade credits reflected the fall in treasury bond yields rather than a rise in actual borrowing costs. However, below investment grade, the spread widening was also associated with a sharp increase in nominal yields. The U.S. credit market may have been particularly vulnerable to a setback, given that prolonged periods of economic expansion such as that achieved by the United States in the 1990s often culminate in excessive borrowing and underpricing of risk.[5] However, corporate bond spreads also appear to have widened in some European markets, though time-series data on these spreads are much more limited. For example, spreads on AA euro sterling bonds over U.K. gilts widened from about 90 basis points to 130 basis points during the same period,[6] and spreads also widened for bonds issued by financial institutions in France and Germany. New debt issuance activity dropped off markedly, most notably in the high-yield market in the United States, where the volume of bonds issued in October fell to about $2 billion, compared with a monthly average of roughly $15 billion in the second quarter (Figure 3.4). A substantial though less pronounced

Figure 3.3 United States: Yields on Corporate and Treasury Bonds[1]
(Percent)

In the wake of the Russian crisis, yield spreads on corporate bonds widened sharply to levels not seen since the early 1990s.

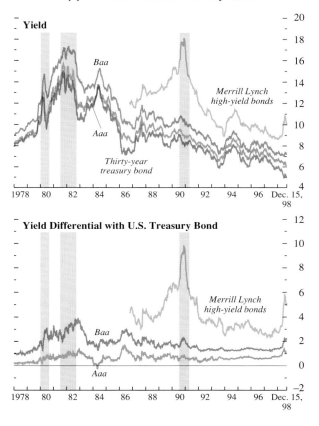

Sources: Board of Governors of the Federal Reserve System; Bloomberg Financial Markets, LP; and Merrill Lynch.
[1]Weekly data; the Moody's ratings of the corporate bonds are shown in the panels. Yields on thirty-year treasury bonds of constant maturities are used for the U.S. treasury bond. The shaded regions indicate recession periods.

---

[5]U.S. credit spreads had become unusually compressed in the past two years amid a marked acceleration in private indebtedness, much of it securitized and held off banks' balance sheets.

[6]Individual U.K. corporate bond spreads also widened significantly during the third quarter. See Bank of England, *Inflation Report* (London: November 1998), p. 6.

Figure 3.4. United States: Corporate Bond Market

The widening in yield spreads was associated with a marked drop-off in new issuance activity, particularly for lower-quality bonds.

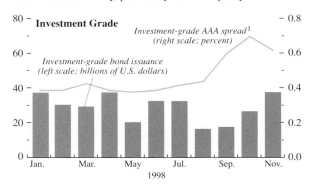

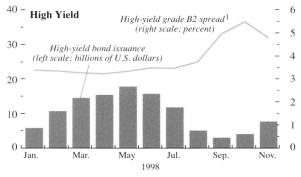

Source: Bloomberg Financial Markets, LP.
[1]Spread between yields on corporate bonds and ten-year U.S. government bonds. Monthly average of daily observations.

drop-off was observed in the issuance of U.S. investment-grade bonds, and there are reports that high-yield corporate bond issuance also slowed sharply in continental Europe.

In September and early October, indications of heightened concern about liquidity and counterparty risk emerged in some of the world's deepest financial markets. As discussed further below, a key development was the news of difficulties in, and ultimately the near-failure of, a major U.S. hedge fund—Long-Term Capital Management (LTCM)—which had large highly leveraged positions across a broad range of markets, and substantial links with a range of U.S. and European financial institutions. Although a private rescue of LTCM, organized with the help of the New York Federal Reserve Bank, was announced on September 23, the market reverberations intensified in the ensuing weeks as previous positions were unwound and as concerns increased about the extent to which other financial institutions might be in trouble or face a need to unload assets into illiquid markets at distressed prices. In response to these developments, market volatility increased sharply, and there were some significant departures from normal pricing relationships among different asset classes.[7] In the U.S. treasury market, for example, the spread between the yield on "on-the-run" and "off-the-run" treasuries widened from less than 10 basis points to about 15 basis points in the wake of the Russian debt restructuring, and to a peak of over 35 basis points in mid-October, suggesting that investors were placing an unusually large premium on liquidity (Figure 3.5).[8] In terms of the value of the bonds, this spread widening was equivalent to a relative price movement of about 4 percentage points—a relatively large differential for bonds of similar duration and the same underlying credit risk. Spreads between yields in the Eurodollar market and on U.S. treasury bills for similar maturities also widened to historically high levels, as did spreads on fixed-for-floating interest rate swaps, pointing to heightened concerns about counterparty risk.

In exchange markets, the U.S. dollar continued to strengthen on a multilateral basis through mid-August, remaining relatively stable against major European currencies but rising further against the Japanese yen and currencies of the major commodity-exporting countries (Figure 3.6). As the emerging market crisis took on global dimensions, however, the dollar began to weaken amid increased concerns about the down-

---

[7]While the observed movements in market prices suggest problems of reduced liquidity and perhaps broader disruption of normal market functioning, reports of such problems remain largely anecdotal (see the next section).

[8]This particular comparison refers to the spread between the 25-year and the 30-year benchmark treasury, but a similar pattern was observed for other maturities. On-the-run securities are the latest issue of a particular maturity. Off-the-run securities are the previous issues of the same maturity.

side risks to U.S. growth and a shift in market expectations about the direction of U.S. monetary policy from modest tightening to significant easing.[9] These developments, combined with signs in Japan of greater progress with long-awaited bank reform[10] and additional moves there toward fiscal and monetary stimulus, significantly altered the balance of risks facing investors with yen-denominated exposures. The initial weakening of the dollar was relatively orderly; it fell by less than 10 percent against both the yen and the deutsche mark between mid-August and early October. However, the situation changed in the week beginning October 5 when the dollar fell by almost 15 percent against the yen in the space of 3 days, including the largest one-day movement in the yen/dollar rate since the collapse of the Bretton Woods system. This latter adjustment mainly reflected a sharp general appreciation of the yen: the dollar fell less than 2 percent against the deutsche mark over the same period (Figure 3.7). It also coincided with an unusually abrupt steepening of mature market yield curves outside Japan, as bond yields rose from their historic lows while short rates continued to fall. Over the same week, for example, the gap between three-month and ten-year rates widened by about 85 basis points in the United States, 50 basis points in Germany, and 60 basis points in the United Kingdom. The coincidence of such dramatic moves in the yen/dollar rate and in major credit markets is difficult to explain in terms of changing economic fundamentals alone, and appears to have reflected a large-scale unwinding of yen-denominated exposures—the "yen carry trade"—amplified by technical factors linked to stop-loss orders and dynamic hedging strategies (Box 3.1, page 43). These developments were a particularly visible manifestation of a global move by investors to close out open positions and reduce leverage in the wake of the heightened market turmoil.

In response to these developments, the U.S. Federal Reserve Board moved to cut interest rates on three occasions beginning in late September. An initial cut of ¼ of 1 percentage point in the target federal funds rate was announced following the Federal Open Market Committee (FOMC) meeting on September 29 but failed to have any significant effect in calming markets; spreads continued to widen, equity markets fell further, and volatility continued to increase. Against this background, the Federal Reserve followed up on October 15 with ¼ of 1 percentage point cuts in both the federal funds target and the discount rate, a move that proved to be the key policy action that stemmed

---

[9]For example, the implied yield on the eight-month federal funds futures contract fell from about 5.6 percent in May and June, to 4.25 percent by mid-October, suggesting that market participants expected a sizable easing over the subsequent months.

[10]Recent developments in the Japanese financial system are discussed in Chapter I (Box 1.2).

Figure 3.5. United States: Developments in Fixed-Income Securities Markets
(Basis points)

Growing concerns about liquidity and counterparty risk were partially alleviated after the second cut in the Fed funds rate target in mid-October.

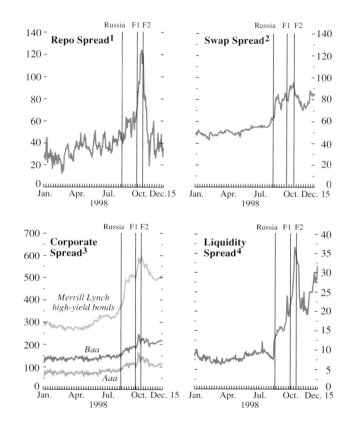

Source: Bloomberg Financial Markets, LP.
Note: The vertical lines represent the following: Russia = Russian debt moratorium (August 17); F1 = Federal Reserve interest rate cut (September 29); and F2 = Federal Reserve interest rate cut (October 15).
[1]Rate on three-month U.S. treasury repos minus yield on three-month U.S. treasury bill.
[2]Spread of fixed-rate leg of 10-year U.S. dollar interest rate swaps over yield on 10-year U.S. treasury bond.
[3]Spread over 30-year U.S. treasury bond.
[4]Spread of 25-year U.S. treasury bond over a 30-year on-the-run U.S. treasury bond.

Figure 3.6. Major Industrial Countries: Effective Exchange Rates
(Logarithmic scale; 1990 = 100)

The U.S. dollar continued to strengthen until mid-August, before a moderate decline associated in part with a sharp rebound in the yen.

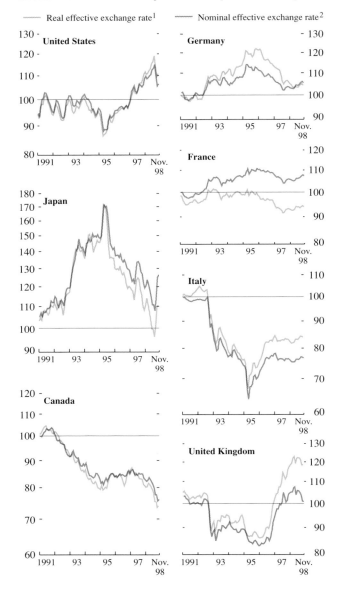

———— Real effective exchange rate[1]   ———— Nominal effective exchange rate[2]

[1]Defined in terms of relative normalized unit labor costs in manufacturing, as estimated by the IMF's Competitiveness Indicators System, using 1989–91 trade weights.

[2]Constructed using 1989–91 trade weights.

and ultimately reversed the deteriorating trend in market sentiment. The second easing was not particularly large, but the fact that it came so soon after the first rate cut and outside a regular FOMC meeting—the first such move since April 1994—sent a clear signal that the U.S. monetary authorities were prepared to move aggressively if needed to ensure normal market functioning. The Federal Reserve subsequently cut both the federal funds target and the discount rate by a further ¼ of 1 percentage point at the next FOMC meeting on November 17, noting that although financial market conditions had settled down materially since mid-October, unusual strains remained. Elsewhere, the Bank of Japan reduced the guideline for the uncollateralized call rate by 25 basis points to ¼ percent on September 9, and official interest rates have been reduced since late September in Australia, Canada, and Europe. While these moves have been motivated primarily by domestic considerations, they have also played a helpful role from a global perspective by contributing to the broad easing of monetary policy in the industrial countries.

Since mid-October, a significant degree of calm returned to financial markets. Indicators of reduced liquidity and heightened counterparty risk were substantially, though not completely, reversed (see Figure 3.5), and exchange rate volatility declined somewhat. Mature equity markets also rebounded, most dramatically in the United States, where the main indices more than regained their earlier losses by late November, before a moderate downward correction. Equity markets in Europe also strengthened, although they remain significantly below their earlier peaks. Sovereign yield spreads over German rates also generally narrowed within continental Europe, particularly in the euro area. In addition to the recent interest rate moves in the industrial countries, further steps in Japan to address the problems in the banking sector and to provide additional fiscal stimulus, and agreement on an economic program in Brazil, played important roles in the restoration of market confidence. In credit markets, spreads on U.S. corporate bonds narrowed by about 90 basis points in the high-yield market and by about 25 basis points on investment-grade bonds; corporate bond spreads also narrowed somewhat in the United Kingdom.

Significance for Economic Activity

The significance for real economic activity of the recent turmoil in mature financial markets remains somewhat uncertain. In credit markets, although spreads have narrowed since mid-October, they remain well above pre-August levels and near levels that in the past have generally been associated with periods of markedly slower growth if not actual recession. By November, there were signs of a significant pickup in new debt issuance in the U.S. high-yield bond market, though volumes remained below their earlier levels. Some further recovery in volumes and narrowing of spreads can reasonably be expected as long as financial market conditions continue to stabilize and economic growth remains well sustained, but a return to the highly compressed credit spreads applying before the Russian crisis is probably neither likely nor desirable. It is worth noting that, except for low-grade credits, actual borrowing costs in mature markets do not appear to have increased significantly during the recent episode and may even have declined for many borrowers.

The risks for real activity will also depend in part on the impact of the turbulence in emerging and mature markets on mature banking systems. Available, but incomplete, balance-sheet data indicate that, as of mid-1998, banking system loan exposures to emerging markets amounted to about $536 billion in the euro area (9 percent of 1997 GDP),[11] $211 billion in Japan (5 percent of GDP), and roughly $120 billion in both the United Kingdom and the United States (9 percent and 1½ percent of GDP, respectively; Table 3.1).[12] These exposures already reflect a substantial pullback in net bank credit outstanding mainly to the Asian emerging market economies, since the beginning of the year. So far, a number of major financial institutions have announced significant profit declines as a result of their losses on emerging market investments and the recent turbulence more generally. For example, in the third quarter of 1998, profits of U.S. money-center banks declined to about half the level recorded a year earlier. However, bank rating agencies presently estimate that the turbulence has had a manageable impact on the mature banking systems, in part because the hardest-hit financial institutions were generally well capitalized going into the turbulence, were reasonably well provisioned (or had state guarantees) on much of their emerging market portfolios (and have in many cases increased provisioning further), and were fairly profitable in the early part of 1998.

The paucity of off-balance-sheet data makes it difficult to assess overall exposures and vulnerabilities, although in some instances these exposures may be relatively large. For example, one estimate suggests that total credit exposure (including off-balance-sheet positions) of foreign banks to Russia may have been 40 to 65 percent higher than on-balance-sheet exposure.[13] In addition, as the recent period of turbulence amply demonstrated, when emerging market financing and leveraged derivatives positions are unwound, the ma-

Figure 3.7. Selected Countries: Bilateral U.S. Dollar Exchange Rates
(Currency units per U.S. dollar)

In early October, the dollar weakened sharply against the yen but more modestly against other major currencies.

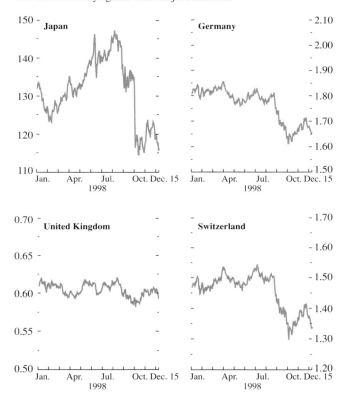

Source: Bloomberg Financial Markets, LP.

---

[11]Exposures for all European Union banking systems totaled about $676 billion (9 percent of GDP).

[12]These data include securities holdings.

[13]Off-balance-sheet exposures may increase or decrease total exposure. For example, counterparty risks increase exposure, since counterparties may default on positions; hedges decrease it, since they decrease the exposure to market risk.

Table 3.1. Claims of Banks in BIS-Reporting Countries on Selected Emerging Markets as of June 1998[1]

(Billions of U.S. dollars)

	All BIS-Reporting Countries	Japan	United Kingdom	United States	Euro Area[2]	France	Germany
Asia	**639.4**	**186.7**	**84.6**	**31.7**	**237.3**	**55.3**	**92.6**
China	59.3	17.5	7.8	2.1	23.5	8.0	7.4
Hong Kong SAR	174.6	54.6	32.8	6.1	59.4	12.6	24.1
Asian-5	210.3	74.3	15.1	16.6	98.9	20.0	26.9
Latin America	**295.7**	**14.8**	**23.1**	**64.2**	**140.7**	**25.1**	**39.5**
Argentina	60.2	1.7	5.2	10.2	34.3	5.2	7.5
Brazil	84.6	5.2	5.8	16.8	37.6	7.9	12.8
Mexico	62.9	4.4	5.7	16.7	24.9	6.1	6.1
Transition countries	**133.4**	**4.1**	**3.9**	**12.4**	**92.4**	**11.1**	**52.5**
Russia	75.9	1.0	1.8	7.8	51.5	6.7	31.3
Middle East	**57.3**	**3.0**	**6.5**	**5.3**	**25.7**	**7.0**	**11.6**
Africa	**58.3**	**2.3**	**3.9**	**4.8**	**39.4**	**18.7**	**9.4**
All emerging markets	**1,184.0**	**210.9**	**122.0**	**118.4**	**535.5**	**117.2**	**205.6**

Sources: BIS; and IMF staff calculations.

[1]On-balance-sheet claims, excluding claims on offshore centers (with the exception of Hong Kong SAR and Singapore, which are included in Asia).

[2]Because data are not reported for Greece and Portugal, data are for Austria, Belgium, Finland, France, Germany, Ireland, Italy, Luxembourg, the Netherlands, and Spain.

ture markets that finance these positions are also affected. Even if the off-balance-sheet exposures of mature banking systems to emerging markets are relatively limited, therefore, they may still have significant consequences for the mature derivatives markets.

Looking ahead, the mature banking systems and the institutions within them face three risks that are particularly relevant to the outlook. First, in addition to the direct exposures described above, financial institutions have significant indirect exposures to emerging market risks, including to counterparties that take on emerging market risks, and to the mature securities markets themselves. As recent events have shown, mature markets can experience sizable turbulence directly related to developments in emerging markets. Second, there are concerns, as discussed further below, that risk management practices continue to lag developments in financial markets, increasing potential vulnerability to turbulence. Third, the fact that the credit cycles in some major countries are in a mature phase, with economies close to potential after several years of strong growth, suggests that banks could face a deterioration in credit quality on domestic exposures, including from a slowdown in economic activity.[14] Available data on bank lending volumes do not point to any broad-based curtailment of credit availability to date, outside Japan, in part because companies have been able to draw down existing bank credit

lines as a substitute for reduced access to the corporate bond and commercial paper markets.[15] However, a Federal Reserve Board survey in November showed that U.S. bank lending practices had tightened significantly, reflecting increased concern about the economic outlook, and with the number of domestic respondents reporting tightened loan standards reaching the highest level since 1990. Some tightening of loan standards is probably a welcome development—indeed, in July 1998 the Federal Reserve expressed concern that standards had become too lax—but a substantial cutback in credit availability clearly would have negative implications for economic growth.

Equity market developments also are likely to have a significant bearing on near-term growth prospects—particularly in the United States, where equity price gains have been a major driving force behind the rapid growth in private consumption in recent years. For example, U.S. consumer confidence fell significantly from the record high reached in June, no doubt at least partly reflecting the downward correction in the stock market, before a partial recovery in November as the stock market rebounded; there have been indications of similar effects in some other countries. Given that equity prices have recovered rapidly since early October, it seems unlikely that the recent relatively short-lived

[14]One credit rating agency takes the view that the U.S. credit cycle has already peaked.

[15]Data for the United States indicate that bank lending growth accelerated in the period after late August, in part reflecting growth in commercial and industrial loans. Similar trends are evident in the United Kingdom.

Box 3.1. Recent Dollar/Yen Exchange Rate Movements

One outstanding feature of foreign exchange market developments in the past few months was the sharp and unprecedentedly sudden appreciation of the yen vis-à-vis most major currencies in early October that ended the trend of yen depreciation since mid-1995. While the recent yen appreciation to some extent may have been warranted by fundamental forces (among them a reassessment of relative monetary policy stances), the timing and the speed of the exchange rate changes strongly suggest that short-term trading conditions (such as the large-scale unwinding of "yen-carry trades") and technical market factors (including repercussions from the expiration of barrier options) contributed significantly to the sharp dynamic adjustments in the yen/dollar market. This box describes these adjustments and the technical features that drove them.

With a brief interruption in mid-1997, the yen depreciated vis-à-vis the dollar by some 40 percent during the past three years and reached an eight-year low at ¥147.26 per dollar on August 11, 1998 (see figure). This long-running appreciation of the dollar was abruptly and sharply reversed in the wake of renewed turbulence in emerging markets. Of particular interest are the developments surrounding the unprecedented, sharp appreciation of the yen during October 6–9, 1998, when the yen appreciated 15 percent vis-à-vis the dollar. This episode was driven by a confluence of factors—some of a fundamental nature, others largely technical but generating positive feedback dynamics.

Various catalysts may have sparked an initial rally in the yen and the 6.2 percent surge in the Nikkei stock index on October 7, 1998. The new draft banking bill was submitted to parliament on that day; there was talk of an additional fiscal stimulus package; and the relative monetary policy stance in Japan, the United States, and Europe was reassessed in part based on the Bank of Japan (BOJ) balance sheet for September, which was interpreted by some market participants as casting doubts on previous hints of extensive monetary easing by the BOJ.

The initial spate of dollar selling, in the wake of some turbulence in U.S. markets and the cut in interest rates by the Federal Reserve, may have induced a change in sentiment that the dollar's long-standing strengthening vis-à-vis the yen had run its course. The impression of a turning point was reinforced by indications of a cascade of dollar selling by institutional investors, including hedge funds. Large financial institutions were reportedly unwinding their yen-carry trade positions,[1] as part of the process of international deleveraging. According to market participants, technical factors stemming from standard hedging

procedures may have contributed to the sudden surge in the yen. In particular, the cancellation of complex options as the yen surged through several trigger levels and dealers' unwinding of hedges against these options, as well as the bunching of limit orders, created additional momentum that boosted demand for yen. Some temporary demand for yen appears to have originated from foreign investors who had short positions in Japanese stocks and decided to cover them ahead of new rules (effective October 23) that bar investors from selling borrowed stock in declining markets. Foreign exchange trading volume surged initially, but liquidity tightened up quickly (see figure) and contributed to large price discontinuities. In these circumstances, market participants took a cautious view, reflecting, among other factors, the very sharp increase in implied foreign exchange volatility.

The dollar eventually stabilized on October 9, 1998, reportedly after market participants began to think that the Federal Reserve was prepared to intervene in support of the dollar. But unlike in June, when a concerted intervention of the Federal Reserve and the BOJ was aimed at boosting the value of the yen, no central bank interventions are reported to have taken place between August and November 1998. In the following weeks, the yen/dollar rate weakened slightly, and liquidity returned to the foreign exchange market. Implied volatility remained high, however, as uncertainty about prospects for Japan and in particular its financial system lingered (see Chapter I, Box 1.2).

Yen-Carry Trade

Tempted by low borrowing costs in Japan, proprietary trading desks of major financial institutions and hedge funds, and even some corporations, had borrowed in yen to invest in U.S., European, and emerging market assets, thereby shorting the yen. The borrowing took various forms. Funds were either raised in the interbank market, through term repo agreements, or by issuing money market paper. Subsequently the funds were swapped for foreign currency or exchanged in the spot market. Owing to the interest rate differentials between Japan and, say, dollar assets and the appreciation of the dollar vis-à-vis the yen, these positions had been highly profitable during the past few years.

Japanese banks also exploited the yen-carry trade by accumulating open foreign asset positions. In the first three quarters of 1998, the net holdings of assets denominated in foreign currencies increased by about $44 billion, while the net holdings of yen-denominated assets abroad declined by $103 billion (see figure). Against the background of the yen depreciation, a shift toward a "long" position in foreign currencies became increasingly attractive to Japanese banks.

---

[1]The yen-carry trade was discussed in detail in the September 1998 *International Capital Markets* report, p. 44; it is also explained below.

(Box continues on next page.)

stock market correction alone will be sufficient to have a significant dampening effect on consumer spending. Indeed, with equity markets back in some cases to near their all-time highs, previous concerns about the sus-

tainability of current market valuations have resurfaced (Box 3.2, page 48; and Figure 3.8), and the possibility of a more pronounced downward correction in equity prices remains an important risk.

Box 3.1 *(concluded)*

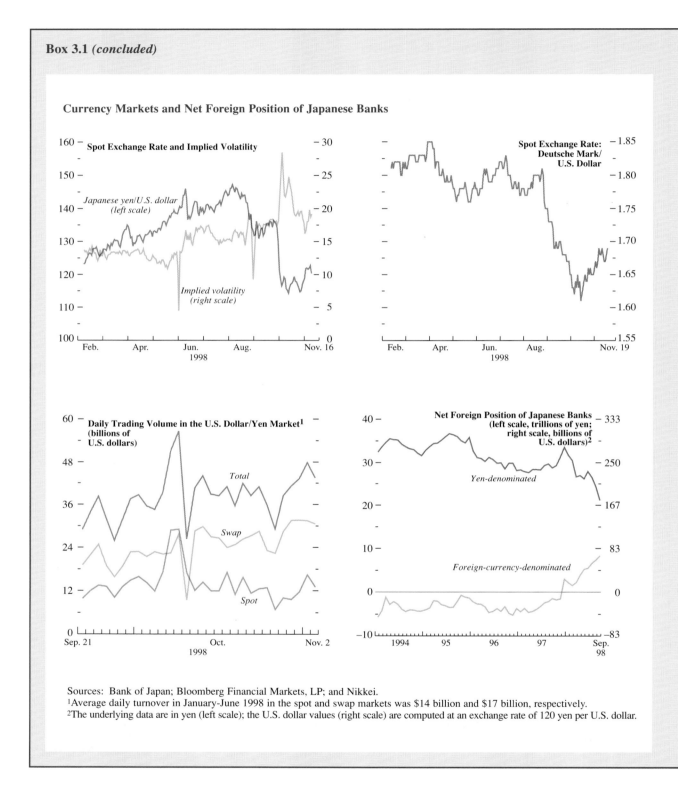

Currency Markets and Net Foreign Position of Japanese Banks

Sources: Bank of Japan; Bloomberg Financial Markets, LP; and Nikkei.
[1]Average daily turnover in January-June 1998 in the spot and swap markets was $14 billion and $17 billion, respectively.
[2]The underlying data are in yen (left scale); the U.S. dollar values (right scale) are computed at an exchange rate of 120 yen per U.S. dollar.

In exchange markets, the most notable by-product of the recent turmoil has been a substantial strengthening of the yen, which by late November was up roughly 20 percent in nominal effective terms from its August low. The multilateral value of the U.S. dollar weakened by about 6 percent over the same period, while that of the deutsche mark was little changed on balance, though it strengthened significantly against the dollar.

Japan: Notional Amounts of Over-the-Counter (OTC) Derivatives Outstanding, End-June 1998

(Trillions of U.S. dollars)

	Grand Total	Of Which: 1 Year or Less	OTC Options	Of Which: 1 Year or Less
Foreign exchange contracts	3.37	2.87	0.40	0.26
With reporting dealers	2.44	2.18	0.31	0.20
With other financial institutions	0.58	0.47	0.07	0.05
With nonfinancial customers	0.35	0.22	0.02	0.02
Single-currency interest rate contracts	9.54	5.27	0.89	0.25
With reporting dealers	7.54	4.42	0.53	0.14
With other financial institutions	1.41	0.72	0.23	0.08
With nonfinancial customers	0.59	0.13	0.13	0.03

Source: Bank of Japan, *Regular Derivatives Market Statistics in Japan* (Tokyo).

Worsening investment opportunities following the turbulence in some emerging markets, and corrections in mature markets during the summer of 1998, prompted a reversal of yen-carry trade positions. In addition to profit taking, the unwinding was also triggered by institutional investors, including hedge funds, that were confronted with margin calls on positions in other markets. Many institutions closed out carry trades because they faced a shortage of liquidity as banks increasingly cut credit lines to leveraged investors—as part of a global reevaluation of the willingness to take risks. Some margin calls on hedge funds might have dampened the yen appreciation as they triggered the sale of liquid yen assets to raise cash, which was subsequently converted into foreign currency.

Japanese institutions began to repatriate funds in light of rising funding costs—including an increasing "Japan premium" and higher rates on basis swaps (currency swaps)[2]—and reportedly deteriorating access to international interbank markets. In this situation, long dollar positions represented a potential source of vulnerability and contributed to unwinding pressures. These pressures were intensified by the need to overcome capital shortfalls on

[2]In a basis swap, a bank swaps principal and interest obligations on a yen liability for dollar principal and interest payments. This arrangement converts yen-denominated debt held by a Japanese bank into dollars and thus helps fund the bank's overseas activities. Basis swaps had offered Japanese banks an attractive source of foreign currency at a time when their credit ratings made it difficult to borrow abroad.

their half-year balance sheets (September 30) and as an increasing number of Japanese banks reconsidered the viability of their overseas business. Selling pressures on the dollar reportedly originated from Japanese investors pulling funds out of U.S. securities as those markets softened and the higher exchange rate volatility increased foreign-currency risk and made hedging more expensive.

Technical Factors

Large dollar-yen movements were likely exacerbated by a series of technical factors, such as stop-loss orders and, more important, by the cancellations of barrier options[3] and the unwinding of associated hedging positions by dealers. Leverage and the hedging of yen positions can often be achieved more cheaply through derivatives. The volume of outstanding yen foreign exchange contracts had grown at end-June 1998 to $3.4 trillion, of which about $400 billion corresponded to options (*see table*). Although no official breakdown by type of options is available, market participants consider barrier options a popular instrument.

Knockout options (a special form of barrier options)[4] are widely used as a hedge of currency risk because they are less expensive than standard options. But knockout options provide protection only against moderate exchange rate changes and leave the investor unhedged against large currency movements, since as soon as the exchange rate breaches a certain level, the knockout option is canceled. A Japanese exporter, for example, might buy dollar knockout put options, which expire prematurely if the dollar exchange rate drops below a certain level, to protect against a (moderate) depreciation of the dollar. A drop of the dollar large enough to trigger the cancellation of the option would, however, expose the exporter to losses. In response, the exporter might be inclined to sell dollars into a falling market to cut his expected losses.

Additional feedback in a falling market may have originated from the dynamic hedging strategies commonly employed by dealers who sell knockout options. As the dollar exchange rate fell and knockout call options were canceled, dealers immediately sold the long dollar positions they held as a dynamic hedge for these options. The hedging of knockout put options typically involves more complex buying and selling of standard options as exchange rates vary. In a down market, standard put option values are bid up even higher by the dynamic hedging and expose dealers to significant losses. These reactions can contribute to an overshooting in the price (and implied volatility) of options.

[3]Barrier options are options that either come into effect or are canceled if the price of the underlying asset crosses a stated level.

[4]Knockout options are barrier options that are canceled as the underlying asset price breaks through a specified level.

As discussed above, the sharp rise in the yen appears to have been at least partly attributable to the sudden unwinding of large short yen positions, amplified by technical factors, and it remains to be seen to what extent the current yen/dollar alignment will persist as the impact of these essentially one-off factors begins to fade.

At a more fundamental level, however, the yen's rise also appears to have reflected expectations of ad-

Figure 3.8. United States: Equity Market Performance

With the latest rebound in U.S. equity prices, several indicators of market valuation have moved further away from their long-term averages; however the yield gap vis-à-vis treasury bonds remains below recent peaks, reflecting the decline in government bond yields.

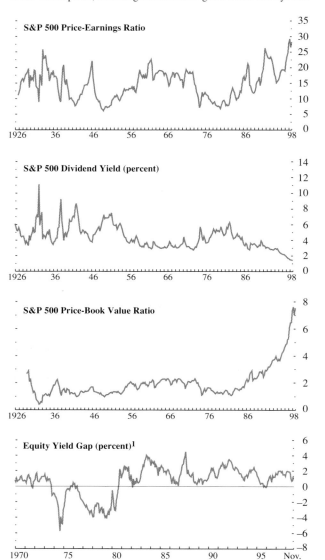

Sources: Board of Governors of the Federal Reserve System; Bloomberg Financial Markets, LP; WEFA, Inc.; and Standard and Poor's.
[1]Difference between the yield on long-term government bonds and the inverse of the price-earnings ratio.

ditional policy steps to boost growth in Japan and of slower growth in the United States, which would imply a narrowing of the current large divergences in relative cyclical positions. So far, there is little evidence of such narrowing in the economic data, however, and the recent abrupt strengthening of the yen could be damaging to prospects for recovery in Japan at a time when domestic private sector demand remains very weak. Indeed, as discussed in Chapter IV, the appreciation of the yen is one of the factors behind the further downward revision in the 1999 staff forecast for Japan. From a global perspective, however, a moderate realignment of the yen/dollar rate also carries several potential benefits. First, by introducing a greater element of uncertainty about the future direction of exchange rates, it has probably reduced the incentives for investors to take on large short-yen exposures that may have contributed to the emergence of exchange market strains and asset price bubbles elsewhere in the global financial system over the past two years. Second, it has helped to alleviate downward pressures on the currencies of other emerging market economies in Asia and elsewhere—particularly those with explicit or implicit links to the U.S. dollar—and thus has provided scope for these economies to pursue somewhat easier monetary policies. Particularly in the current environment where global deflationary pressures remain relatively strong, such cautious monetary easing is generally helpful in terms of reducing the risks of a more pronounced slowdown in world growth. Third, it has provided additional scope for the Japanese authorities to pursue an aggressively expansionary monetary policy aimed at boosting domestic demand and easing strains in the financial sector. Nonetheless, a further significant strengthening of the yen or weakening of the dollar in the short term would also carry risks, in terms of both the prospects for economic recovery in Japan and the scope for further interest rate cuts in the United States.

Systemic Aspects of Mature Market Turbulence

Recapping some of what has already been discussed, the turbulent dynamics in mature markets had been preceded by a steady buildup of prices in the mature equity and bond markets during the years and months preceding the Russian crisis in mid-August 1998. The long-standing rise in asset values was supported by several important developments in the mid-to-late 1990s—including the widespread reduction in inflation rates in the world economy; the continued noninflationary expansion in the United States, and the belief by some that the U.S. economy had entered a new, high-productivity growth age; continued flows of funds into U.S. and other mature equity and bond markets; and the relatively successful convergence process toward EMU. All of these developments continued through the early summer, amid earlier warning signs that many advanced country equity markets, not just in the United States, were reaching record and perhaps unsustainable levels. In addition, as early as mid-1997, differences in the cost of borrowing between high- and low-risk borrowers began to narrow to the point where several advanced country central banks sounded warnings that credit spreads were reaching relatively low levels and that lending standards had been relaxed in some countries beyond a reasonable level.

In mid-July 1998, equity markets in the advanced countries began to decline somewhat on reports of poor corporate earnings and concerns about a slowdown in U.S. economic growth. At the same time, some mature markets—notably the U.S. fixed-income markets—began experiencing a widening of interest rate spreads between low- and high-quality borrowers, in part the result of concerns over growth prospects and what this might imply for the ability of higher-risk debtors to service obligations in the future and in part the result of the continued flight to quality and liquidity (and away from Asian emerging markets). This relatively small widening of interest rate spreads between low- and high-quality fixed-income securities was then followed by a more dramatic widening of spreads, and subsequently by a period of severe turbulence in mature and international financial markets, triggered, and driven, by several related events—including the Russian unilateral restructuring of GKOs (ruble-denominated discount instruments); the immediate partial closing out, and deleveraging, of positions in other emerging markets; and later in mid-September the near collapse of a highly leveraged hedge fund, LTCM.

Dynamic adjustments in other emerging markets related to the Russian crisis necessarily entailed some adjustments in the mature markets as well, reflecting the important role of these markets in financing and leveraging investments in Russia and in other emerging markets. But it would normally be expected that such adjustments would occur relatively smoothly and without the kind of severe financial turbulence that occurred in September and October 1998 in some of the deepest and most liquid markets in the world. By definition, deep and liquid markets, such as those in the United States, might have been expected to be able to absorb the after-effects of what were relatively moderate shocks with relatively limited price and liquidity effects.

However, the financial turbulence in the mature markets appeared out of proportion to the events that triggered it. The events surrounding the Russian unilateral debt restructuring led to large investment and trading losses and changed market perceptions of default and convertibility risk, which together affected the balance of risks and returns in international portfolios. Because of the new financial calculus that re-

sulted, the internationally active financial institutions and other asset managers appear to have engaged in a wholesale reassessment and repricing of financial risk, which was accompanied by a rebalancing and deleveraging of international portfolios in a short period of time, accented by risk avoidance, market illiquidity, and extreme price movements.

As a result, and contrary to what would normally be expected, the mature markets subsequently experienced dramatic, and in some cases unprecedented, price and liquidity adjustments that cut across mature equity, fixed-income, currency, and derivative markets and caused some of them to become illiquid, and at times to seize up temporarily; liquidity spreads reached record highs.[16] Despite the apparent concentration of mature market turbulence in U.S. financial markets and the focus of attention on some newsworthy U.S. financial institutions, internationally active European and Japanese financial institutions were involved in similar leveraged risk taking, in some cases on a very large scale, and, as of end-November 1998, appear to be undergoing a similar process of risk reassessment and rebalancing. The negative impact on asset values during the most turbulent subperiod—between mid-September and mid-October—was sufficiently severe that it triggered fears of significant negative spillover effects on world economic growth.

The severe nature of the mature market turbulence raises several issues about private risk and portfolio management, banking supervision, financial market surveillance, the management of systemic risk, and the operation of the international financial system. The remainder of this section examines several features of international financial markets that provide an understanding of why there was a reassessment of risks and rebalancing of mature market portfolios in the period from mid-August through mid-October 1998. These features include the following: (1) the unilateral debt restructuring in Russia challenged underlying assumptions of investors in mature markets about sovereign risk and potential international financial support; (2) mature markets financed a significant share of emerging market exposures; (3) a large number of diverse financial institutions, not just hedge funds, had

---

[16]The turbulence was also affected by a number of features of the structural transformations that have occurred in financial markets during the past 10–15 years, some of which contributed to, and magnified the effects of, the turbulence, and some of which moderated the turbulence and its impact. These features include the expanded opportunities for unbundling and repackaging components of financial risk, and advances in trading and portfolio management techniques (stop-loss orders, portfolio insurance, dynamic hedging) afforded by advances in information and computer technologies; the evolution of commercial and investment banks into financial conglomerates with global reach; and the growing importance of institutional investors (insurance companies, pension funds, hedge funds). For analyses of some of these changes see "Globalization of Finance and Financial Risk," Annex 5 of the September 1998 *International Capital Markets* report.

Box 3.2. What Is the Implied Future Earnings Growth Rate that Would Justify Current Equity Prices in the United States?

Since its peak in July 1998, the U.S. stock market has experienced a significant correction and then a rebound. The Standard & Poor's 500 index fell some 19 percent from peak (July 17) to trough (October 8). The S&P 500 index has since rebounded by about 24 percent (having reached a new high on November 27). The correction was triggered in part by reports of lower corporate earnings and reevaluations of earnings expectations. At the same time, long-term bond yields declined markedly. A key question is: At present levels of interest rates, what is the implied growth rate of future nominal earnings that would justify equity prices in early December as the present value of discounted future earnings? The answer provided by the analysis below is that, assuming an unchanged risk premium, the implied nominal earnings growth rate (7½ percent) is about the same as in late 1997, when the S&P 500 index was significantly lower than in early December 1998. The decline in long-term interest rates thus makes the 20½ percent higher S&P 500 consistent with unchanged expected earnings growth. The analysis supports the view that current equity valuations are unsustainably high, especially in light of the relatively late stage of the U.S. business cycle, by showing that the implied earnings growth rate adjusted for inflationary expectations is at a post–World War II peak.

Calculation of Implied Earnings Growth Rates

The relationship between equity prices and the implied growth of future nominal earnings can be derived from the hypothesis that the current equity price, P_t, is equal to the discounted present value of future earnings, E_{t+j} ($j \geq 1$), with discount factor ρ_t.

$$P_t = \sum_{j=1}^{\infty} \left(\frac{1}{1+\rho_t}\right)^j E_{t+j}. \tag{1}$$

Assuming that future earnings grow at a constant rate, g_t, such that $E_{t+j+1} = (1+g_t)E_{t+j}$, equation (1) becomes:

$$P_t = E_t \sum_{j=1}^{\infty} \left(\frac{1+g_t}{1+\rho_t}\right)^j. \tag{2}$$

This implies the following relationship between the current price earnings ratio, (P_t/E_t), the discount factor, and the future earnings growth rate:

$$\frac{P_t}{E_t} = \left(\frac{1+g_t}{\rho_t - g_t}\right). \tag{3}$$

Given a suitable discount factor, equation (3) can be solved for the implied earnings growth rate, g_t. The discount factor, ρ_t, is equal to $(r_t + e)$, where r_t denotes the 30-year U.S. treasury bond yield and e is a constant equity risk premium (assumed to be 6 percentage points).[1]

Assessment

The S&P 500 price index on December 2, 1998, although 20½ percent higher than at the beginning of the year, is underpinned by about the same earnings expectations as at the end of 1997 (see figure). The drop in long-term interest rates (by about 90 basis points) can, according to this approach, almost fully explain the gains in the S&P 500. Had interest rates not fallen but remained at their end-1997 levels, the implied earnings growth rate as of early December would be consistent with the S&P 500 being 235 points (20¼ percent) lower. Alternatively, to support current equity prices at end-1997 interest rates, the implied earnings growth would need to be about 90 basis points higher indefinitely into the future (see figure).[2]

From a historical perspective, implied earnings growth rates[3]—at about the same level as in the 1980s—can be considered high (see the bottom panel of the figure). The implied earnings growth rates, g_t, may not provide the best comparison of equity valuations over a long time horizon because they depend in part on the discount factor, ρ_t, and thus on the bond yield, r_t, (see equation (3)). Bond yields are influenced by many factors that may distort intertemporal comparisons and are sensitive to market participants' inflationary expectations. A measure of implied earnings growth independent of expected inflation is the ratio of the (gross) nominal earnings growth rate to the (gross) nominal bond yield, which can be approximated by the spread between the earnings growth rate and the bond yield. This spread was at an all-time high in November 1998 (see bottom panel of the figure), raising questions about the sustainability of current high equity valuations.

---

[1]R. Mehra and E. C. Prescott, "The Equity Premium: A Puzzle," *Journal of Monetary Economics*, Vol. 15, (1985), pp. 145–61, and J. Y. Campbell, A. W. Lo, and A. C. MacKinlay, *The Econometrics of Financial Markets* (Princeton, New Jersey: Princeton University Press, 1997), find a risk premium of about 6 percentage points. An 8 percent risk premium (instead of 6 percent) would shift the level of the earnings growth path plotted in the figure up by approximately 2 percentage points. Thus, the choice of risk premium would not affect the comparisons of earnings growth between end-1997 and November 1998 so long as the risk premium did not change over this interval of time.

[2]Consider the following scenario that telescopes the needed changes in earnings into 1999. Assume that in 2000 and thereafter the paths for interest rates and earnings revert back to the paths implied at the end of 1997; in this case earnings would need to be about 5½ times larger in 1999 than in 1998 in order to justify the S&P 500 level in early December.

[3]Owing to data limitations, the historical implied earnings growth rates for 1954–98 were derived based on the 10-year U.S. treasury bond yield, rather than the 30-year bond yield.

---

similar risk exposures and became vulnerable to a continued widening of interest rate spreads; (4) risk management models did not prevent the buildup, and modern portfolio management exacerbated the unwinding, of the preponderance of credit risk convergence plays; and (5) a disorderly unwinding and deleveraging, if it

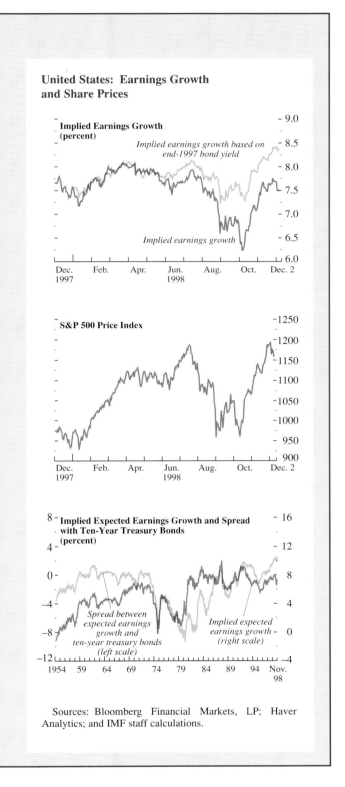

United States: Earnings Growth and Share Prices

Implied Earnings Growth (percent)

Implied earnings growth based on end-1997 bond yield

Implied earnings growth

Dec. 1997 — Feb. — Apr. — Jun. 1998 — Aug. — Oct. — Dec. 2

S&P 500 Price Index

Dec. 1997 — Feb. — Apr. — Jun. 1998 — Aug. — Oct. — Dec. 2

Implied Expected Earnings Growth and Spread with Ten-Year Treasury Bonds (percent)

Spread between expected earnings growth and ten-year treasury bonds (left scale)

Implied expected earnings growth (right scale)

1954 — 59 — 64 — 69 — 74 — 79 — 84 — 89 — 94 — Nov. 98

Sources: Bloomberg Financial Markets, LP; Haver Analytics; and IMF staff calculations.

had been allowed to continue to build momentum, would have posed systemic risks in international financial markets.

Although these features provide some understanding of why the mature market adjustments occurred, taken together they do not provide an understanding of why the recent mature market turbulence was so extreme. The turbulence was extreme enough that it was judged to have posed threats to internationally active financial institutions, and potential systemic problems in the mature and international financial markets. The apparent under-estimation of the extent to which these vulnerabilities and risks had accumulated raises a number of systemic concerns, which are raised briefly in the third and final subsection.

Why Did the Russian Crisis Create More Mature Market Turbulence than the Asian Crises?

The depth and scale of the recent financial market turbulence certainly cannot be explained by the potential direct impact of the unilateral debt restructuring in Russia. First, the value that could be lost from an outright default was relatively small, and only one-third of it was held by nonresident investors. Second, interest rates on Russian GKOs in the period leading up to the unilateral restructuring were high relative to the cost of borrowing by other emerging market sovereign credits. This suggests that investors were aware of the risks of lending to Russia, as reflected in the significantly higher returns that were necessary to compensate for the higher perceived risks. Indeed, financial markets should have realized that the economic and financial problems faced by Russia were significantly more protracted than in many other emerging markets. Finally, Russia was perceived as unique among emerging markets in one significant regard: long-standing political and foreign policy considerations implied to many investors that Russia might continue to receive the funds it required from the international community to finance the required adjustments. In effect, Russia was perceived as "too big to fail." Overall, these factors suggest that it is not obvious why the Russian unilateral restructuring would trigger a wholesale exit from emerging markets and a period of unprecedented turbulence in mature and international markets.

Nevertheless, for market participants the Russian unilateral restructuring seems to have been a defining event. The restructuring appears to have challenged fundamental assumptions about emerging market finance—widely held by the major financial institutions and priced into all but the safest investments—perhaps including a presumption that countries would not unilaterally restructure sovereign debt obligations. In the event, and regardless of the subjective reasons, the Russian crisis drove risk managers and investors to question the validity of their assumptions and the balance of financial risks in their international portfolios made up of investments in both emerging and mature markets.

Accordingly, risk reassessments implied that many portfolios might be riskier than risk management models had previously indicated, and that even mature market portfolios with even relatively low-risk combinations of emerging and mature market investments might be riskier than perceived before August 17. In addition to affecting emerging markets, developments in mid-to-late August, including the unwinding of mature market financing, led to a further widening of interest rate spreads between relatively low-quality advanced country fixed-income securities (such as asset-backed securities and low-grade corporate bonds) and very high-quality government (U.S. and German) debt securities, as the general flight to quality proceeded.

Unlike the Asian crises, the Russian financial problems triggered mature market turbulence because of differences in the nature of the shock. The Russian crisis was a unilateral restructuring of sovereign debt—a traded financial market instrument—that in a mark-to-market environment would immediately trigger the unwinding of leveraged positions by large, internationally active, financial institutions. In the Asian crisis, by contrast, the bulk of the financial contracts that immediately became at risk consisted of (nontradable) interbank loans. In addition, Russia's unilateral restructuring was a sudden and defining event, whereas the Asian crises developed more slowly in several stages. But the Asian crises, of course, contributed to the recent turbulence by already reducing appetites for risk. Another difference is that the Russian crisis occurred amid greater concerns about the health of the U.S. economy and the sustainability of the valuation of U.S., and other mature, equity markets.

Ultimately, the Russian unilateral debt restructuring triggered an abrupt, post-Asian-crisis flight from a wide range of emerging financial markets, a sharp widening of emerging market interest rate spreads to 1,700 basis points, and a drying up of liquidity in international capital markets. The related flights to quality and liquidity in international capital markets set off a process of deleveraging of financial transactions and virulent turbulence in mature financial markets that rapidly and sharply affected many investors and a wide range of mature financial markets.

Mature Markets Financed and Leveraged Emerging Market Investments

At least some of the immediate impact on mature markets of the unilateral debt restructuring in Russia reflected the fact that a significant share of financing for Russian and other emerging market investments had been arranged and leveraged in the mature markets, in particular U.S. financial markets. For example, some investors had purchased Russian GKOs, on margin, through investment banks that had funded the purchases with short-term repurchase agreements and commercial paper in U.S. markets. Other Russian and emerging market securities purchases had been funded in Japan and swapped into local currencies or dollars. Accordingly, the initial unwinding of financing for emerging market positions, hedges, and leverage meant that mature market positions related to these investments also had to be unwound or hedged, because the Russian restructuring triggered margin calls and led to a widespread increase in margin requirements. Because many of the investments that needed to be unwound were highly leveraged, the downward price adjustments were unusually sharp in a wide range of markets. The leveraging of investments magnifies returns when asset prices are appreciating, but it also magnifies losses, and requires the expenditure of scarce capital to meet margin calls, when adverse price movements occur, thereby forcing market participants to liquidate positions as rapidly as possible. Thus, the simultaneous presence of a high degree of leverage in a wide range of interconnected markets forced a large number of investors simultaneously to sell assets into declining markets. This contributed to the rapid speed and heightened intensity of the downward price pressures and adjustments in September and October 1998 (Box 3.3).

The widening of spreads and liquidity pressures that immediately followed the Russian crisis and the flight from emerging markets destroyed value in fixed-income positions that had been predicated on the perception that "credit risk" spreads between low-quality (mortgage-backed securities and corporate debt, for example) and high-quality (sovereign) borrowers in the advanced countries had widened beyond sustainable levels because of the "Asian contagion." These so-called credit-risk "convergence plays" (not to be confused with EMU currency and interest rate convergence plays) were widely held. They were made up of financial positions in advanced country fixed-income markets in which the investor would simultaneously be "long" in relatively high-risk debt securities (such as U.S., German, and Danish asset-backed and corporate securities)—expecting their value to appreciate—and "short" in sovereign debt instruments of similar currency denomination and maturity (such as U.S., German, and Danish government bonds)—expecting their value to depreciate. The plays were calculated gambles that, once Asian contagion dissipated, credit spreads would narrow to more normal (historically consistent) levels and would be associated with the expected price movements. Instead of narrowing, however, credit risk spreads widened further. Depending on how the transactions were financed, these adverse price movements were associated with further margin calls, liquidations, and hedging, leading to further significant demands on the shrinking pool of liquidity. This led

---

Box 3.3. Leverage

Leverage is the magnification of the rate of return (positive or negative) on a position or investment beyond the rate obtained by a direct investment of own funds in the cash market. It is defined as the ratio of assets to equity. Leverage is achieved by increasing the investment through either outright borrowing or derivative instruments. In the former case, a loan (including repurchase agreements) is used to supplement the equity investment, which is expected to have a rate of return higher than the interest rate on the loan. Instead of cash, the loan could consist of a security (as in short-selling operations). In the latter case, derivative positions (such as futures and options) allow the investor to earn the return on the notional amount underlying the contract by committing a small portion of equity in the form of initial margin or option premium payments.[1] To measure precisely the use of leverage by a firm, one needs to know all of the firm's positions. This is frequently not possible because activities such as repurchase agreements and derivatives take place off the balance sheet and are therefore not observable to an outsider.

Leverage is of concern because of two effects. By definition it creates and enhances the risk of default by market participants; furthermore, rapid deleveraging—the unwinding of leveraged positions—can cause major disruptions in financial markets by exaggerating market movements.[2]

If the rate of return on an investment to which borrowed funds have been committed turns out to be less than expected, the investor's equity may very quickly diminish and become insufficient to cover the loans. In response to an adverse price movement, a leveraged position will be closed faster by an investor (with a given loss tolerance) than if it were not leveraged. The larger the leverage, the smaller is the needed price change to trigger an unwinding of the position. The need to quickly unwind large positions in response to margin calls following exogenous price movements can magnify these movements in a destabilizing manner. That is, a "long" leveraged position will be sold as a result of an exogenous price decline, thus contributing to the price movement even further. Conversely, a "short" position needs to be covered in a rising market by buying the security, therefore contributing to upward price pressure. While any (unleveraged) position would require similar actions, leveraged positions may increase volatility more rapidly.

If there are many similar leveraged positions, if there is a single large position, or if the underlying market is not very liquid, rapid deleveraging can create price disconnects (large price moves resulting from temporarily one-sided markets). These price movements in a mark-to-market environment will trigger margin calls or cause other investors to reevaluate their positions. This, in turn, will force the liquidation of more leveraged positions, resulting in a knock-on effect, which can send ripples through diverse financial markets spawned by leveraged positions.

Some institutional investors, such as hedge funds, employ leverage in various ways, aimed at designing strategies to bet on developments in many different markets by committing as little of their own equity as possible. The following hypothetical scenario illustrates how an institution can lever up its equity several times. It also shows how seemingly exogenous events can cause this strategy to unravel, magnifying the turbulence in financial markets (*see figure*). The example is inspired by, but does not necessar-

---

[1]The degree of leverage for a futures contract can be defined as the ratio of the notional value (assets) to the margin posted (equity). The degree of leverage for an option contract can be defined as the delta times the underlying price, times the notional value, divided by the option premium.

[2]Leverage also has benefits not only to participants but to the system as a whole. It can be usefully employed to hedge an existing commitment in a cost-saving manner. It also facilitates speculation, which is necessary for the efficient functioning of markets and enhances liquidity. Furthermore, commercial banks are by their nature highly leveraged without necessarily building up leveraged positions as described in this box.

(Box continues on next page.)

---

to even wider spreads in some markets as more positions were liquidated to make margin calls in other markets.

This adjustment process ultimately posed potential systemic risks because of its impact on market liquidity and dynamics. Market liquidity dried up temporarily even in the deepest and most liquid markets as risks were repriced and positions deleveraged. Anecdotal evidence suggests that this occurred in the U.S. treasury securities markets (in both August and September), the U.S. repo market (in October), and the yen/dollar market (during October 7–9). The drying up of liquidity had a visible impact on prices and flows, and there were repeated instances when concerns about liquidity were heightened, with markets becoming one-sided until prices declined enough to bring buyers back into the fray. There also appears to have been unusual

concern about counterparty risk in collateralized markets, although this can be explained by the uncertainty surrounding the turbulence, most notably around the time of the near collapse of LTCM and in the early weeks of the unwinding of LTCM's positions. It was not clear how far asset prices needed to fall, or how badly counterparties' balance sheets had been damaged by the turbulence.

The potential for these dynamics to have systemic consequences was especially visible in U.S. dollar markets, the center of gravity for much of the portfolio rebalancing and deleveraging. Moreover, the dollar is the principal financial vehicle for international financial transactions and for managing liquidity, engineering leverage, and speculation. As noted in previous *International Capital Markets* reports, financial institutions and markets in the United

Box 3.3 *(concluded)*

Hypothetical Example of Leverage

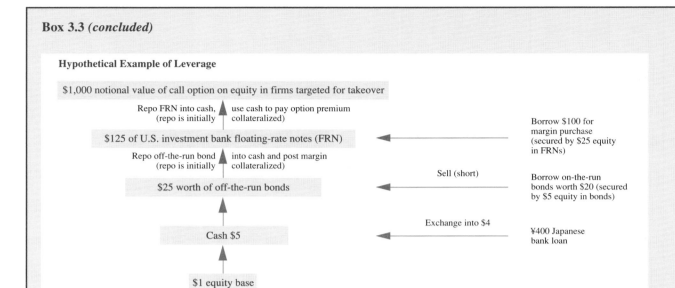

ily accurately reflect, positions alleged to have been taken by Long-Term Capital Management (LTCM). It is by no means unique; similar leveraged positions might also be taken by many hedge funds and investment banks alike.

The first layer involves an outright loan, using a small amount of equity to secure a yen-denominated loan in order to take advantage of the interest differential between Japan and the United States. The proceeds from the loan are exchanged into U.S. dollars and used as collateral to short-sell on-the-run government bonds.[3] The

proceeds from this sale finance the purchase of off-the-run government bonds in the expectation that the yield spread between the two bond types would narrow. In the third layer of leverage, the fund would then use its long position in off-the-run government bonds as collateral to borrow funds under a repurchase agreement.[4] The pro-

---

[3]On-the-run securities are the latest issue of a particular maturity. Usually they are the most actively traded issues for a particular maturity. Off-the-run securities are the previous issues of the same maturity. For example, in October 1998 the on-the-run 30-year treasury bond matures in August 2028; the most recent off-the-run 30-year treasury bond matures in November 2027.

[4]The lender of cash in a repo may also demand a "haircut" (margin payment) to limit his credit exposure resulting from a decline in the price of the collateral. This margin payment would reduce leverage. While stock margins are 50 percent and exchange-traded futures margins are between 2 and 8 percent, haircuts on repos are between 1 and 2 percent. Hedge funds are often able to negotiate a zero margin. Without any cushion to accommodate fluctuations, a 4 percent price movement (see the text) on a few trillion dollars of assets serving as collateral in a repo would cause massive margin calls and result in a major market movement.

States have played the critical role of international financial intermediary. Some have interpreted this role as bestowing benefit on the U.S. economy: developments between August and October suggest that there are also significant costs and risks. However, although U.S. markets were most visibly affected by the turbulence, other mature financial systems were also at risk if the disorderly unwinding had continued to escalate.

The resulting dynamics experienced in the mature markets—in particular, dollar financial markets and yen/dollar currency markets—reflected the very high degree of leverage that accumulated in these markets through the late summer 1998. This high degree of leverage itself reflected the relatively low margin requirements on over-the-counter derivative transactions and the increasingly accepted practice of very

low, or zero, "haircuts" on repo transactions. These and other features of modern finance may have increased the vulnerability of the involved markets, and the investors trading in them, to the kind of selling pressures, liquidity needs, rapid price adjustments, and illiquidity that ultimately occurred. These features and market dynamics ultimately exposed the international financial system to unexpected and unwarranted risks.

A Large Number of Diverse Financial Institutions, Not Just Hedge Funds, Drove the Turbulence: An Asian Lesson Revisited

Partly because of the near collapse of LTCM and the publicity it attracted, there has been a tendency to exaggerate the role that hedge funds played in the ma-

ceeds of the repo could be invested in floating-rate notes (FRNs) issued by U.S. investment banks, earning a higher return than would be paid under the repo. The investor could lend these FRN securities back to the investment bank from which it had bought them through another repo agreement. As is common under repo agreements, the investor would continue to earn the floating-rate coupon on the FRN, which by assumption is higher than the rate the investor has to pay for the repo. Furthermore, the last repo frees up cash that can in turn be used for another investment, facilitating the increase in leverage through a derivative instrument. For example, the fund could buy a call option on equity of firms targeted for a takeover, which represents the fourth layer of leverage.[5]

At each stage of this strategy the assets of the institution are increased without committing further equity, leveraging up its equity base through a series of investments on margins, short sales, repurchase agreements, and derivative securities. It allows the firm to bet on yen depreciation, narrowing U.S. treasury yield spreads, rising U.S. investment bank FRN prices, and rising equity prices of takeover targets. Furthermore, some of these activities are not recorded on the firm's balance sheet. The initial loans and U.S. treasury positions will be booked on the balance sheet. However, the repos and the derivative transaction will facilitate off-balance-sheet activity.

The investment strategy illustrated in this example would have unraveled after the Russian debt restructuring when the flight to quality and liquidity widened the yield spread between on-the-run and off-the-run U.S. treasury bonds, and the turbulence and losses dampened prospects for the U.S. investment banking industry. The widening of the liquidity spread not only implied a loss on the second leg of the transaction, owing to relative price movements, but also triggered a margin call on the first repo as the value of off-the-run bonds serving as collateral was reduced. This meant the fund would not only have to buy on-the-run bonds when their price was rising to cover its short position, but also to sell off-the-run bonds in a falling market to meet the margin call. Similarly, the FRN securities in the second repurchase agreement dropped in price and would therefore also trigger a margin call. To raise the cash needed to meet the margin calls, the investor would likely sell the FRNs in the rapidly declining market. As rumors spread that a financial institution was in a liquidity crisis, counterparties would raise the "maintenance" margin to the level of the initial margin to ensure that the loss in value of collateral would not expose counterparties to credit risk. This in turn would accelerate the unwinding of leveraged positions, causing even sharper price movements. The FRN market seized up completely at the beginning of October. Similarly, the bond market experienced significant turbulence in the period of October 7–9, around the time that much of this deleveraging may have been going on. Furthermore, the continuous appreciation of the yen prior to October would have squeezed the fund on the first leg of the transaction, triggering a rush into yen to repay the initial loan, which is consistent with the observed sharp yen appreciation in the first week of October. This illustrative scenario shows how leveraged positions may have amplified the exogenous price movement triggered by the Russian crisis and spread the turbulence to other markets.

---

[5]Balance sheet leverage is limited by two factors: underlying equity and requirements to hold capital against the assets created from the equity, which limits the number of times equity can be lent out. Leverage accumulated through off-balance-sheet derivative contracts is limited by the amount of margin payments counterparties require. If there is no margin payment, leverage can be unlimited.

ture market turbulence. Within the large universe of 3,000 hedge funds, LTCM was a unique institution (Box 3.4). Like other bond arbitrage operations, its strategy was to profit from small price discrepancies in the safest securities markets in the world, a strategy pursued by other hedge funds and other financial institutions. LTCM was unique, however, in the way that it tried to magnify the value of seemingly low-risk, low-profit gambles by taking very high-volume and highly leveraged positions to a greater extent than most other hedge funds. It was viewed in the markets as having a large appetite for risk. Single LTCM trades would involve large positions (for example, one trade of $10 million worth of U.S. treasury securities) financed on 10 percent (or smaller) margin, in order to profit from interest rate spread changes of 1 or 2 basis points. By employing this strategy—high

leveraging, with supposedly low-risk and low-return investments—a small profit from each trade potentially would be magnified, and the same trade would be repeated over and over again. Few hedge funds employed the scale of leverage that LTCM assembled.[17] In the end, both the leverage and the positions ultimately destroyed LTCM.

Although LTCM was the best-known loser from the kind of low-profit-margin, fixed-income position taking that became exposed to a widening of credit risk and liquidity spreads, other, much larger institutions took similar positions, in some cases with consider-

---

[17]See Barry Eichengreen, Donald Mathieson, and others, *Hedge Funds and Financial Market Dynamics,* Occasional Paper 166 (Washington: IMF, 1998).

Box 3.4. The Near Collapse and Rescue of Long-Term Capital Management

Long-Term Capital Management (LTCM) manages an investment fund[1]—a hedge fund—that attempts to profit from (often small) discrepancies in the relative value of government bonds, fixed-income derivatives, equities and equity derivatives primarily in the U.S., Japanese, and European markets. The fund also invests in a few markets outside the G-7 countries. LTCM's traders are legendary for being the best and brightest technicians in the hedge fund community, and the firm is reported to have recorded total returns, after fees, of 43 percent in 1995, 41 percent in 1996, and 17 percent in 1997.[2]

In the week of September 21—amid market rumors about LTCM and some of its major creditors and counterparties, and concerns over potential liquidity problems in financial markets—the Federal Reserve Bank of New York (FRBNY) helped to organize and coordinate a $3.6 billion private rescue of LTCM by a consortium of 14 major international financial institutions. All of these institutions are either counterparties, creditors, or investors of the hedge fund. According to press reports and FRBNY press statements at the time, the rescue was seen as necessary for two reasons: LTCM's financial condition had deteriorated to the point where it might not be able to make either loan repayments or margin calls on its highly leveraged positions in U.S., Japanese, and European bond markets, and might require either recapitalization or liquidation; and immediate closure of LTCM would have worsened the financial condition of some already weakened international financial institutions and could have triggered a massive simultaneous sale of LTCM's collateral (securities) by creditor institutions. This would have further strained the stability of the world's major bond markets, creating the potential for debilitating and widespread spillovers and contagion, including in emerging markets.

What Brought LTCM to the Brink of Collapse?

LTCM specializes in fixed-income and equity convergence strategies, taking complex and leveraged positions in order to profit from (often small) discrepancies in the relative price of bonds, swaps, options, and similarly in the relative price of equities and their derivative instruments. The bulk of LTCM's investments are convergence trades in U.S., Japanese, and European bond markets—essentially gambles that interest rate spreads had widened beyond a sustainable level and would narrow and return

to more normal spreads. These transactions typically have horizons of 6 to 24 months. These so-called convergence trades are based on the judgment, probably supported by asset-pricing models, that markets have been undervaluing relatively risky bonds (mortgage-backed securities, for example) and overvaluing low-risk bonds (G-7 government securities).[3] LTCM purchased or borrowed large volumes of relatively risky bonds and sold short G-7 government bonds. These positions were leveraged using borrowed funds from internationally active commercial and investment banks. At the beginning of 1998, on capital of just $4.8 billion, LTCM managed balance sheet positions totaling about $120 billion, implying a leverage ratio of 25-times-capital. At the same time, LTCM was managing total gross notional off-balance-sheet derivative contracts amounting to about $1.3 trillion. These leverage ratios and off-balance-sheet transactions did not change significantly in the months leading up to the August 1998 crisis.

LTCM's trading book was "long" in relatively illiquid, low-quality securities (mortgage-backed securities, advanced country junk bonds) and "short" in liquid, high-quality securities (U.S. treasuries and other G-7 sovereign credits). It was also short volatility in the main equity markets. Contrary to LTCM's judgment, interest-rate spreads widened throughout 1998 in most of the theaters of its operations—earlier in the year, as the intensification of the financial crises in Asia encouraged a flight to quality in the G-7 government securities markets and, later in the year, as the Russian involuntary restructuring of GKOs (ruble-denominated discount instruments) led to an even greater widening of credit spreads.[4] Similarly, implied volatilities reached all-time

---

[3]Bankers familiar with LTCM's portfolio suggested that LTCM engaged in a lot of transactions involving total return swaps, which allow investors to profit or to lose from price movements on securities without actually purchasing them. For example, for an obligatory financing charge, LTCM would borrow asset-backed securities and receive both interest and capital gains or losses. The securities would have to be returned and the finance charge paid regardless of the value of the securities. LTCM's expectation was that they would lock in relatively high interest payments and at the same time receive capital gains as the value of these securities rose as the markets' assessment returned to normal.

[4]In 1997, LTCM is reported to have borrowed aggressively, and on relatively favorable terms, to increase its exposure and leverage as spreads widened, presumably on the strong belief in its technical judgment that spreads would ultimately narrow and that it would be able to manage its growing exposure.

---

[1]The fund is Long-Term Capital Portfolio.

[2]By comparison, the return to the S&P 500 was 34 percent in 1995, 20 percent in 1996, and 34 percent in 1997.

---

able leverage.[18] These institutions included internationally active commercial and investment banks, bro-

kers and dealers, and other institutional investors. While LTCM was alleged to have had $80 billion dol-

---

[18]According to an analysis by Salomon Smith Barney, balance sheet data indicate that investment banks are highly leveraged institutions. Gross leverage ratios (ratio of gross assets to equity) for the

top firms range between 25 and 35, while net leverage ratios (ratio of gross assets excluding matched-book financing to equity) range between 10 and 20. These ratios exclude off-balance-sheet activities.

highs. During these flights to quality, liquidity dried up in the high-yield (high-risk) sectors of U.S., Japanese, and European bond markets, driving spreads even higher. Because of the illiquidity of its positions, and difficult market conditions, LTCM was unable to reduce the size of its positions and strategies. The losses associated with this divergence of spreads and increased volatilities reduced the hedge fund's equity (net asset value) from $4.8 billion in January 1998 to $2.3 billion in August. This resulted in an increase of leverage to 50-times-capital on its balance sheet positions alone.

In a September 2 letter to investors, LTCM informed investors that the value of the fund was down 44 percent in August and 52 percent for the year. LTCM also reported that losses occurred in a wide variety of strategies, distributed approximately 82 percent to relative value trades and 18 percent to directional trades; only 16 percent of losses were attributed to emerging market investments. On average, spreads continued to diverge in September. Through Friday, September 18, LTCM was meeting margin calls, in part by drawing on a long-standing $580 million credit facility headed by Chase Manhattan Corporation.

After it was determined that LTCM's financial condition had deteriorated to the point where it might not be able to service its debt obligations and make margin calls during the week, the FRBNY organized a meeting of LTCM creditors and counterparties and began helping to coordinate a private consortium to rescue LTCM. As of Tuesday, September 23, LTCM's equity position stood at just $600 million and was supporting balance sheet positions in excess of $100 billion, implying balance sheet leverage of 167 times capital; the hedge fund's losses on its highly leveraged positions (but not necessarily on the securities that it was holding) had wiped out 90 percent of its equity.

Why Was LTCM Rescued?

At some point—probably culminating on Sunday, September 20, when staff at the FRBNY and the U.S. Treasury visited LTCM headquarters in Greenwich, Connecticut—the assessment was made that the potential for market disruption supported facilitating a private-sector solution, given the similarity of position taking by other large internationally active financial institutions and the large number of other institutions (including brokers and dealers) that held large inventories of securities across the credit spectrum. It was known by the banks and U.S. authorities that LTCM's exposure was large enough, and cut across a suffi-

cient number of important markets, that if the fund were forced into a sudden and disorderly liquidation, markets around the globe could be disrupted as LTCM's illiquid securities were dumped at prices well below face value. The further widening of spreads and dramatic price dynamics that might have accompanied an immediate closing out and deleveraging of LTCM's positions would have entailed a simultaneous and massive trading of a large volume of securities by the large international financial institutions in New York, Japan, and Europe, posing risks of systemic proportions. The process could have led to many technical insolvencies. Given the number of institutions involved in these transactions, even a small probability of this occurring posed the serious systemic risk broadly encompassing financial markets.

The threat of a massive "fire sale" of LTCM's collateral did exist. Repurchase and reverse repurchase agreements are governed by a provision of the bankruptcy law that would have allowed LTCM's creditors to sell immediately the collateral that secured repos and swaps used extensively by LTCM if it were allowed to fail. With LTCM's large balance sheet exposures and additional large off-balance-sheet positions, a bankruptcy filing could have touched off a simultaneous and potentially destabilizing effort by all creditors to buy and sell the securities that were backing these huge repo and swap positions, at a time when markets were already strained and jittery. In the days before the rescue was arranged, the $1 trillion U.S. repo market was showing strains on market rumors and concerns about the credit quality of some leading investment banks. A liquidation of collateral would have had repercussions in the underlying repo and swap markets themselves—in New York, Japan, and Europe. There was growing evidence that liquidity in these important funding markets was drying up, and the mounting nervousness might have encouraged the FRBNY to arrange the rescue in order to avoid a panic and the potential for systemic problems. The private rescue by creditors was orchestrated, in part, to allow for a more orderly unwinding of positions and to remove the potential for a rapid draining of liquidity in the world's major securities markets, and the systemic risks that such an event might entail.

Most if not all of the credit supplied to LTCM by the major financial institutions was fully collateralized with high-grade paper, in most cases U.S. treasury securities (probably some of it off-the-run issues). Never-

(Box continues on next page.)

lars in balance-sheet arbitrage positions in U.S. treasury security markets, commercial banks alone were estimated to have had $3 trillion in similar exposures. The widespread position taking, the complexity of the layers of derivative and leveraged spot market transactions, and the relatively closed circle of counterpar-

ties created a potentially unsustainable balance and distribution of financial risks. The confluence of these institutions' positions led to a situation in which a rapid unwinding of LTCM's portfolios in fixed-income and equity markets might have meant not only that direct creditors and counterparts could have had

Box 3.4 *(concluded)*

theless, potential losses on bank loans to LTCM might have resulted from adverse movements in the market values of this collateral were LTCM to default. There was also concern that many of the world's largest internationally active institutions stood to lose from a massive sell-off of positions and the liquidity problems it might create. But the predominant consideration seems to have been that a very large number and variety of financial institutions could have been affected by such a wave of selling and repricing. This could have disrupted financial markets around the world. One way to contain the potential systemic risk was to organize a private consortium of LTCM's main creditors and counterparties, in part to engineer a more orderly process of unwinding and deleveraging, but also to internalize many of the risks. The pooling and internalization of risk was possible because the consortium included many, if not all, of the financial institutions that would necessarily have been involved in the closing out and deleveraging of positions in the markets, because they are the major market makers, dealers, brokers, and counterparties. An additional benefit might be that some share of the transactions could be netted within the consortium, and others could be closed out and deleveraged within the consortium rather than in the markets, which would help to reduce selling pressures in the major markets. Alternative solutions could have been found with similar benefits. For example, a single buyer might have been found for LTCM, and there was at least one such interested party. In the short time available for finding solutions, however, such alternatives were not agreed by LTCM's partners and potential buyers.

The rescue of LTCM can be seen as an out-of-court bankruptcy-type reorganization of LTCM in which its major creditors have become its new owners in charge of every aspect of the business, with the objective of salvaging as much value from the wreckage as they can. With the benefit of hindsight, it is safe to conclude that the outright failure of LTCM would have posed significant risks of systemic problems in international financial markets, and that it was necessary to restructure LTCM. A more rapid and disorderly unwinding of LTCM's very large and highly leveraged fixed-income positions and related positions of other institutions could have triggered an even more destructive forced deleveraging in U.S., German, and Japanese fixed-income markets and in the major currency markets. This would have necessarily included equally disruptive selling pressures in the associated derivative markets, where the volume and notional value of transactions are several multiples

of the volume and face value of the underlying securities. One can only speculate how much worse the market turbulence would have been had LTCM been allowed to collapse.

Two counter arguments against the Federal Reserve System's involvement in facilitating the private rescue of LTCM have been suggested. First, it has been argued, because LTCM was not subject to the Federal Reserve's supervisory and regulatory jurisdiction, it was inappropriate for the Federal Reserve to risk its reputation and goodwill. Second, the involvement of the central bank in facilitating the private rescue might entail moral hazard for institutions not ordinarily regulated or supervised by the central bank, or for institutions that ordinarily take on high leverage in their activities. Moral hazard clearly is a concern with any central bank or other official interventions in individual financial institutions. Because no public funds were necessary in rescuing LTCM, the moral hazard implications of this particular intervention would be limited to the signals implicit in the Federal Reserve's involvement. It is not possible to evaluate objectively the potential costs of these signals against the benefits of the Federal Reserve's involvement.

Who Are LTCM's New Owners?

A total of $3.625 billion was injected as equity into LTCM by 14 international financial institutions, many of them creditors: 11 institutions took equity stakes of $300 million (Banker's Trust, Barclays, Chase Manhattan, Credit Suisse First Boston, Deutsche Bank, J.P. Morgan, Goldman Sachs, Merrill Lynch, Morgan Stanley Dean Witter, Travelers, and Union Bank of Switzerland); 2 institutions took a $125 million stake (Société Générale, Lehman Brothers); and 1 institution took a stake of $100 million (Paribas).[5]

The new owners together own 90 percent of LTCM's equity for a period of three years (the remaining 10 percent is held by the original partners) and have the option to obtain 50 percent of the management company for a nominal fee of $1. Most new investors are reported to be hoping to be bought out before then. The terms of the agreement provide the private consortium with full authority over the investment strategy, capitalization structure, credit and market risk management, compensation, and all other significant decisions.

---

[5]Among the new owners, Union Bank of Switzerland had already announced the writing down of its original equity stake in LTCM of $685 million.

difficulties collecting on their contracts, but also that the wide array of other institutions holding similar positions could have been adversely affected by sharp price movements.

Some of the proprietary trading operations of commercial and investment banks rival in scale the opera-

tions of large hedge funds and at times may have more risky proprietary trading books than many hedge funds. In addition to taking positions on their own account, the globally active commercial and investment banks may encourage clients to take similar positions, and so the volumes of trades and capital these institutions place are larger than their proprietary positions, and than the positions taken by hedge funds.[19] Much of this investment and trading activity takes place in the relatively safe fixed-income markets in the advanced countries.

Nevertheless, the hedge funds together have enough capital and are sufficiently highly leveraged to have a noticeable impact on market liquidity when they withdraw from markets during turbulence: they often are the first to exit a market, but they also often are the first to reenter.[20] However, it is doubtful that any single hedge fund, or small group of hedge funds, alone could pose a risk of systemic problems. Rather it was the simultaneous and interrelated involvement of a large number of players, including both hedge funds and many internationally active commercial and investment banks, that recently raised the potential for such risks.

Why Did Risk Management Models Not Prevent the Buildup of Positions and Leverage?

The ultimate impact of the turbulence on bank balance sheets and profitability, and on the financial condition of other financiers and investors, raises questions about why so many sophisticated institutions may have engaged in similar positions. A key issue is: Why did risk management technologies (models, stress tests, and scenario analyses) and internal operational control mechanisms apparently not warn risk managers and top management about the growing vulnerabilities?

Modern risk management models are designed (and are used along with stress testing) to measure and assess the riskiness of portfolios on the basis of assumptions about the likelihood of outcomes that might put a firm's capital at risk and ultimately risk its solvency. Value-at-risk (VaR) models are one way of achieving this objective.[21] One problem with relying on these techniques is that they may provide a false sense of precision, in part because the output of models depends on inputs that depend on human judgment. Faulty assumptions—about the probability of adverse events, the structure of markets, cross-market price correlations, and within stress tests and scenario analyses— might have impaired the usefulness of models. The models also assume that market liquidity will be sufficient to allow positions to be closed out without ex-

tremely large price changes or market disorder. Moreover, because they usually rely on historical relationships between price movements in many markets, the models can break down during times of unusual stress and turbulence, particularly when structural breaks occur in cross-market relationships. Such structural shifts, even if temporary, may imply dramatic shifts in risk in portfolios, and call for a rapid portfolio rebalancing. Even asset managers who only employed normal principles of portfolio diversification might have called for reductions in emerging market and similar risk exposures and for increases in low-risk or risk-free assets (Box 3.5). If many investors adjust large portfolios simultaneously in the same direction, market liquidity would tend to be adversely affected.

High-tech computer-driven portfolio management techniques, such as portfolio insurance[22] and dynamic hedging,[23] are supposed to have helped firms to minimize their losses and maximize their gains when these techniques worked, but they probably also exacerbated large volumes of sell orders flowing into declining markets where buyers and sellers were uncertain about who owned what risks and how they should be priced. Risk components that in normal circumstances would have remained isolated became blurred, and liquidity and counterparty risk considerations came to the fore as key concerns. At a time when there already may have been heightened concern about credit, market, and settlement risks, market participants appear to have intensified their focus on whether securities could be liquidated quickly if necessary (liquidity risk) regardless of the quality of the paper. It is this kind of blurring of risks, the intermittent, absolute focus on market liquidity, and the almost automatic nature of some position-unwinding and liquidity-seeking trades that could explain unusual developments in some market segments. One such example is the sharp rise in the premium on off-the-run over on-the-run U.S. treasury securities, which increased to more than 35 basis points in at least one segment of the market (possibly when LTCM was liquidating its long position in off-the-run U.S. treasuries).

Threat of Systemic Problems: Accelerated Deleveraging and Widening of Spreads Surrounding the Near Collapse of LTCM

By late August 1998 the initial widening of credit risk spreads likely contributed to pressures on the port-

---

[19]Hedge funds obtain most of their operational financing from, and place their trades with, the large commercial and investment banks. The banks are seen by hedge funds as "front-running" the hedge funds' own position taking. Because of this front-running behavior, many hedge funds see commercial and investment banks as a threat to their returns. This is one of the reasons why hedge funds are so secretive about their positions and use complex trading strategies and tactics.

[20]See the 1997 *International Capital Markets* report.

[21]VaR models measure how much of the firm's capital could be lost because of swings in the value of its portfolio.

[22]Portfolio insurance is a technique that changes a portfolio's market exposure systematically in reaction to prior market movements, with the objective of avoiding large losses and securing as much participation as possible in favorable market movements.

[23]Dynamic hedging is a position-risk management technique in which option-like return patterns are replicated by adjusting portfolio positions to offset the impact of a price change in the underlying market on the value of an options position (the "delta"). Dynamic hedging relies on liquid, continuous markets with low transaction costs.

Box 3.5. Risk Management: Progress and Problems

The most familiar risk management model is the value-at-risk (VaR) model.[1] The VaR model measures how much of the firm's capital could be lost owing to swings in the value of its portfolio, given a host of assumptions about correlations among security prices, the way that security prices move over time, and so forth. More technically, the VaR model estimates the loss on the firm's portfolio that should be exceeded with no more than a certain probability, given a model for changes in the prices of all the assets in the portfolio. For example, a firm's VaR might indicate that its losses over the coming week should exceed $10 million with no more than 5 percent probability.[2] Financial institutions base VaR calculations on historical data, and some also use stress tests, in which scenarios are simulated. Regardless of the methodology, if the potential loss is too large, the firm might rebalance, or hedge, part of its portfolio to reduce the value at risk. Some financial institutions also allocate capital on the basis of results of VaR and similar models.

Prevailing risk management practices focus on market risk, for which modeling is advanced and has reached a reasonable level of performance. Modeling of market risk entails formal models of the behavior of the prices of the assets making up the portfolio. A simple VaR model might assume that changes in the value of each asset in the portfolio are normally distributed and independent across time, with correlations and variances that change slowly. Such models would also tend to assume that the structure of markets is relatively simple and stable; for example, that the relationship between stock and bond prices is simple and does not change sign or magnitude, or that the complex relationship of a derivative security to its underlying security can be well approximated by a simpler relationship.

However, models of market risk have, over time, revealed weaknesses, owing primarily to their heavy reliance on historical data and relationships. Such analysis tends to understate the likelihood of extreme events and often involves the assumption that the processes generating market prices are stable. Recent events have underscored that rare, "fat-tailed" events can occur more frequently than expected, that correlations can increase and change sign suddenly, and that volatility can increase sharply without warning. Moreover, it is also presumed that market liquidity will be maintained so that positions can be closed out when necessary without adverse price declines.

Significant gaps also remain in the modeling of other types of risk, particularly credit and liquidity risks.[3] Credit risk modeling is still in its infancy, in part because credit risk is difficult to model: defaults are rare, and the risk of default evolves over time in a complicated fashion. However, the bulk of risk on balance sheets consists of credit risk; indeed, credit losses have been the key source of financial distress.

Even less advanced is the modeling of liquidity risk—the risk that transactions cannot be executed without

---

[1]For further discussion of recent advances in risk management, see the September 1998 *International Capital Markets* report, Annex V.

[2]Philippe Jorion, *Value at Risk* (New York: McGraw-Hill, 1997) provides technical details of risk management models.

[3]Other types of risk—which for the most part remain to be quantitatively addressed—include legal and operational risks; see Jorion, *Value at Risk*.

---

folios of the major financial institutions and LTCM, and the rebalancing and deleveraging of mature market portfolios accelerated. Although the Russian unilateral restructuring might have been perceived as a significant event for traders in New York, London, and Frankfurt, an important wake-up call for mature market position takers occurred in early September, when LTCM announced that 52 percent of its capital had been spent on margin calls, only 16 percent of which were related to emerging market investments (see Box 3.4). This apparently triggered rounds of speculation, selling, and counterparty concerns in the international markets. At that time, LTCM also had engaged in fund raising to try to increase capital to sustain its convergence plays long enough for interest rate spreads to converge.

Fears in the markets that many other institutions might be holding similar positions created substantial uncertainty about counterparty risk and generated rumors, which probably contributed to heightened market turbulence even after LTCM's rescue by a private consortium of its creditors and counterparties had been

agreed. In the week beginning October 5, while the consortium was beginning to unwind and sell off LTCM's complex positions, there were several waves of turbulence (especially during October 7–9). The yen/dollar market, in particular, experienced extreme turbulence as the financing of global investments from Japan was abruptly unwound and the dollar fell sharply against the yen. As discussed earlier (see Box 3.1), this unprecedented yen/dollar adjustment was partly the result of the unwinding of the "carry-trade," in which investors around the world borrowed yen cheaply, swapped into other currencies (probably mostly dollars), and then purchased assets with higher returns in a wide range of countries and markets, including U.S. government securities. Much of the liquidity-driven (and large volumes of) trading that accompanied the further widening of spreads, the dramatic depreciation of the dollar, rumors of failing financial institutions, and other uncertainty-creating events was probably partly driven by the actual unwinding and deleveraging of positions by the consortium on behalf of LTCM and by consortium members.

unsettling markets. Liquidity risk may have been the most significant type of risk in the recent turbulence, since a lack of liquidity may have been responsible for some of the price disconnects that occurred.[4] Liquidity risk can make risk management extraordinarily difficult. For example, firms that take positions under the assumption that the positions can be unwound smoothly if events turn against them sustain larger-than-expected losses when they attempt to unwind in illiquid markets.

There are likewise significant gaps in the modeling of the nexus of market, credit, and liquidity risks, gaps that came into sharp focus during the Asian crises and in the aftermath of the Russian devaluation and moratorium.[5] For example, in the recent turbulence, market risk itself gave rise to credit and liquidity risks. In some cases, firms that had significant paper gains vis-à-vis emerging market counterparties were unable to collect these gains as counterparties went bankrupt: while market risk had moved in banks' favor, counterparty risk had moved just as strongly against them. Similar problems arose when large market moves sharply reduced the value of collateral. In other instances, large market moves created selling pressures, which in turn impaired market liquidity and gave rise to liquidity risk.

---

[4]There is also a different type of liquidity risk (the ability to roll over funding). See Jorion, *Value at Risk*.

[5]For an approach to modeling both market and credit risk, see Theodore M. Barnhill, Jr., and William F. Maxwell, "Modeling Correlated Interest Rate and Credit Risk" (unpublished; Washington: George Washington University and Georgetown University, October 1998).

These problems—the unstable nature of market risk, the difficulty of modeling credit and liquidity risk, and the highly complex relationship between them—also undercut attempts to hedge. Banks that hedged the ruble exposure in GKOs (ruble-denominated discount instruments) through forward contracts with Russian banks faced losses on both the GKOs and hedges. Also, during the recent market stresses, assets that usually were uncorrelated or negatively correlated, and hence offered diversification or hedging, declined together as liquidity evaporated.

Successful risk management requires human judgment, including a balanced (lack of) respect for statistical models built on historical data. Another human factor is the interaction between the risk management and business functions in banks; sometimes, the dictates of risk models are overridden by business units in pursuit of, for example, a strategic relationship.[6] Indeed, within financial institutions there is a tension between taking risk during market upturns and managing the risk from market downturns.

There are two lessons for risk management from the market turbulence of the past summer and fall. First, risk management should promote a conservative and comprehensive approach to risk; a piecemeal approach clearly can miss significant risks and the interactions among them. Second, in risk management as in other areas, complex, formal models can complement but cannot fully substitute for judgment and experience.

---

[6]See Bank for International Settlements, "On the Use of Information and Risk Management by International Banks: Report of a Working Group Established by the Euro-Currency Standing Committee of the Central Banks of the Group of Ten Countries" (Basle, October 1998).

Some trading was also likely to have been generated by the uncertainty over whether the emerging market contagion would spread to Latin America, in particular Brazil. It was not until after the U.S. Federal Reserve's second interest rate cut on October 15 that market pressures began to ease.

It is uncertain how much more deleveraging will occur in the period ahead. The manner in which markets adjusted; the apparent price disconnects in usually deep and liquid, but temporarily thin, markets; the panic-driven rumors; and other aspects of the turbulence strongly suggest that the unwinding that had to be accomplished to reach more comfortable risk levels was unusually large relative to underlying balance sheet positions. However, given the limited availability of transaction data, and the infrequency and incompleteness of the reporting of derivatives market transactions, it is not possible to assess the degree of leverage remaining in the system that might create further turbulent dynamics in the future. Considering that the process of deleveraging that followed the bond market turbulence in early 1994 took some eight

months to complete, and that the price and flow adjustments at their nadir in the more recent episode were in many respects unprecedented—in particular the massive shifts out of relatively risky and illiquid assets—it would seem that the process of deleveraging may still have some distance to go, although presumably not with the extreme tensions that developed in September and early October.

While the preceding analysis provides some understanding of why the Russian crisis and some features present in mature markets might lead to a reassessment of risks and rebalancing of emerging and mature market portfolios, this understanding is not entirely reassuring. In particular, the associated surprisingly large flights to safety and liquidity, the rapid drying up of liquidity in international capital markets, and turbulence in a wide range of mature markets—defined at times by price disconnects and near seizures in some markets—all appear to have been out of proportion to the factors that triggered them. Thus, the overriding concern is not that the reassessments and portfolio adjustments occurred; instead, it is that they were so violent and widespread that they might have posed systemic risks for world financial markets and significant downside risks to the world economic outlook.

Shortcomings in Risk Management and Implications for Prudential Regulation and Supervision

As has been suggested, deficiencies in both private and systemic risk management probably contributed to the recent financial market turbulence. In private markets, a large number of diverse market participants were apparently surprised by sharp adverse price movements in asset markets, and this suggests that they engaged in excessive risk taking, excessive leverage, and ultimately an unsustainable structure of financial positions.[24] In addition, they may have paid insufficient attention to the interplay of market and credit risk. This confluence of mistakes might have created an accident waiting to happen. On the public side, although public systemic risk management in the period September–November 1998 alleviated the threat of a systemic problem in international markets, at least two lines of defense—banking supervision and market surveillance—that would ordinarily safeguard against the buildup of such a threat did not appear to provide sufficient warnings.

Weaknesses in Private Risk Management

Financial systems have several lines of defense against systemic problems. The first are the risk management systems and internal management control mechanisms of private financial institutions that are designed to prevent them from taking excessive risks that could ultimately threaten their capital position and viability. In view of the extent of losses suffered by a number of large institutions, the degree of surprise associated with those losses, and the reaction of equity prices for these institutions, risk management systems appear to have not worked very well for a large number of diverse and systemically important financial institutions, including many of the internationally active commercial and investment banks, proprietary trading desks, market makers, broker/dealers, and foreign-exchange traders/dealers. Bank loan books had already become somewhat weakened by the Asian crises and were eroded further by the Russian crisis in August 1998. The profitability of trading books was also affected by the emerging market turbulence through the Asian and Russian crises, which induced a shift to advanced

country fixed-income markets and the currency markets, and most notably the yen/dollar market. Many players appear to have been involved in convergence plays, in part because yield curve plays were not lucrative given the compression of the term structure.

The evidence suggests that many market participants did not adequately anticipate or understand the risks that were realized in the period mid-August through mid-October 1998. Several systemically important internationally active financial institutions appear to have made similar, if not the same, misjudgments in their risk assessments, risk management, and investment strategies. This suggests that management command and control systems now used by these financial institutions may be flawed, and raises concerns about the adequacy of risk and portfolio management systems and operational controls within some international financial institutions. The systems now in use apparently have not adequately incorporated some of the lessons of the 1994–95 Mexican crisis—some mistakes appear to have been repeated in the 1997 Asian crises—and some deeper-seated problems surfaced in the recent management of advanced country portfolios during the most recent turbulence. During the Mexican crisis, some investors made significant paper gains on their trading books by shorting the peso with Mexican entities, but they could not collect their sizable gains because the Mexican counterparty did not survive the peso devaluation. In the most recent turbulence, similar mistakes appear to have been made. Internationally active banks extended credit to LTCM and also were counterparties to some of LTCM's transactions without adequately understanding the size, complexity, and riskiness of LTCM's balance sheet and off-balance-sheet positions. As is now known, some creditors held many of the same positions as LTCM. At least some of the turbulence in 1998 probably could have been avoided if a more integrated approach to market and credit risk management and position taking had been the normal practice when the positions were being taken weeks, months, and years ago. This also was a lesson apparently not learned during the Asian crises. Greater diligence in credit risk assessment and oversight of credits to LTCM and other hedge funds also might have diminished the extent to which their exposures made creditor and counterparty institutions vulnerable to this kind of turbulence.

Risk management models and modern techniques of portfolio management typically presume that positions can be closed out in orderly, liquid, continuous markets, with low transaction costs. These conditions are unlikely to be present during times of stress and turbulence. Similarly, although market risk assessment and management appear to have reached a sophisticated level, and have met with some success in containing private risk in normal markets, such systems can break down in times of stress and turbu-

---

[24]During the past two years, central banks have voiced concerns about credit standards, the relaxation of loan covenants, and compressed interest rate spreads.

lence, when market correlations suddenly shift. In addition, the near collapse of LTCM, and the potential counterparty risk its failure posed, can be seen as a warning sign that some banks may not be devoting sufficient attention to credit risk assessment and management. Moreover, previous crises, and now the mature market turbulence, strongly suggest that sophisticated financial institutions with diverse ranges of semi-independent operations have not yet found a fully satisfactory way to assess the level of consolidated risks at the institutional level, and in particular do not yet fully incorporate (into their position taking, financing, and leverage) an adequate understanding of the impact of market risk events on credit risk assessments. Finally, the recent turbulence in the mature markets indicates that liquidity risk is an important area that also may not be sufficiently well understood.

It is tempting to blame the shortcomings in the application of modern quantitative approaches to risk assessment, risk management, and portfolio management to failures in the risk management technologies and systems themselves. The technical details of models, the sensitivities to assumptions, including the assumed probabilities of adverse events in stress testing, and the excessive risk tolerance limits may all be part of the problem. But an equally important shortcoming may be the element of human judgment required to implement these technologies and systems and to assess the economic and financial environment. Also relevant are the incentives within these organizations to maximize short-term gains and individual bonuses, at times at the expense of the firm's overall risk exposure and longer-term profit. In this regard, greater diligence, especially surrounding creditor and counterparty relationships between the major financial institutions and the hedge fund LTCM, was probably called for.

The recent turbulence also appears to have extended beyond the aggregation of the individual responses to margin calls and the need to unwind, deleverage, and hedge positions as protection against the adverse consequences of owning assets in declining markets. In particular, the impact of the simultaneous rush of many investors to close out positions and deleverage seemed to have been magnified by the inability of international financial markets to absorb the first round of the Russian unilateral restructuring. The process of adjustment seems to have taken on a life of its own through the structure of linkages between the relatively small circle of counterparties; the high, and perhaps excessive, degree of short-term competitive pressures; the complex manner in which the positions were originally financed, leveraged, and hedged; and the diversity of mature markets, currency denominations, and maturity structures that facilitated these transactions. In short, there also seemed to be systemic components that contributed to the virulence of the mature

market turbulence that few, if any, participants fully anticipated. Accordingly, the market turbulence, and the issues raised by it, also need to be examined at the systemic level.

Public Systemic Risk Management

An important line of defense against systemic problems is financial supervision and regulation. Modern financial institutions are complex organizations, and the risks taken by them may not always be fully understood by those who manage them. How, then, can supervisors be expected to make informed judgments about whether institutions are financially sound? Finding operational answers to this difficult question for the industrial countries of North America, Europe, and Japan, of a form that can be applied with reasonable consistency for a wide range of internationally active commercial banks, is the continuing task of the Group of Ten (G-10) banking supervisors under the auspices of the Basle Committee on Banking Supervision. The established approach, which relies on quantitative rules, such as the Basle capital ratio, has proved useful in providing enhanced discipline for risk taking by covered institutions—although there have been instances where the rules have apparently not been rigorously applied. However, it is also widely recognized (Box 3.6) that the established Basle approach has significant deficiencies, especially in the area of off-balance sheet activities, which are of substantial and growing importance for most, large, internationally active commercial banks.[25] This has led the Basle Committee to consider alternative approaches that would supplement present rules with supervisory assessments of the adequacy of risk management systems and systems of operational controls (see Box 3.6). In this regard, the recent experience suggesting significant deficiencies in the performance of risk management and operational control systems in at least some systemically important institutions clearly raises important concerns upon which the Basle Committee and others interested in effective bank supervision will need to reflect.

It is not evident that any system of supervision or surveillance could have identified these problems as they were actually developing. Nevertheless, it seems plausible that some of the excessive risk taking and leveraging could have been avoided if home national supervisors, and those responsible for market surveillance, knew more about the buildup of both balance sheet and off-balance-sheet positions, leverage, and both the aggregate amount and distribution of risk taking in national and international markets. For example, LTCM was known, and even advertised, to have a

---

[25]These deficiencies have been discussed in previous IMF *International Capital Markets* reports.

Box 3.6. Supervisory Reforms Relating to Risk Management[1]

Structural changes in financial markets have encouraged international bank supervisors and the Basle Committee on Banking Supervision to shift gradually from "rules-based" to "risk-focused" methods of supervision, particularly in setting capital requirements for market and credit risks. Despite some progress in the treatment of market risk, recent events have exposed shortcomings in the treatment of credit risk, as laid out in the 1988 Basle Accord. These shortcomings are primarily in three areas: the distortions arising from risk weights, including on interbank claims and sovereign debt of OECD countries; the disregard of the effects of the business and credit cycles on credit risk; and the neglect of the broader operating environment for banks in emerging markets. Measures to address such shortcomings are under discussion by members of the Basle Committee and other international groupings of financial supervisors.

Encouraged by the rapid changes in the structure of financial markets and perceived shortcomings of past approaches, supervisors are gradually changing emphasis, focusing less on static concepts of risk and more on the systems and procedures that firms use to measure and manage risk. Leading the way within this new paradigm have been supervisory changes to capital requirements relating to market risk. The Basle Committee's 1996 guidelines on capital requirements for market risk, which became applicable and mandatory for internationally active banks on January 1, 1998, represent a watershed in the regulatory treatment of capital. The new requirements allow banks to use their own internal models for the determination of market risk capital. While only a few countries have banks with models that pass muster, their sanctioned use has raised issues about the role of regulatory capital more generally.

Notwithstanding this recent progress, three shortcomings remain in the regulatory treatment of credit risk. First, distortionary effects of the capital accord arise from the arbitrary manner in which the risk weights are assigned. For instance, under the 1988 Basle Accord, short-term claims on banks from any country carry a relatively low (20 percent) risk weight, leading to a lower cost of borrowing in the interbank market and a heavier reliance on interbank funding.[2] Also, the accord assigns a zero risk weight to instruments issued or guaranteed by OECD governments. It has been suggested by some Basle Committee members that the OECD designation has served as a "stamp of approval" and has encouraged banks to steer funds to OECD emerging markets rather than to non-OECD countries with equivalent or lower sovereign risks.

The second shortcoming is the arbitrary and unchanging 8 percent minimum capital assigned to risk-weighted assets. The constancy of this capital requirement over the business and credit cycles is viewed by some as unnecessary and undesirable. An alternative is to require banks to hold a higher ratio of capital to risk-weighted assets during the cycle's upswing, for two reasons. First, some cushion above the 8 percent minimum would be in place when the business cycle turns down. Although capital may be above the required minimum at the peak of the cycle, the additional buffer may not be sufficient in light of the increased risk. Second, at the peak of the cycle, the riskiness of banks' assets may be well above the average for the cycle, but the 8 percent minimum does not adjust upward as the cycle matures to take account of the increase in risk. Indeed, the risk of a sharp downturn in asset quality is probably highest at the peak of the business cycle, but current capital standards do not account for this dynamic. There is also a well-documented "credit cycle" in most countries, with banks moving down the credit curve as the cycle expands, taking on more and more risk. To the extent that the credit cycle tends to coincide with the business cycle, as it likely does, this would tend to augment the risk of a sharp downturn in asset quality during the mature phase of the business cycle. A minimum capital requirement that acknowledged these dynamics in credit risk and varied with risk over the business cycle would help to accommodate these risks.

[1]This box draws heavily on the September 1998 *International Capital Markets* report, Chapter V.

[2]See Box 5.8 in *International Capital Markets*, September 1998, for the accord's current risk-weighting scheme for on-balance-sheet assets.

large appetite for risk.[26] If the institutions that provided credit to facilitate LTCM's position taking and leverage had been encouraged to come to the judgment that LTCM was an excessively risky counterparty, then LTCM might not have gone as far as it did in taking risk. Likewise, had LTCM's counterparties not been so exposed to high-risk positions with as many high-risk players, the buildup would have been more limited.

Another line of defense against systemic problems is financial market surveillance. For example, the U.S. Federal Reserve's involvement in the markets means that it has continuous access to market intelligence and information. Moreover, to fulfill its mandate to ensure U.S. financial system stability, it has over the years de-

[26]LTCM's original prospectus warned investors that "it is expected that the Portfolio Company will generally be very highly leveraged, and that such leverage will generally be higher than that of other typically leveraged investment funds" and that "returns are anticipated to be volatile, especially on a monthly and quarterly basis."

A third shortcoming is the neglect of the banking system's larger operating environment. The 8 percent minimum was set with the industrial countries' banking systems in mind. The accord's adoption by many developing countries, where economic business cycles have larger swings and the operating environment for banks is much riskier, means that these banking systems are less protected than those in industrial countries. These problems argue for a more flexible approach toward capital requirements for credit risk in which a broader view about risk is incorporated.

Members of the Basle Committee recognize such deficiencies and are discussing the merits of a possible revision to risk weights. Members' suggested revisions to the capital accord include promoting better implementation, altering risk weights to better reflect actual risk, and incorporating portfolio-based risk models along the lines of capital requirements for market risk. U.S. Federal Reserve Board Chairman Alan Greenspan has advocated an increase in the risk weight on short-term interbank claims, which would raise the cost of borrowing, discourage excessive use of interbank funding, and encourage securitization of short-term claims. Other suggestions have included additional requirements that would need to be met before a zero risk weight could be applied to OECD sovereign debt, such as transparency and disclosure about the financial sector and implementation of the Basle Core Principles. The International Swaps and Derivatives Association (ISDA) has promoted a mixed approach involving the current accord, a modified version of the current accord, and a portfolio-modeling approach to capital requirements. Despite the pressures to move on the topic, the Basle Committee is likely to maintain its consensus-oriented deliberateness.

A reevaluation of the role of capital is also under way within the International Organization of Securities Commissions (IOSCO) and many of the securities commissions it represents. In the former regime, capital protected securities firms against unexpected liquidity shortages, allowing them to meet daily settlement flows and initiate an orderly windup if necessary. As banks and securities firms become increasingly involved in similar products and business activities, it has become less clear whether the different motives for capital requirements for the two types of firms still make sense.

Level playing fields and regulatory arbitrage mean that capital requirements for banks and securities firms are unlikely to be far different for long.

Since market risk is the dominant risk faced by securities firms, capital requirements for market risk are likely to be a significant part of any unified approach. For example, the U.S. Securities and Exchange Commission (SEC) is already trying to determine how best to gain experience with the use of VaR models in the determination of capital requirements. In the United Kingdom, the Securities and Futures Authority (SFA), to be merged into the Financial Services Authority, has released a consultative paper outlining the impact of the introduction of the European single currency on its regulatory capital regime. The SFA is using this opportunity to revisit a number of issues.

While credit risk capital requirements are beeing debated, supervisory guidance dealing with operational and other risks is also being considered by both the Basle Committee and IOSCO. Recognizing that operational failures are the most common cause of financial institution failures, the two organizations are promoting operational controls and guidelines. Previous guidance issued by the Basle Committee has covered internal controls associated with specific areas of banks' activities, while the recent document, "Framework for the Evaluation of Internal Control Systems,"[3] provides a framework for a complete evaluation of internal controls for all on- and off-balance-sheet activities. The IOSCO initiative, "Risk Management and Control Guidance for Securities Firms and their Supervisors," combines risk management and operational controls as part of a larger goal of managing all types of risk—market, credit, legal, operational, and liquidity—noting that risks can come from both internal (for example, insufficient internal controls) and external sources (for example, sharp price changes). The principles of good risk management and control systems are intended as benchmarks against which firms and supervisors in each jurisdiction can judge the adequacy of their control systems.

---

[3]Basle Committee on Banking Supervision, "Framework for the Evaluation of Internal Control Systems" (Basle, January 1998).

veloped sophisticated research and surveillance functions, which include aspects of banking supervision as well. Given the turbulence that occurred, and its statutory mandate for ensuring financial stability, the Federal Reserve reached the judgment that it needed to facilitate a private rescue of LTCM as well as reduce the cost of liquidity. Together these measures fenced in an important aspect of the ongoing turbulence—by internalizing some of the unwinding of the positions of LTCM and the other financial institutions that had similar positions—and eased liquidity pressures in the

markets when such action was most needed. The final cut in mid-November probably was taken, in part, as insurance against a relapse.

Probably no system of market surveillance, in particular of the U.S. financial system, could have accurately foreseen what unfolded during the turbulence in September and October. However, the bouts of turbulence, illiquidity, price disconnects, and other features of the sharp dynamics strongly suggest that the turbulence that erupted in the aftermath of the flight from emerging markets in mid-1998 may have been partly the result of pressures that accumulated over a long period of time—in particular, during the long "bull" runs in fixed-income markets. The potential risks associated with these developments—which could have been triggered by some event that threatened the positions held by the large and diverse group of financial institutions—clearly should have received greater attention. Moreover, disclosure requirements for the unregulated hedge funds are limited, and so their activities are not transparent to all stakeholders. Indeed, market behavior during the summer and fall suggest that there may not be sufficient disclosure and transparency for even the most sophisticated players to know enough about the credit and counterparty risks they are taking.

Another observation is that public systemic risk management did not become proactive about the potential accumulation of financial vulnerabilities and disturbances until some of their adverse consequences were becoming painfully apparent. Warning signs were present almost two years ago when some central banks suggested that equity valuations were beginning to look unsustainable (irrational exuberance), credit risk spreads were unusually narrow and compressed, and loan covenants and nonfinancial terms were being relaxed. With the benefit of hindsight, it is possible to suggest that absent from these concerns were warnings that the degree of (off-balance-sheet) leverage was potentially becoming excessive, that credit extension to high-risk enterprises (hedge funds) was widespread and also possibly excessive, and that there was an excessive amount of position taking on the faith that mature market credit risk spreads would narrow once the "Asian contagion" dissipated. This suggests that there should be a more heightened awareness about potential financial vulnerabilities and disruptions when they are least expected—when economic and financial conditions are favorable and, in particular, when expansions in economies are reaching a mature stage. It is at the top of business and credit cycles as credit risk spreads narrow, when there are strong incentives to improve asset returns through leverage, and when bank capital appears ample.

* * *

The difficulties encountered in September and October 1998 suggest that financial markets can be adversely affected by the manner in which individual financial institutions react to market pressures, stress, and turbulence, particularly when many of them hold similar highly leveraged positions. Mistakes appear to have been made by systemically important, internationally active financial institutions, and it appears that management command and control systems should be reassessed to better cope with the risks inherent in modern financial markets. It is a necessary first step to enhance disclosure of the financial activities of financial institutions, particularly the least regulated among

them. This can enhance the ability of both private and public sector stakeholders to assess financial risks and to understand where the risks reside. The widespread application of private risk management systems, which could benefit from greater disclosure, also should be reassessed in light of recent experience. These systems appear to have not incorporated some lessons from the Mexican and Asian crises, which could have aided institutions in avoiding vulnerabilities exposed by the most recent bout of turbulence in mature markets. Because many of the involved institutions are part of their national financial safety nets, supervisors and regulators need to be closely involved in this reassessment.

In addition to the adverse developments related directly to behavior of individual financial institutions, the mature market turbulence also seemed to have reflected features of the international financial system, including the highly integrated and complex nature of financial position taking, institutions, and markets, and in particular the linkages of financial positions across national and international markets. These linkages derive in part from basic elements of financial transactions, such as the need or desire to finance, leverage, hedge, and risk-manage diversified portfolios of claims. The linkages themselves, the dramatic nature of the position unwinding and deleveraging, and the severe price dynamics and illiquidity in the interconnected markets together revealed the possibility of significant problems in how the international financial system—composed of the interconnected national and international financial markets—performs in the presence of heightened financial vulnerability, stress, and ultimately excessive turbulence. Particularly disturbing is the revelation that otherwise deep and liquid mature (dollar-based) and international (yen/dollar) markets experienced difficulties in absorbing what appeared initially to be relatively moderate shocks.

The feedback effects of the growing market tensions, illiquidity, and rapid market dynamics intensified pressures on market participants to shed risk and acquire liquidity rapidly, which apparently impaired the ability of the mature financial markets to smoothly and efficiently facilitate the closing out and deleveraging of positions and exposures. Distinctions between credit, market, liquidity, and operational risks apparently became blurred as replenishing liquidity became the driving force behind risk assessment, asset pricing, and portfolio rebalancing. Ex ante, few would have expected this to occur in deep and liquid financial markets. This suggests that private risk models and their underlying principles of risk management and portfolio management have a tendency during periods of stress and turbulence to accelerate dynamics in declining markets, which in this most recent episode led to a temporary drying up of liquidity in even the most liquid markets.

The role of banking supervisors and those responsible for market surveillance in warning about the accumulation of increasing levels of risk and leverage in the mature markets is also an issue of concern. The argument often heard in the aftermath of the Asian crisis was that no one could see through the opaque financial structures and markets. Yet the markets and institutions that experienced the turbulence this summer and fall are the most open and transparent in the world. Why then were potential dangers not more accurately perceived at an earlier stage?

The features of the international financial system revealed by the turbulence in the period mid-August through mid-October 1998 suggest that neither private market participants nor the institutions in charge of prudential supervision and market surveillance have a full understanding of the ever-changing nature, structure, and dynamics of the rapidly changing international financial institutions and markets.[27] This, of course, is not an entirely new problem, and it is not a problem that possesses a complete and final solution. Rather, the difficulties revealed by recent financial market turbulence testify to the urgency of continuing efforts, in the private and public sectors, to improve the performance and enhance the stability of the international financial system.

----

[27]U.S. Federal Reserve Board Chairman Alan Greenspan made this observation in his remarks, "Risk Management in the Global Financial System," before the Annual Financial Markets Conference of the Federal Reserve Bank of Atlanta, in Miami, Florida, on February 27, 1998. In referring to the dramatic changes that have occurred in what was characterized as "the global financial system," Chairman Greenspan observed, "We do not as yet fully understand the new system's dynamics. We are learning fast, and need to update and modify our institutions and practices to reduce the risks inherent in the new regime."

IV

Implications for the World Economy: Revisions and Risks to the Projections

Global growth in 1999 seems likely to be in the range of 2–2¼ percent for the second consecutive year, well below the historical average of nearly 4 percent. This underscores the continuing costs of the Asian crisis, its repercussions, and the crises that have afflicted financial markets more broadly in 1998. However, the most serious downside risks to the global economy that emerged as a result of the turbulence in global financial markets in the wake of the Russian crisis in August now seem to have subsided, and the relatively modest scale of the further downward revisions to the global growth outlook since early September suggests that the situation may have begun to stabilize. At the same time, the balance of risks still seems to be predominantly on the downside. The consequences of some of these risks materializing are explored in an alternative scenario below.

Key Revisions to the Projections

Projected growth in the world economy in 1999 has been lowered only modestly from the October 1998 *World Economic Outlook* to 2.2 percent, about the same growth rate as estimated for 1998 (Table 4.1). Nevertheless, there are significant downward revisions to projected growth in particular countries and regions, notably in Japan, where the recession now appears deeper and longer than previously projected, and in other countries reflecting the crisis in Russia and the subsequent contagion to other emerging markets, including Brazil. Recent changes in exchange rates, interest rates, and commodity prices, which affect assumptions underlying the projections, have also contributed to forecast revisions. Chief among these are a stronger yen (which, in real effective terms, is now assumed to be 12½ percent more appreciated in 1999 compared to the October 1998 *World Economic Outlook*), lower short-term interest rates in the United States and Europe, and lower real oil and nonfuel commodity prices (see Table 4.1 and Figure 4.1). Net private capital flows into emerging market economies are projected to increase by about one-third in 1999 to about $90 billion, but this represents a downward revision of about $40 billion compared with the October projection, and it would still be well below the levels seen in 1990–97. The timing

Figure 4.1. Prices of Crude Petroleum and Nonfuel Commodities[1]
(Quarterly averages, 1990 = 100)

Prices of oil and nonfuel commodities have declined further in 1998, in both nominal (U.S. dollar) and real terms. Petroleum prices are assumed to recover somewhat in 1999.

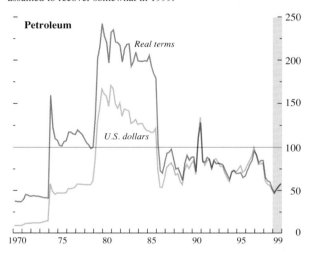

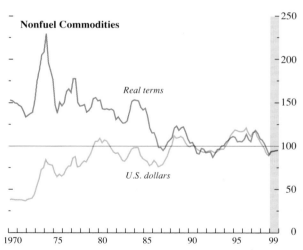

[1]Shaded areas indicate IMF staff projections.

Table 4.1. Overview of the *World Economic Outlook* Projections

(Annual percent change unless otherwise noted)

	1996	1997	Current Projections 1998	Current Projections 1999	Differences from October 1998 Projections 1998	Differences from October 1998 Projections 1999
World output	**4.3**	**4.2**	**2.2**	**2.2**	**0.2**	**−0.3**
Advanced economies	3.2	3.2	2.0	1.6	—	−0.3
Major industrial countries	3.0	3.0	2.1	1.5	—	−0.4
United States	3.4	3.9	3.6	1.8	0.1	−0.2
Japan	5.0	1.4	−2.8	−0.5	−0.3	−1.0
Germany	1.3	2.2	2.7	2.0	0.1	−0.5
France	1.6	2.3	3.0	2.6	−0.1	−0.2
Italy	0.7	1.5	1.3	1.9	−0.8	−0.6
United Kingdom	2.6	3.5	2.6	0.9	0.3	−0.3
Canada	1.2	3.8	2.8	2.2	−0.2	−0.3
Other advanced economies	3.8	4.2	1.5	2.0	0.1	−0.3
Memorandum						
Industrial countries	3.0	3.0	2.3	1.7	—	−0.3
Euro area	1.6	2.5	2.8	2.4	−0.2	−0.4
Newly industrialized Asian economies	6.3	6.0	−2.6	0.5	0.3	−0.2
Developing countries	6.5	5.7	2.8	3.5	0.5	−0.1
Africa	5.8	3.2	3.6	3.8	−0.1	−0.9
Asia	8.2	6.6	2.6	4.3	0.8	0.4
China	9.6	8.8	7.2	6.6	1.7	1.1
India	7.4	5.7	4.7	4.8	−0.1	−0.1
ASEAN–4[1]	7.1	3.7	−10.6	−1.4	−0.2	−1.3
Middle East and Europe	4.7	4.5	3.3	2.9	1.0	0.2
Western Hemisphere	3.5	5.1	2.5	1.5	−0.3	−1.2
Brazil	2.8	3.2	0.5	−1.0	−1.0	−3.0
Countries in transition	−1.0	1.9	−0.8	−1.9	−0.6	−1.7
Central and eastern Europe	1.6	2.8	2.5	2.2	−0.9	−1.4
Excluding Belarus and Ukraine	3.7	3.2	2.9	3.2	−0.8	−0.9
Russia	−5.0	0.7	−5.7	−8.3	0.3	−2.3
Transcaucasus and central Asia	1.6	2.2	2.1	3.0	−2.0	−0.8
World trade volume (goods and services)	**7.0**	**9.9**	**3.3**	**4.4**	**−0.4**	**−0.2**
Imports						
Advanced economies	6.5	9.2	4.6	4.6	0.1	−0.1
Developing countries	9.5	10.4	−0.7	5.7	−1.7	1.1
Countries in transition	10.0	8.2	1.0	1.3	−2.5	−2.2
Exports						
Advanced economies	6.3	10.4	3.3	3.7	−0.3	−0.5
Developing countries	8.7	11.3	2.9	5.4	−1.0	−0.1
Countries in transition	7.0	6.9	3.5	5.1	−1.8	−0.8
Commodity prices						
Oil[2]						
In SDRs	23.7	−0.2	−29.7	5.6	−0.5	−4.8
In U.S. dollars	18.4	−5.4	−30.5	8.4	0.6	−0.9
Nonfuel[3]						
In SDRs	3.3	2.0	−14.5	−3.2	−2.9	−4.6
In U.S. dollars	−1.2	−3.3	−15.6	−0.6	−1.7	−1.0
Consumer prices						
Advanced economies	2.4	2.1	1.6	1.6	−0.1	−0.1
Developing countries	14.1	9.2	10.2	8.4	−0.1	0.1
Countries in transition	41.4	27.9	21.0	30.2	−8.5	−4.4
Six-month LIBOR (in percent)[4]						
On U.S. dollar deposits	5.6	5.9	5.5	5.1	−0.2	−0.8
On Japanese yen deposits	0.7	0.7	0.7	0.5	0.1	—
On deutsche mark deposits	3.3	3.4	3.7	...	—	...
On Euro deposits	...	...	...	3.3	...	−0.4

Note: Real effective exchange rates are assumed to remain constant at the levels prevailing during October 19–November 4, 1998 except for the bilateral rates among ERM currencies, which are assumed to remain constant in nominal terms.

[1]Indonesia, Malaysia, Philippines, and Thailand.

[2]Simple average of spot prices of U.K. Brent, Dubai, and West Texas Intermediate crude oil. The average price of oil in U.S. dollars a barrel was $19.27 in 1997; the assumed price is $13.39 in 1998 and $14.51 in 1999.

[3]Average, based on world commodity export weights.

[4]London interbank offered rate.

Table 4.2. Advanced Economies: Real GDP, Consumer Prices, and Unemployment Rates
(Annual percent change and percent of labor force)

	Real GDP				Consumer Prices				Unemployment Rate			
	1996	1997	1998	1999	1996	1997	1998	1999	1996	1997	1998	1999
Advanced economies	**3.2**	**3.2**	**2.0**	**1.6**	**2.4**	**2.1**	**1.6**	**1.6**	**7.3**	**7.0**	**6.9**	**7.0**
Major industrial countries	3.0	3.0	2.1	1.5	2.2	2.0	1.3	1.5	6.9	6.7	6.5	6.7
United States	3.4	3.9	3.6	1.8	2.9	2.3	1.6	2.2	5.4	4.9	4.5	4.8
Japan	5.0	1.4	−2.8	−0.5	0.1	1.7	0.4	−0.7	3.3	3.4	4.2	4.9
Germany	1.3	2.2	2.7	2.0	1.5	1.8	1.0	1.2	10.4	11.5	10.9	10.5
France	1.6	2.3	3.0	2.6	2.0	1.2	0.7	0.9	12.4	12.7	11.7	11.3
Italy	0.7	1.5	1.3	1.9	3.9	1.7	1.7	1.6	12.1	12.3	12.2	12.0
United Kingdom[1]	2.6	3.5	2.6	0.9	2.9	2.8	2.6	2.5	7.3	5.5	4.7	5.1
Canada	1.2	3.8	2.8	2.2	1.6	1.4	1.2	1.8	9.7	9.2	8.4	8.4
Other advanced economies	3.8	4.2	1.5	2.0	3.2	2.5	2.7	2.2	8.3	8.0	8.3	8.2
Spain	2.4	3.5	3.8	3.4	3.6	2.0	1.9	2.0	22.2	20.8	18.9	17.7
Netherlands	3.1	3.6	3.8	2.5	2.1	2.2	1.8	1.6	7.6	6.6	5.3	5.3
Belgium	1.3	3.0	2.9	2.2	2.1	1.6	1.0	1.2	9.8	9.3	8.8	8.4
Sweden	1.3	1.8	2.9	3.0	0.5	0.5	0.5	0.7	8.0	8.0	6.6	5.7
Austria	1.6	2.5	2.9	2.5	1.9	1.3	1.1	1.3	6.3	6.4	6.4	6.3
Denmark	3.5	3.5	2.5	1.9	2.1	2.2	1.9	2.1	8.6	7.6	6.4	6.2
Finland	3.6	6.0	4.9	3.3	0.6	1.2	1.5	1.7	14.6	12.6	11.3	10.2
Greece	2.7	3.5	3.3	3.6	8.2	5.5	4.8	2.6	10.3	10.3	10.2	10.0
Portugal	3.6	4.0	4.2	3.5	3.1	2.2	2.7	2.5	7.3	6.7	5.1	5.0
Ireland	7.4	9.8	9.1	6.8	1.6	1.5	2.8	2.8	11.5	10.2	8.9	8.2
Luxembourg	3.5	4.8	4.1	3.9	1.4	1.4	1.6	1.7	3.3	3.7	4.1	4.5
Switzerland	—	1.7	2.1	1.4	0.8	0.5	0.1	0.9	4.7	5.2	3.9	3.5
Norway	5.5	3.4	2.5	2.6	1.3	2.6	2.3	3.5	4.8	4.1	3.2	3.6
Israel	4.6	2.2	1.5	2.0	11.3	9.0	5.5	9.1	6.7	7.7	9.0	9.5
Iceland	5.5	5.0	5.0	4.0	2.3	1.8	2.2	3.0	4.5	3.9	3.3	3.0
Korea	7.1	5.5	−7.0	−1.0	4.9	4.4	7.8	3.8	2.0	2.7	7.0	8.0
Australia[2]	3.7	3.3	3.5	2.0	2.7	1.7	1.7	2.3	8.6	8.6	8.1	7.7
Taiwan Province of China	5.7	6.8	4.9	3.9	3.1	0.9	1.5	2.0	2.6	2.7	2.7	2.4
Hong Kong SAR	4.6	5.3	−5.0	−1.0	6.0	5.7	3.0	−1.8	2.8	2.2	5.0	6.4
Singapore	6.9	7.8	0.7	−0.8	1.4	2.0	−0.2	0.3	2.0	1.8	3.4	3.9
New Zealand[2]	3.2	2.4	−0.7	1.6	2.3	1.7	1.6	1.4	6.1	6.6	7.5	8.4
Memorandum												
European Union	1.8	2.7	2.8	2.2	2.5	1.9	1.5	1.6	11.2	11.0	10.2	9.9
Euro area	1.6	2.5	2.8	2.4	2.4	1.7	1.3	1.4	12.3	12.4	11.6	11.2

[1]Consumer prices are based on the retail price index excluding mortgage interest.
[2]Consumer prices excluding interest rate components; for Australia, also excluding other volatile items.

and strength of the recovery in capital flows to emerging markets is one of the key uncertainties in the outlook.

Apart from Japan, the largest downward revisions to projected growth in 1999 are for various emerging market countries across all regions. These downward revisions are slightly offset by an upward revision for China. The major industrial countries, excluding Japan, have been affected relatively little so far by the crisis, in part because of the limited importance, relative to overall activity, of trade with emerging market economies, and also because of generally robust domestic demand, especially in the United States. In 1999, output growth is expected to slow somewhat in the euro area and to a greater extent in the United States, but the risk of more pronounced slowdowns has been reduced by recent monetary policy actions.

Japan and Emerging Market Economies in Asia: When Will the Recessions End?

The outlook for *Japan* has deteriorated further since the October assessment, with output now expected to fall by 2¾ percent in 1998 and by ½ of 1 percent in 1999 (Table 4.2). The downward revisions reflect the continued stagnation of private domestic demand, which is linked to difficulties in the financial sector, as well as implications for net exports of the appreciation of the yen since September. These factors are expected to be only partially offset by additional countercyclical policy measures. The appreciation of the yen, in particular, represents a tightening of monetary conditions that could, on its own, reduce GDP by about 1 percent over a one- to two-year period (Figure 4.2).

Recent data point to a continued deepening of the recession. Retail sales have continued to decline, while

Table 4.3. Selected Advanced Economies and Regions: Importance of Merchandise Export Markets in 1996

(Exports to partner countries as a percent of exporter's GDP)

Exporters	Importing Partners			
	Asia[1]	Western Hemisphere[2]	Countries in transition	World[3]
North America	1.5	1.3	0.1	9.9
European Union	1.6	0.5	1.4	23.5
Japan	3.9	0.4	—	8.9
Asia[1]	12.3	0.7	0.4	30.0
Western Hemisphere[2]	0.7	2.7	0.1	13.6
Transition economies	1.5	0.2	8.4	23.6

Sources: IMF, *Direction of Trade Statistics*, and *World Economic Outlook* database.

[1]Excludes Japan, Australia, and New Zealand.

[2]Developing countries.

[3]Total exports as a ratio to total GDP. For the European Union, intraregional trade is included. Excluding this reduces the export share in GDP by about one-half.

employment contracted again in the third quarter, and unemployment rose to 4¼ percent, contributing to consumer apprehension. GDP fell in the third quarter, by 2.6 percent at an annual rate, owing to declines in private consumption and investment that were partially offset by a boost from net exports and marginal increases in public spending. Industrial production shows no sign of sustained improvement; machine orders are low, signaling further declines in investment, as does the accelerating decline of bank lending; land price declines have picked up again; and business sector confidence remains depressed (Figure 4.3). The external sector contributed to growth in 1998 entirely through import compression. Looking ahead, it is unlikely that exports will contribute much to Japan's recovery in the near term, owing to the weakness of activity among many of Japan's trading partners, especially in Asia, and the recent yen appreciation. Indeed, uncertainties about the strength and timing of recoveries in the Asian crisis economies are an important risk factor for Japan, just as recovery in Japan will be critical for recovery in the rest of Asia (Tables 4.3 and 4.4).

The government announced a new fiscal stimulus package in mid-November, which will begin to be felt in the current fiscal year, although most of the impact is expected by IMF staff to be concentrated in FY 1999, which starts next April. The stimulus to be provided by fiscal policy as a whole in FY 1999, as measured by the change in the structural deficit from FY 1998, is now projected to be 1 percent of GDP. This is about ½ of 1 percent of GDP more than assumed in the October 1998 *World Economic Outlook,* where part of the stimulus in the November package was anticipated in the staff's projection.[1] Also in November, the Bank

Figure 4.2. Major Industrial Countries: Indices of Monetary Conditions[1]

Monetary conditions—reflecting changes in both real interest rates and real exchange rates—have recently eased in North America and the United Kingdom but have tightened in Japan.

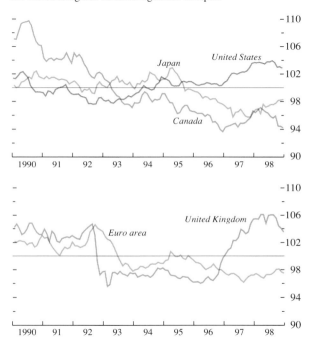

[1]For each country and the euro area, the index is defined as a weighted average of the percentage point change in the real short-term interest rate and the percentage change in the real effective exchange rate relative to a base period (Janaury 1990 to December 1997). Relative weights of 3 to 1 are used for Canada and the United Kingdom; 6.25 to 1 for the euro area; and 10 to 1 for Japan and the United States. The weights are intended to represent the relative impact of interest rates and exchange rates on aggregate demand; they should be regarded as indicative rather than precise estimates. For instance, a 3-to-1 ratio indicates that a 1 percentage point change in the real short-term interest rate has about the same effect on aggregate demand over time as a 3 percent change in the real effective exchange rate. For more details, see the October 1998 *World Economic Outlook*, Figure 2.7. For the euro area, a synthetic euro is constructed. For details, see the October 1998 *World Economic Outlook*, Box 5.5.

---

[1]The actual stimulus is estimated to be below the "headline" figures largely because the package replaces temporary measures

Figure 4.3. Selected European Countries, Japan, and the United States: Indicators of Consumer and Business Confidence[1]

Consumer confidence has continued to improve in France and Germany but has declined in the United Kingdom and the United States. Falling business confidence has been widespread.

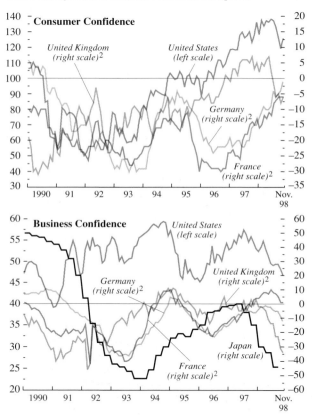

Sources: Consumer confidence—for the United States, the Conference Board; for European countries, the European Commission. Business confidence—for the United States, the U.S. Department of Commerce, Purchasing Managers Composite Diffusion Index; for European countries, the European Commission; for Japan, Bank of Japan.

[1]Indicators are not comparable across countries.

[2]Percent of respondents expecting an improvement in their situation minus percent expecting a deterioration.

of Japan announced new measures to alleviate corporate funding difficulties, broadening the scope of its repurchase operations by raising the maturity ceiling of eligible commercial paper to one year. These and other related measures are intended to alleviate the effects of the credit crunch caused by large volumes of nonperforming or substandard loans in banks' portfolios, but their impact on the economy is difficult to judge given the uncertainties about banks' ability and willingness to lend and about the demand for new loans. There has been some progress in establishing a framework to resolve Japan's banking problems, but there is a need for strong implementation.

The crisis-afflicted economies in east Asia—*Indonesia, Korea, Malaysia,* and *Thailand*—have suffered deep recessions in 1998, with output declines through the first half of the year, and probably also in the second half, in all countries (Table 4.5). Prospects for 1999 are better, with small declines in output or modest recoveries in prospect for all countries except Indonesia, where the reform process is less advanced and political uncertainties have complicated the economic difficulties (Table 4.6). The Philippines has fared better, with only a negligible decline in output in the year to the third quarter of 1998, in part reflecting the benefits of past stabilization and reform policies, but also the country's stronger export ties to North America, where import demand has remained robust.

In Korea and Thailand, financial markets have already recovered significantly: the exchange rate collapses of late 1997 and early 1998 have been partly reversed, international reserves have been substantially replenished, and stock markets have rebounded. Key factors behind the return of confidence in financial markets are the significant progress with policy programs in both countries and the emergence of large external current account surpluses, which provide assurance that external obligations can be met. The depreciation of the U.S. dollar since September and reductions in short-term interest rates throughout the industrial countries in recent months have also alleviated financial market pressures. Beyond the financial markets, however, there are few signs of incipient recovery, although there are some signs of bottoming out. The rate of decline in industrial production has begun to moderate in recent months; the unemployment rate in Korea has declined slightly after reaching over 7½ percent in July; and sales of new vehicles in Thailand, which have been an indicator of consumer confidence and of the strength of the nonbank financial sector, which extends the loans to buyers, rose in October on a 12-month basis for the first time since the beginning of the crisis. However, these signals are tenuous, and activity may well remain quite weak in

introduced in the FY 1998 budget. Estimates of structural budget positions in the major industrial countries are contained in the Statistical Appendix, Table 4.

Table 4.4. Selected Regions: Importance of Merchandise Export Markets in 1996

(Exports to partner countries as a percent of exporter's GDP)

	Importing Partners					
Exporters	Japan	Russia	Brazil	North America	European Union	World[1]
Asia[2]	3.9	0.2	0.2	6.2	4.4	30.0
ASEAN-4	6.2	—	0.1	6.7	5.2	34.0
Newly industrialized economies	5.2	0.3	0.4	11.5	7.3	53.6
China	3.8	0.2	0.1	3.5	2.4	18.3
Western Hemisphere[3]	0.5	—	0.6	7.0	2.1	13.6
Argentina	0.2	0.1	2.2	0.7	1.5	7.9
Brazil	0.4	0.1	—	1.3	1.7	6.1
Chile	3.6	—	1.4	3.9	5.3	21.5
Mexico	0.4	—	0.3	25.1	1.1	29.1
Venezuela	0.4	—	1.4	18.4	2.5	30.3
Countries in transition	0.4	2.1	0.1	1.1	9.9	23.6
Russia	0.7	—	—	1.5	6.3	19.1
Ukraine	0.3	12.8	0.1	1.2	3.8	31.1
Africa, Middle East, and Europe[3]	3.1	0.2	0.4	2.9	8.1	24.4

Sources: IMF, *Direction of Trade Statistics*, and *World Economic Outlook* database.
[1]Total exports as a ratio to total GDP.
[2]Excludes Japan, Australia, and New Zealand.
[3]Developing countries.

1999. In Malaysia, signs of an end to the recession, which has been as deep as that in Korea, also remain tentative. However, financial markets appear to have stabilized, and there are some indications of a turnaround in demand.

The return of financial market confidence has allowed monetary and fiscal policies to become quite supportive of activity in all the affected countries. Short-term market interest rates in Korea, Thailand, and the Philippines have fallen below precrisis levels, although lending rate spreads remain high owing to problems in the financial sectors. In Malaysia, capital and exchange controls introduced in September may have facilitated the easing of interest rates, but controls could be an impediment to recovery. Interest rates have also come down somewhat in Indonesia. Fiscal policy has helped to dampen the recession and lessen its impact on the poor in these countries in 1998, and some additional stimulus is assumed for 1999.[2] Recovery will also be aided by further easing of monetary policy to the extent that exchange market conditions permit; however, a sustainable rebound will also require financial sector reforms and corporate sector restructuring. Export market growth, which declined sharply in 1998, is expected to recover somewhat in 1999 but to remain well below trend, underscoring the external constraints on the pace of recovery.

Real GDP in *China* in the third quarter of 1998 is estimated to have been 7.6 percent higher than in the corresponding period of 1997, suggesting that growth has been better sustained than appeared likely at the time the October 1998 *World Economic Outlook* projections were prepared. As a result, the 1998 growth estimate has been revised up, to 7.2 percent. The stronger than expected growth in 1998 partly reflects policy measures—including a fiscal stimulus package equivalent to 2½ percent of GDP, consisting primarily of infrastructure projects, as well as reductions in domestic interest rates—that will continue to support growth in 1999. These measures appear to have more than offset the significant drags on the economy originating from the impact of the Asian crisis on exports, and severe flooding, but evidence of overbuilding and inventory accumulation, as well as financial sector fragilities, raise questions about the sustainability of growth at its recent pace. For these reasons, the staff projects some further slowdown in 1999, to 6½ percent. It should also be noted that the various signs of weakness in domestic demand may not be fully captured in the official GDP statistics (Box 4.1, page 78).

In *Hong Kong SAR* output is estimated to have contracted by 5 percent in 1998, reflecting the impact of the regional crisis and sharp falls in property and stock market prices; there have also been clear indications of declines in consumer prices and labor earnings. The authorities have responded to the weakening in activity with a fiscal stimulus of about 3 percent of GDP and measures to support the property market, including a suspension of government land sales. In addition, the authorities intervened in the stock market in August, purchasing about $15 billion of shares and significantly reducing the free float for many issues.

---

[2]See the October 1998 *World Economic Outlook*, Box 2.5, for a discussion of fiscal policies in the crisis economies.

Table 4.5. Selected Asian Economies: Macroeconomic Indicators

(Percent change from four quarters earlier unless otherwise noted)

	1997				1998		
	Q1	Q2	Q3	Q4	Q1	Q2	Q3
Hong Kong SAR							
Real GDP	5.7	6.9	6.1	2.8	−2.7	−5.2	−7.0
Consumer prices	6.1	5.7	6.1	5.5	5.0	4.4	2.8
Trade balance (billions of U.S. dollars)[1]	−6.2	−6.2	−4.0	−4.1	−4.2	−4.5	−0.8
Import value[2]	4.2	4.7	5.5	5.8	−5.1	−6.1	−15.4
Export value[2]	2.0	4.0	2.5	7.4	−0.9	−3.2	−10.3
Export volume	4.0	6.2	4.4	9.6	1.4	−0.5	−7.3
Indonesia							
Real GDP	8.5	6.8	2.5	1.4	−7.9	−16.5	−17.4
Consumer prices	5.2	4.9	6.0	10.1	29.9	52.1	79.7
Trade balance (billions of U.S. dollars)[1]	1.7	2.4	3.6	4.0	3.4	4.3	5.4
Import value[2]	11.0	−7.8	−2.6	−10.1	−31.3	−26.7	−46.4
Export value[2]	10.4	7.5	9.6	2.4	−1.0	−8.8	−3.4
Export volume	26.2	20.4	33.5	33.0	32.8	19.1	27.6
Japan							
Real GDP	3.8	1.0	1.7	−0.8	−3.6	−1.8	−3.5
Consumer prices	0.6	2.0	2.1	2.1	2.0	0.3	−0.2
Trade balance (billions of U.S. dollars)[1]	11.6	21.0	22.2	27.2	22.8	27.0	27.0
Import value[2]	2.2	−2.8	−3.9	−10.0	−13.3	−19.4	−20.3
Export value[2]	−1.6	6.0	3.5	0.2	−2.8	−12.2	−13.1
Export volume	12.1	16.5	10.9	7.6	2.2	−3.5	−1.6
Korea							
Real GDP	5.7	6.6	6.1	3.9	−3.9	−6.8	−6.8
Consumer prices	4.7	4.0	4.0	5.1	8.9	8.2	7.0
Trade balance (billions of U.S. dollars)[1]	−7.3	−1.8	−1.5	2.2	8.4	11.7	9.3
Import value[2]	3.9	0.8	−3.8	−14.8	−35.5	−36.7	−39.6
Export value[2]	−5.6	7.1	15.6	3.5	8.5	−1.8	−9.6
Export volume	17.3	24.1	35.6	23.1	32.4	20.7	11.4
Malaysia							
Real GDP	9.2	8.4	7.5	6.0	−2.8	−6.8	−8.6
Consumer prices	3.2	2.5	2.3	2.7	4.3	5.7	5.7
Trade balance (billions of U.S. dollars)[1]	0.8	−1.9	0.5	0.5	2.1	3.4	4.1
Import value[2]	1.0	11.2	1.4	−8.2	−18.7	−33.1	−29.3
Export value[2]	6.2	0.1	2.0	−5.7	−11.3	−9.6	−10.0
Philippines							
Real GDP	5.5	5.6	4.9	4.8	1.6	−0.8	−0.1
Consumer prices	5.1	5.3	5.9	7.2	7.9	9.9	10.4
Trade balance (billions of U.S. dollars)[1]	−2.9	−2.8	−3.1	−2.4	−1.1	−0.3	0.5
Import value[2]	14.2	8.3	20.9	12.9	−5.9	−17.4	−10.6
Export value[2]	17.0	26.5	24.7	22.2	23.8	14.4	15.2
Singapore							
Real GDP	4.2	8.5	10.6	3.9	5.6	1.8	−0.7
Consumer prices	1.7	1.7	2.3	2.3	1.0	0.3	−0.9
Trade balance (billions of U.S. dollars)[1]	−0.2	0.8	−0.2	0.7	2.7	4.0	4.4
Import value[2]	−2.6	2.7	8.8	−5.2	−16.3	−24.4	−23.4
Export value[2]	−3.2	4.0	3.2	−4.0	−6.8	−14.0	−9.3
Export volume	−0.3	8.8	10.5	7.8	7.6	−2.1	−1.8
Taiwan Province of China							
Real GDP	6.6	6.1	7.0	7.2	5.9	5.2	4.7
Consumer prices	1.7	1.0	1.1	−0.2	1.5	1.7	0.6
Trade balance (billions of U.S. dollars)[1]	1.6	1.8	1.6	2.5	−0.1	1.3	3.5
Import value[2]	5.8	3.6	7.0	6.4	−5.4	−6.9	−15.4
Export value[2]	5.8	4.9	17.1	7.1	−0.3	−7.8	−9.6
Export volume	9.3	5.6	9.7	11.4	3.8	0.8	. . .
Thailand							
Manufacturing production	7.0	7.5	−4.2	−11.5	−16.8	−15.3	−11.3
Consumer prices	4.4	4.3	6.1	7.5	9.0	10.3	8.1
Trade balance (billions of U.S. dollars)[1]	−3.2	−3.1	−0.9	2.5	3.1	2.6	3.1
Import value[2]	−7.7	−7.6	−11.4	−27.5	−39.8	−38.2	−34.2
Export value[2]	−0.9	2.2	7.1	6.7	−2.9	−5.3	−8.7
Export volume	−1.7	4.0	11.7	16.2	14.1	12.8	5.7

Sources: Country authorities; IMF, *International Financial Statistics (IFS)*, and IMF staff estimates.

[1]On national accounts basis calculated as exports (f.o.b.) less imports (c.i.f), except balance of payments basis for the Philippines, Singapore, and Thailand. 1998:Q3 trade data for Indonesia exclude oil and gas.

[2]In U.S. dollar terms, on a national accounts basis, except balance of payments basis for the Philippines, Singapore, and Thailand.

Table 4.6. Selected Developing Countries: Real GDP and Consumer Prices
(Annual percent change)

	Real GDP			Consumer Prices		
	1997	1998	1999	1997	1998	1999
Developing countries	**5.7**	**2.8**	**3.5**	**9.2**	**10.2**	**8.4**
Median	**4.4**	**4.1**	**4.4**	**6.2**	**5.0**	**4.7**
Africa	**3.2**	**3.6**	**3.8**	**11.0**	**8.5**	**7.8**
Algeria	1.3	3.6	3.4	5.7	5.5	9.0
Cameroon	5.1	5.0	5.2	4.2	2.1	2.0
Côte d'Ivoire	6.0	6.0	6.0	5.6	3.0	2.5
Ghana	3.0	5.6	5.8	27.9	15.5	8.0
Kenya	2.1	1.5	3.5	11.2	9.6	6.7
Morocco	−2.0	6.8	4.0	1.0	2.8	2.5
Nigeria	3.9	2.0	—	8.5	10.2	8.0
South Africa	1.7	0.2	1.3	8.6	7.0	6.8
Sudan[1]	6.6	5.2	5.5	46.7	20.0	14.0
Tanzania	3.4	4.3	5.6	17.1	14.5	8.0
Tunisia	5.4	5.1	5.5	3.7	3.6	3.6
Uganda	5.4	6.2	7.0	8.2	5.0	5.0
SAF/ESAF countries[2]	4.8	4.6	6.0	8.7	7.1	5.1
CFA countries	5.5	5.7	5.4	4.3	2.7	2.5
Asia	**6.6**	**2.6**	**4.3**	**4.7**	**7.9**	**6.4**
Bangladesh	5.7	4.2	3.4	4.8	7.9	8.1
China	8.8	7.2	6.6	2.8	−0.8	2.0
India	5.7	4.7	4.8	6.3	7.2	7.6
Indonesia	4.6	−15.3	−3.4	6.6	61.1	26.8
Malaysia	7.7	−7.5	−2.0	2.7	5.2	5.8
Pakistan	−0.4	5.3	3.0	11.8	7.8	10.7
Philippines	5.2	0.2	2.5	6.0	9.8	8.8
Thailand	−0.4	−8.0	1.0	5.6	8.0	2.5
Vietnam	8.8	3.5	3.5	3.2	8.0	8.0
Middle East and Europe	**4.5**	**3.3**	**2.9**	**22.8**	**23.6**	**20.5**
Egypt	5.1	5.3	5.0	6.2	3.8	4.0
Iran, Islamic Republic of	2.6	1.7	2.0	17.3	22.0	12.0
Jordan	2.2	0.5	2.0	3.0	5.0	3.5
Kuwait	2.5	2.2	−2.0	0.7	0.5	1.6
Saudi Arabia	1.9	0.4	0.4	−0.4	—	0.7
Turkey	7.6	4.4	2.9	85.7	84.7	81.0
Western Hemisphere	**5.1**	**2.5**	**1.5**	**13.9**	**10.3**	**8.3**
Argentina	8.6	5.2	3.0	0.8	1.3	1.4
Brazil	3.2	0.5	−1.0	7.9	3.9	. . .
Chile	7.1	4.5	2.0	6.1	5.1	4.5
Colombia	3.1	2.7	1.9	18.5	18.8	14.4
Dominican Republic	8.1	7.0	7.3	8.3	4.6	6.2
Ecuador	3.4	0.5	1.5	30.6	36.2	34.4
Guatemala	4.1	4.8	4.0	9.2	6.0	7.0
Mexico	7.0	4.6	3.0	20.6	15.3	13.8
Peru	7.2	3.0	6.0	8.5	7.5	5.6
Uruguay	5.1	2.7	1.0	19.8	10.2	7.0
Venezuela	5.1	−2.5	0.1	50.0	36.1	29.6

[1]The inflation figures published in the May 1998 *World Economic Outlook* were end-of-period data.
[2]African countries that had arrangements, as of the end of 1997, under the IMF's Structural Adjustment Facility (SAF) or Enhanced Structural Adjustment Facility (ESAF).

Over the past few months the authorities have also adopted several measures to discourage speculation in the futures market, strengthen the regulatory framework for securities, and modify the discount window facility to buffer the effects of temporary market pressures on interest rates. Interest rates have come down as pressure on the currency has subsided. While activity is expected to remain weak in the first half of 1999, partly reflecting the impact of high real interest rates associated with falling prices, growth may pick up in the second half of the year. Considerable downside risks remain, however, given the economy's openness and exposure to developments in Japan and mainland China.

Effects of the Russian Crisis on the Domestic Economy and Other Countries in Transition

Economic and social conditions in *Russia* have deteriorated dramatically since the August crisis. The decline in output in 1998 is estimated at almost 6 percent, and projections for 1999 have been revised down further since the October *World Economic Outlook,* to show an 8 percent output decline (Table 4.7). There is clearly a risk of an even larger decline, however, given the continuing fiscal imbalances, banking sector problems, and signs of reversals in the reform process. Monthly inflation, which had accelerated to 38 percent in September, receded to 4½ percent in October, as new foreign exchange controls contributed to a stabilization of the exchange rate and as price controls limited open inflation. Inflation is projected to accelerate in 1999, however, because support to the banking system and the continuing large budget shortfall are expected to be financed largely through monetary expansion.

Russia's external current account is likely to have swung into surplus in the second half of 1998, owing to a sharp compression of imports that reflects import financing problems and the collapse of the ruble. Indications are that capital flight is also on the rise and, together with the collapse of private and official capital inflows, is putting pressure on the overall external position. In 1999 the current account surplus is expected to reach 6½ percent of GDP.

The financial crisis in Russia has significantly affected developments and prospects in many other transition countries, especially those that are dependent on external private financing or have maintained strong trade and financial ties with Russia. *Ukraine,* in addition to facing reduced trade with Russia, has been confronted with the consequences of persistent budgetary imbalances and inadequate reform efforts, which have contributed to a drying up of new financing and the need to repay some of its maturing external debt. The country has, however, managed to avert a complete cutoff from private financing by obtaining agreement to a voluntary conversion of a substantial part of its

Table 4.7. Countries in Transition: Real GDP and Consumer Prices

(Annual percent change)

	Real GDP			Consumer Prices		
	1997	1998	1999	1997	1998	1999
Countries in transition	**1.9**	**−0.8**	**−1.9**	**28**	**21**	**30**
Median	**3.4**	**4.2**	**3.7**	**15**	**11**	**8**
Selected countries						
Central and eastern Europe	2.8	2.5	2.2	38	18	16
Excluding Belarus and Ukraine	3.2	2.9	3.2	41	16	10
Albania	−7.0	8.0	8.0	32	21	8
Belarus	10.4	7.0	2.0	64	53	75
Bulgaria	−6.9	5.0	3.7	1,082	23	7
Croatia	6.5	2.4	1.3	4	5	4
Czech Republic	1.0	−1.5	1.0	8	11	8
Estonia	11.4	5.1	3.6	11	11	6
Hungary	4.4	5.2	4.8	18	15	11
Latvia	6.5	6.0	5.0	8	5	4
Lithuania	6.1	5.3	4.0	9	5	5
Macedonia, former Yugoslav Rep. of	1.5	5.0	5.0	2	2	3
Poland	6.9	5.6	5.1	15	12	8
Romania	−6.6	−5.5	−2.0	155	60	31
Slovak Republic	6.5	4.0	2.0	6	8	8
Slovenia	3.8	4.4	4.5	9	8	5
Ukraine	−3.2	−1.7	−3.5	16	11	32
Russia	0.7	−5.7	−8.3	15	26	56
Transcaucasus and central Asia	2.2	2.1	3.0	31	20	12
Armenia	3.1	5.5	4.0	14	9	10
Azerbaijan	5.8	8.0	7.5	4	4	5
Georgia	11.0	4.0	2.0	7	3	8
Kazakhstan	2.0	−1.5	—	17	8	8
Kyrgyz Republic	6.5	6.0	4.6	26	12	10
Mongolia	4.0	3.5	3.5	27	12	10
Tajikistan	1.7	3.4	4.0	88	64	19
Turkmenistan	−25.9	3.6	12.1	84	17	26

treasury bills held by nonresidents into Eurobonds and to a rescheduling of some loans from international banks. Following the adoption of a new exchange rate band in early September, the hryvnia depreciated by around 35 percent (against the U.S. dollar) before stabilizing at the limit of the band in mid-October, as administrative controls on the foreign exchange market were tightened. The depreciation has put upward pressure on inflation, which accelerated to 6½ percent on a monthly basis in October. Ukraine has not experienced positive growth in any year since transition began, and output is projected to continue to contract in 1999 (see Table 4.7).

In *Kazakhstan*, sharply reduced access to international financial markets has exacerbated the impact of the slowdown in trade with Russia, and output is estimated to have declined by 1½ percent in 1998. In *Belarus* and *Moldova*, which both rely on Russian markets for 60–70 percent of their exports, the main impact of the Russian crisis is occurring through trade. The effects of the decline in exports to Russia are expected to be more limited, but still significant, in the *Caucasian and Central Asian states* that have made progress in reorienting their trade toward new markets.

The three *Baltic countries*, in addition to being affected by reduced access to private external financing, are expected also to face significant direct effects from the Russian crisis through banking sector and trade links. Estonia and Lithuania, with current account deficits of around 10 percent of GDP in 1998, are particularly vulnerable to changes in sentiment in global financial markets. Latvia, whose commercial banks have around 10 percent of their assets loaned to Russia, with the two banks with the largest exposure already being restructured, is also substantially affected by spillovers from the Russian crisis.

The least affected transition countries are those in *central and eastern Europe*, where fundamentals are relatively strong. In these cases, financial market pressures in the wake of the Russian crisis have been mostly short-lived. Nevertheless, there are downward revisions of the growth projections for some countries. For the *Czech Republic*, continued weakness in domestic demand and economic activity in recent months, following the tightening of macroeconomic policies in 1997, suggests that real GDP is likely to have contracted by 1½ percent in 1998, and activity is expected to remain subdued in 1999. In *Hungary* and *Poland*, less favorable prospects for exports are projected to lead to some slowdown in growth in 1999, but not to much less than 5 percent in either case.

Brazil and Other Emerging Market Economies: Effects of the Global Crisis

Among the regional groups of developing countries, near-term growth prospects have weakened the most

for the Western Hemisphere, reflecting the particularly severe impact of the emerging market crisis on *Brazil*, the largest economy in the region (see Tables 4.6 and 4.8). Growth projections for Brazil have been revised down sharply, with a small decline in output now projected for 1999. The policy program adopted by the authorities to reduce the fiscal deficit, address structural weaknesses, and restore investor confidence is discussed in Chapter I (Box 1.1). Effects of the reduced availability and increased cost of external finance, and tight domestic credit, have begun to show in the real economy, as indicated by a sharp fall in industrial production in September. The economy has also been adversely affected by a recent contraction of export earnings, reflecting lower commodity prices—notably for soya, sugar, and coffee—and a drop in demand for manufactured goods from trading partners (Figure 4.4). Even after the downward revisions, considerable downside risks to the outlook remain, including in relation to conditions in international financial markets and the possibility of steeper-than-projected slowdowns in export demand from partner countries. The projections assume that the policy program will be fully implemented and that investor confidence and willingness to roll over public debt will be maintained.

Spillover effects from the Russian crisis to the other large countries in Latin America have been less severe, and their output growth in 1999 is projected to be in the 2–3 percent range (except in Venezuela), little different from the previous projections. As reported in the October *World Economic Outlook*, the slowdowns in *Colombia* and *Venezuela* in 1998 have been due in part to the drop in world oil prices and declines in domestic oil production. For Venezuela, however, projected oil production has been revised upward, with the result that activity is no longer projected to decline further in 1999. For *Chile*, projected growth in 1999 has been revised to 2 percent from 3 percent, reflecting the external financial environment and the tightening of macroeconomic policies implemented in recent months.

Although pressures in financial markets appear to have eased, risks to the projections appear to remain predominantly on the downside for the countries in the region. First, access to international capital may not improve as assumed, and diminished access would necessitate further adjustment and lower domestic demand in the near term. Second, important export markets could turn out to be weaker than projected in the baseline. A sharper slowdown in North America would have particularly adverse implications for Mexico, whose exports there represent 25 percent of its total output (see Table 4.4). Activity in Argentina has already been adversely affected by the emerging market crisis, and output growth in 1999 is expected to slow to 3 percent.

Several countries in Central America—*El Salvador, Guatemala, Honduras,* and *Nicaragua*—were severely

Table 4.8. Selected Latin American Economies: Macroeconomic Indicators
(Percent change from four quarters earlier unless otherwise noted)

	1997:Q1	1997:Q2	1997:Q3	1997:Q4	1998:Q1	1998:Q2	1998:Q3
Argentina							
Real GDP	8.0	8.3	9.9	8.2	7.2	6.9	3.8
Consumer prices	0.7	0.7	0.6	0.0	0.6	1.2	1.1
Trade balance							
(billions of U.S. dollars)[1]	−0.7	−0.3	−1.3	−1.9	−1.7	−0.6	−1.9
Import value[2]	29.6	30.8	23.6	26.3	15.6	9.2	3.8
Export value[2]	20.2	8.2	6.4	4.0	1.1	5.5	−4.1
Export volume	17.3	14.8	12.7	6.9	10.0	10.6	3.3
Brazil							
Real GDP	3.8	4.8	2.7	1.9	0.9	1.5	. . .
Consumer prices	9.2	8.4	6.7	7.4	6.1	4.4	3.3
Trade balance							
(billions of U.S. dollars)[1]	−2.5	−1.3	−2.0	−2.6	−1.5	−0.5	−1.8
Import value[2]	22.2	23.5	19.0	0.3	2.2	−5.5	−9.7
Export value[2]	3.6	12.0	15.0	11.9	11.7	−0.5	−9.5
Export volume	4.2	10.9	13.8	10.8	10.6	5.8	−1.6
Chile							
Real GDP	3.6	6.0	11.2	10.6	7.9	4.6	. . .
Consumer prices	6.8	5.3	6.0	6.0	5.3	5.4	4.8
Trade balance							
(billions of U.S. dollars)[1]	0.6	0.2	−0.7	−1.3	−0.6	−0.5	−1.1
Import value[2]	5.3	7.3	12.6	15.3	15.3	7.2	−5.1
Export value[2]	14.3	2.1	13.7	11.9	−13.0	−8.6	−14.3
Export volume	3.3	4.1	8.2	14.7	5.3	12.5	. . .
Mexico							
Real GDP	4.9	8.6	7.9	6.7	6.6	4.3	5.0
Consumer prices	24.5	20.3	18.8	15.7	15.3	15.3	15.9
Trade balance							
(billions of U.S. dollars)[1]	8.4	5.0	2.4	−0.1	−1.9	−2.2	−4.6
Import value[2]	18.6	25.2	23.1	21.0	25.7	14.9	7.9
Export value[2]	10.3	15.5	15.1	11.1	15.6	10.5	6.6
Export volume	16.4	16.2	18.9	19.0	19.9	16.3	7.4
Venezuela							
Real GDP	0.5	7.5	7.4	4.9	7.6	−0.7	. . .
Consumer prices	83.1	52.5	39.7	38.1	37.3	39.4	36.2
Trade balance							
(billions of U.S. dollars)[1]	3.3	2.7	2.4	3.0	1.4	0.9	. . .
Import value[2]	21.3	7.0	39.3	37.0	28.3	8.4	. . .
Export value[2]	17.2	4.7	1.0	−11.9	−21.2	−25.3	. . .
Export volume	9.5	11.0	10.4	7.5	9.0	−0.2	. . .

Sources: Country authorities; and IMF, staff estimates (for GDP) and *IFS* (for inflation, trade balance, import value, export value, and export volume, except where noted).

[1]On a national accounts basis.

[2]In U.S. dollars terms on a national accounts basis.

hit in late October by Hurricane Mitch. The hurricane caused the most damage in *Honduras* and *Nicaragua* where, apart from causing large-scale loss of life, it took a heavy toll on infrastructure and the agricultural sector. At this stage, it is difficult to assess the impact on economic prospects, but the devastation of productive capital in agriculture and other sectors is likely to reduce output significantly in the short term. Emergency financial assistance to support rehabilitation and recovery is being arranged by bilateral and multilateral agencies, including the IMF.

Turning to other regions, growth in *India* is projected to slow to some 4½–5 percent in both 1998 and 1999, from almost 6 percent in 1997. Industrial growth has slowed markedly, with output during April–September 1998 only 3½ percent higher than in the corresponding period a year earlier. The slowdown in growth reflects a number of factors—slow progress in implementing key structural reforms; high real interest rates for the industrial sector; a decline in exports, owing to weak international demand and sector-specific factors; and fragile sentiment, which has been further undermined by the intensified weakness in the equity market since the revelation of financial problems in India's largest mutual fund (which may also have fiscal implications). Meanwhile, inflation has picked up to over 8 percent as a result of agricultural supply problems and an acceleration in broad money growth.

Output growth in *Pakistan* is projected to decline to 3 percent in 1999 after 5 percent growth in 1998, reflecting the deterioration in 1998 of the country's external financial situation, partly owing to the economic sanctions imposed after the nuclear tests in May and the ensuing loss of investor confidence. By end-November, the government had prepared a program of substantial macroeconomic adjustment and structural reforms designed to promote a sustainable improvement in growth performance. The program, which seeks to restore investor confidence and regularize Pakistan's relations with creditors, would require exceptional financing from the international community.

Among developing countries in the Middle East and Europe region, and in Africa, direct spillover effects from the Russian crisis have been largest in the countries with relatively developed capital markets. In *Turkey,* output growth is projected to slow further in 1999, reflecting both the tightening of macroeconomic policies over the past year, aimed at reducing inflation, and contagion from the emerging market crisis. Its international reserves have stabilized since early September, but real interest rates remain high, affecting the likely costs of the refinancing of almost one-third of the government's debt scheduled for early next year. In *South Africa,* interest rates were increased sharply around the middle of the year to defend the rand, but a strengthening of the exchange rate more recently has allowed monetary policy to be eased somewhat. Reflecting the tightening of financial conditions, GDP contracted in the third quarter. In *Kenya,* several commercial banks have been closed in recent months, owing to increases in nonperforming loans related to the economic slowdown this year. Repercussions of the bank failures have so far been limited to runs on deposits at the affected banks.

In the oil-exporting countries of the Middle East and Africa, the decline in world oil prices has worsened external balances and forced cutbacks in public expenditure that have contributed to the slowing of growth. In *Nigeria,* where output is expected to be flat in 1999 after weak growth in 1998, the authorities are implementing cuts in public expenditure to contain the fiscal deficit, given the limited scope for increasing non-oil revenues in the short term. There has been some spillover into neighboring countries, where growth has declined owing in part to reductions in worker remittances. Most other African countries are oil importers and have benefited from lower fuel import bills, but the majority are also non-oil commodity exporters facing losses in export earnings. In *Tanzania* and other neighboring countries, for example, export earnings declined in 1997–98, reflecting both the drop in primary commodity prices and weather-related production shortfalls. On balance, many countries in

Figure 4.4. Selected Economies: Export Market Growth[1]
(Percent)

Export market growth fell sharply in 1998 for most countries. The effect of the crisis in Russia can be seen particularly clearly in Ukraine's declining export market growth.

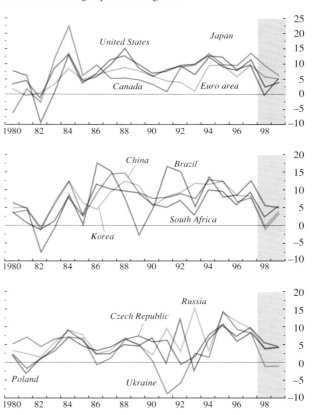

[1]Export market growth is a weighted average of trading partners' import growth. Shaded areas indicate IMF staff projections.

Box 4.1. Is China's Growth Overstated?

Over the past year, China's economy has been increasingly affected by the Asian crisis, as reflected in a sharp slowdown in exports. In addition, domestic demand slowed markedly in the first half of 1998, owing to the direct and indirect effects of rising unemployment, as well as the impact of serious flooding during the summer. As a result, GDP growth has weakened in 1998 but nevertheless has remained very high—indeed, GDP in the third quarter was 7.6 percent higher than in the third quarter of 1997. Some observers—pointing to the very low growth in electricity consumption (according to preliminary estimates), freight traffic, and other indicators of activity—have questioned whether official statistics may be overestimating the true growth rate.

Between 1992, when extraordinary growth of 14 percent was recorded, and 1997, China's growth rate was on a steadily declining trend, reflecting the authorities' efforts to reduce overheating. By 1997, GDP growth had fallen to 8.8 percent, broadly in line with past staff estimates of potential growth. In the first half of 1998, as the effects of the Asian crisis began to be felt, the GDP growth rate fell to 7 percent (relative to the first half of 1997), the lowest level since 1990. While the authorities do not publish quarterly data on the components of demand, this appears mainly to have reflected the weakening contribution of net exports. In addition, indicators of private consumption growth slowed, partly owing to rising unemployment. In response to these developments, the authorities reduced domestic interest rates twice during the first half of 1998, and in midyear announced a fiscal stimulus of Y 200 billion (2½ percent of GDP), financed equally through the budget and by domestic banks. During the third quarter, the stimulus package began to take effect. GDP growth rose to 7.6 percent in the third quarter, relative to the corresponding period of 1997, and this was reflected in a strong pickup in the growth of public investment, which increased from 13.7 percent in the first half of 1998 (relative to the same period of 1997) to 20 percent in the first three quarters of 1998 (relative to the corresponding period of 1997).[1] It was also reflected in a pickup in the growth of

industrial production, from 9.3 percent in June 1998 on a 12-month basis to 12.8 percent in September 1998. GDP was also boosted by rising industrial inventories, although their contribution to growth has declined relative to last year.[2] With public investment and industrial production continuing to expand rapidly in October, GDP growth is likely to remain strong in the fourth quarter as well.

Taking all these factors into account, the staff has revised upward its growth projection for 1998 to 7¼ percent, well above the 5½ percent projection in the October 1998 *World Economic Outlook,* and close to the official target of 8 percent. For 1999, while the external environment will remain very difficult, China will benefit from lower U.S. interest rates, as well as from the recent appreciation of the yen. While export growth is expected to remain weak, the continued implementation of the fiscal stimulus package, combined with rebuilding following the flooding, should allow GDP to grow by about 6½ percent. However, this projection is subject to downside risks, especially with respect to demand in major trading partners.

Although much progress has been made in recent years, the quality of Chinese statistics remains a major difficulty for both policymakers and outside analysts, both in the national accounts and in other areas. For example, many analysts have argued that official statistics overstated GDP growth by 1 to 2 percentage points during the reform period: a study by the World Bank found that GDP growth may have been 1¼ percentage points lower than official figures suggest over the period 1978 to 1995, owing to an underestimation of consumption and investment deflators.[3] Beyond technical problems, misre-

---

world.) This does not provide sufficient basis for accurate estimation of quarterly developments in GDP, or to adjust appropriately for seasonal factors.

[2]Data on overall inventory accumulation—including agricultural inventories—are available only on an annual basis. Data on industrial inventories are available at a monthly frequency. Over the past 15 years, overall inventory accumulation has averaged 6 percent of GDP. Since a significant proportion of this has proved to be unsalable, the growth generated by inventory accumulation is of very low quality from an economic perspective.

[3]See World Bank, *China 2020: Development Challenges in the New Century* (Washington, 1997). In addition, valuation procedures for new goods, as well as for inventories, may also give rise to upward bias in growth estimates.

---

[1]GDP data are provided on a cumulative quarterly basis during the year, and estimates for previous periods are not revised. (The data are published about two weeks after the end of each quarter—probably faster than in any other country in the

---

Africa will gain from developments in commodity markets because losses in export earnings are offset by lower oil import bills.[3] Output growth in most of the larger countries in Africa is expected to remain close to rates observed in 1998, or to pick up somewhat in 1999, partly, in a number of cases, owing to the abate-

ment of weather-related problems. For countries in central Africa, however, regional conflicts are adversely affecting growth performance and prospects.

North America and Europe: To What Extent Is Growth Slowing?

The widespread financial market turmoil during August–October raised concerns that growth in many

---

[3]See the October 1998 *World Economic Outlook,* Chapter II, for a more complete analysis of the impact of lower commodity prices on these countries.

porting of data may also be an issue, although any tendency to overreporting may be partly offset by the fact that official statistics do not fully capture the development of the nonstate sector, which has likely been more dynamic than the state sector during much of the reform period. (A 1997 investigation by the State Statistical Bureau found misreporting at the local and provincial levels to be an important problem, although they found examples of both under- and overreporting during the period they examined.)

From an immediate policy perspective, however, a key question is whether the degree of any overstatement or understatement may have widened in 1998, so that trends in key variables may have provided misleading signals. In this context, it is instructive to examine the changes in the relationship between growth in GDP and industrial production, on the one hand, and electricity consumption and freight traffic on the other.[4] On the basis of past trends, the slowdown in the growth of electricity consumption and freight traffic during 1998 would normally have been accompanied by somewhat lower GDP and industrial production growth rates (*see figure*). Beyond the important caveat that the statistics on electricity consumption and freight traffic may themselves not be entirely reliable, a number of specific factors can help to explain this apparent anomaly. These include the declining share of industry and of state-owned enterprises, which are both heavily energy-intensive, combined with the fact that the rapid-growth sectors are not heavy users of electricity; the substantial increase in the relative price of electricity in recent years, which has increased incentives for conservation; and declining output in the coal industry, which accounts for around 40 percent of freight traffic. In addition, electricity output from recently established small-scale power plants, and freight traffic carried by the private sector, may also not be fully captured in the official statistics. Notwithstanding these possible explanations—and the fact that movements over short periods can be misleading—the Chinese authorities themselves are concerned by the discrepancies and are currently studying them in more detail.

---

[4]The relationship has been significantly stronger for electricity output than for freight traffic.

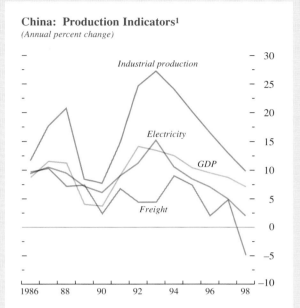

China: Production Indicators[1]
(Annual percent change)

[1]For 1998, cumulative growth rates from corresponding periods of 1997, January to September.

In general, GDP growth rates in China provide an important indicator of broad economic trends—for the third quarter of 1998, all indicators, including electricity consumption and freight traffic, as well as industrial production and money and credit growth, confirm a pickup in the rate of growth of activity. However, they have to be interpreted with care, taking into account the underlying statistical methodologies used and developments in other indicators. The composition of growth, and its underlying quality, also remains an important issue. The ongoing debate about China's GDP statistics highlights the urgent need for continued efforts to improve the quality, coverage, and timeliness of China's economic statistics, for the benefit of both policymakers and outside analysts.

of the industrial countries would slow sharply. This risk seemed most acute in the *United States*, where private consumption had been strong and saving rates low and where market-sensitive equity holdings account for a relatively large share of household wealth. Also troubling, because it could be viewed as threatening a credit crunch, was the widening of yield spreads in corporate bond markets, which are a much larger source of corporate finance in the United States than in other industrial countries. In the event, how-

ever, declines in government bond yields and the three reductions in the federal funds rate between late September and mid-November fostered a rebound in U.S. and other equity markets and contributed to a narrowing of spreads on corporate bonds, allaying concerns of a credit crunch and of a slowdown in demand induced by negative wealth effects.

Recent indicators of economic activity in the United States show continued strength despite some mixed signals. Third-quarter GDP growth, at almost 4 per-

Figure 4.5. Major Industrial Countries: Output Gaps[1]
(Actual less potential output, as percent of potential)

Output in the United States and the United Kingdom has recently exceeded potential levels. In Japan, output is falling further below capacity.

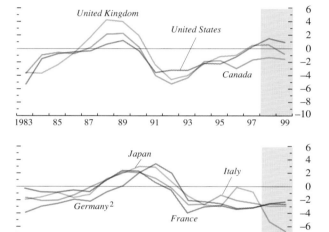

[1]Shaded areas indicate IMF staff projections. The estimates of output gaps are subject to a significant margin of uncertainty. For a discussion of approaches to calculating potential output, see Paula R. De Masi, "IMF Estimates of Potential Output: Theory and Practice," in *Staff Studies for the World Economic Outlook* (Washington: IMF, December 1997), pp. 40–46.
[2]Data through 1991 apply to west Germany only.

cent, was higher than expected, but there was a large increase in business inventories that may portend weaker future production. Industrial production in 1998 has shown the slowest growth in seven years, while durable goods orders fell by almost 2 percent in October, reflecting plummeting orders for machinery and heavy equipment. In contrast, private consumption remained strong in the third quarter, and net exports were less of a drag on the economy than earlier in the year owing to a high, but probably temporary, level of aircraft deliveries. Export volumes are likely to be lower in the fourth quarter. More recently, retail sales showed a further solid gain in October, but gains in personal income have slowed, so that the household saving rate has declined further, turning negative in September and October. Consumer confidence fell from its peak reached in June, recovering partially in November; but with the likelihood of a turnaround in personal saving, consumer spending is expected to moderate in 1999.

The projections assume that the interest rate reductions during September–November, the depreciation of the dollar, and the modest fiscal stimulus provided by the rise in spending implied in this year's federal budget (approximately ¼ of 1 percent of GDP) will moderate the cyclical slowdown, such that the pace of the expansion will slow below potential in 1999 but remain above 1½ percent. With output estimated to be above capacity currently in the United States, this slowing is expected to reduce, but not to eliminate, the positive output gap (Figure 4.5).

Seen against the surprisingly strong performance of the U.S. economy in recent years, it may be argued that the long expansion may continue at a stronger pace than in the baseline projections. However, some slowdown seems both inevitable and desirable on cyclical grounds. While subdued inflationary pressures indicate that at least some of the imbalances often associated with cyclical peaks are not pronounced, other, quite marked, imbalances have emerged. Thus, not only has the household sector's overall saving rate fallen to unusually low (recently negative) levels, but the private sector's saving-investment balance has recently fallen into an extraordinarily large deficit. In fact, strong private domestic demand over the past four years has caused net private saving—that is, household and corporate saving less investment, or the private sector's financial balance—to fall into uncharted waters at least by the standards of the past 40 years (Figure 4.6). This shift is the counterpart to the combination of the improvement in the U.S. fiscal balance (an increase in public saving), which has allowed a "crowding in" of investment in the 1990s, and the deterioration in the current account balance (reflecting an increased reliance on foreign saving) more recently.

A key risk to the projections is that the recent pattern of saving-investment balances will prove unsustainable, and that it will be corrected. For example, if investors increasingly view the U.S. current account deficit and accumulation of external debt as unsustainable, dollar assets would become less attractive, which would result in a weaker dollar, raise U.S. import prices, and increase the cost of capital. Alternatively, or in combination, there is a risk of a significant, renewed correction in U.S. equity prices. Either case would trigger an adjustment process that would tend to weaken private consumption and investment and reduce the current account deficit. In all probability, the private sector's financial balance will need to be brought back toward historic norms sooner or later, but this need not involve a hard landing. From this perspective, a slowdown in domestic demand in the near term that would reduce the private sector's financial deficit could prove beneficial.

Canada has been significantly affected by the Asian crisis, mainly through its impact on global commodity prices. The associated adverse shift in Canada's terms of trade was reflected in steady downward pressure on the Canadian dollar through the first eight months of the year. Concerned that intensified pressure on the currency in August and an adverse swing in long-term interest rate differentials between Canada and the United States signaled a shift in market confidence in the Canadian dollar, the Bank of Canada raised short-term interest rates by a full percentage point in late August. Subsequently, the value of the Canadian dollar has recovered somewhat, and interest rates have come down—especially at the long end of the term structure—facilitated by the central bank's reversal of most of its earlier rate increase, in line with cuts in U.S. interest rates. In 1999, output growth is expected to slow to 2¼ percent, as further small declines in the terms of trade and softening consumer confidence work to reduce domestic demand growth.

In the *euro area,* the weakening of the economic outlook reflects largely external developments, although indicators of domestic demand have recently seemed less robust (Figure 4.7). Business confidence has turned down noticeably in France and Germany, though consumer confidence has continued to rise. Confidence indicators have turned down more generally in Italy. In each of these countries, there are no signs of a credit crunch. In *Germany,* credit growth has been well-maintained, and spreads between loan and deposit rates in the banking system have been declining. In *France,* however, corresponding spreads remain very large, which may reflect the burden of bad loans in the banking system. While the effective appreciation of euro-area currencies in 1998 and lower inflation tended to tighten monetary conditions, notwithstanding the downward convergence of interest rates among the member countries of the future euro area, the interest rate reductions in early December served essentially to reverse this tendency.

Figure 4.6. United States: Private, Public, and Foreign Net Saving[1]
(Percent of GDP)

Private saving net of investment has declined sharply and, on the assumptions used for the projections (including constant real exchange rates), is projected to remain in deficit, well below levels experienced since 1960.

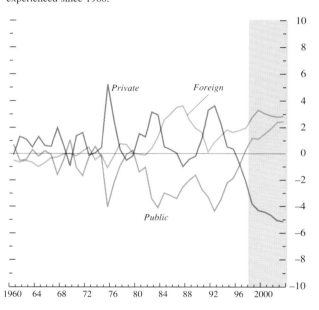

[1]Public net saving is the general government current balance less government net investment, as defined in the national accounts. Foreign net saving is the current account balance, shown with opposite sign; a positive value reflects capital inflows into the domestic economy. Net private saving is the sum of public and foreign net saving, with opposite sign. It represents household disposable income less expenditure, plus after-tax corporate profits, less investment. The net saving of a sector is also known as its financial balance. Shaded area indicates IMF staff projections.

Figure 4.7. Selected European Countries: Real Total Domestic Demand
(Percent change from four quarters earlier)

Domestic demand growth has strengthened since 1996 in France and Germany but has weakened since 1997 in Italy and the United Kingdom.

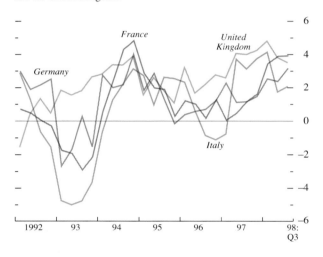

Recent indications of weakening domestic demand were preceded by signs of weaker export performance, especially in Germany beginning in early 1998. This reflects the sharp fall in export market growth for the euro area as a whole in 1998, which is not expected to improve in 1999. The recent appreciation of the euro-area currencies against the U.S. dollar will also affect exports adversely, although it is offset to some extent by the depreciation of these currencies against the Japanese yen. Apart from questions relating directly to foreign demand, risks to euro-area growth include possible inventory corrections (especially in Germany and *Italy*) which could become more likely if the outlook for the external sector weakens further; a greater-than-assumed drag on consumer spending from the phase-out of auto loan incentives (Italy); and a weakening of consumer confidence and spending if, for example, the recent declines in unemployment in a number of countries are halted or reversed. Overall, in France and most of the smaller euro-area countries, growth is expected to be maintained at or slightly above potential in 1999. However, growth is projected to be less vigorous in Germany and Italy, with the implication that the negative output gaps in these countries may stabilize at close to 2 percent of GDP (see Figure 4.5). Inflation in the euro area is projected to be around 1½ percent in 1999–2000, below the target ceiling of 2 percent. In December, the European Central Bank's governing council announced a quantitative reference value for monetary growth (M3) of 4½ percent. The latest monetary data are in line with this reference value.

In the *United Kingdom,* following several years of expansion at above-potential rates, growth has slowed markedly during 1998 and is expected to weaken further in the period ahead, with growth in 1999 as a whole now projected at just under 1 percent, the slowest in the EU. The slowdown stems from the sharp tightening of monetary conditions between late 1996 and early 1998 arising from the tightening of monetary policy and the substantial appreciation of sterling (see Figure 4.2), the impact of fiscal consolidation undertaken in recent years, and the deceleration of global growth. The weakening of net exports apparent since mid-1997 has been accompanied this year by a marked slowdown of domestic demand growth, and business confidence reached an 18-year low in October. The projected slowdown implies that output in the United Kingdom will fall below potential in the period ahead. With price inflation recently at its target and inflationary pressures weakening, the Bank of England has cut interest rates by 1¼ percentage points since early October. As with the other European countries, there is little evidence of a credit crunch: the gap between lending and deposit rates at banks has not widened, and bank lending has continued to grow strongly. Some pickup in demand is expected in the second half of 1999, spurred by the recent effective depreciation of sterling, cuts in short-term interest rates, and also declines in long-term rates that have been the largest among the major industrial countries in 1998.

Global Financial Flows and Current Account Balances

The large shifts in global financial flows since the onset of the Asian crisis have led to substantial adjustments in the external positions of many countries. Net private capital flows to emerging market economies (comprising for this purpose all developing countries, countries in transition, and the newly industrialized Asian economies except Hong Kong SAR) are estimated to have fallen by nearly $150 billion in the two years from 1996 to about $70 billion in 1998, with the decline in flows to the Asian developing and newly industrialized economies more than accounting for this change (Table 4.9). In 1999, net flows to emerging market economies are assumed to rise, mainly owing to a reduction in outflows from Asia, whereas flows to the countries in transition and to the developing countries of the Western Hemisphere are expected to remain near levels experienced in recent years. (Among the transition countries, Russia is assumed to experience a decline in net private inflows.) Following the virtual drying up of capital flows to emerging market countries in general in the wake of the Russian crisis, the baseline projections for 1999 assume, in effect, that the more recent stabilization of financial market conditions will be consolidated, with capital flows recovering from late 1998 through 1999. (See Chapter II for details on recent market conditions and private flows in 1998.)

The reversal of private capital flows to emerging market economies in Asia in 1997–98 has led to dramatic swings toward surplus in the current account balances of these economies (Table 4.10). In the five crisis-afflicted Asian economies, the combined current account balance is estimated to have swung by $118 billion in this direction between 1996 and 1998, with deficits of 3½–8 percent of GDP turning into surpluses of 1–13½ percent of GDP. The turnarounds have resulted mainly from import compression; large increases in export volumes to non-Asian markets, partly owing to gains in competitiveness, have been partially offset by falling intra-Asian trade and declines in export prices. A similar adjustment pattern, but much smaller in scale and thus with smaller implications for world trade, is occurring in Russia, where a small current account deficit in 1997 is expected to swing into a surplus of almost 7 percent of GDP in 1999. In Brazil, however, official financing and drawdowns in reserves are expected to contain the impact of smaller private capital inflows on the current account, which is projected to remain in deficit in 1999.

For the industrial countries as a group, the current account position is estimated to deteriorate by $123 billion between 1997 and 1999 (see the Statistical Appendix, Table 6). This is more than accounted for by the growing deficit of the United States, where export growth has slowed sharply, but domestic demand and imports have been buoyant. Elsewhere, the current account surplus of Japan is projected to increase by $45 billion between 1997 and 1999 because of weak domestic demand and lower commodity prices, while the current account surplus of the euro area is projected to remain largely unchanged at $100 billion.

As in the October 1998 *World Economic Outlook,* the projections for current account balances imply a widening of the current account discrepancy—in the revised projections, to $101 billion in 1999 from $57 billion in 1996. The increase in the discrepancy to levels beyond historical norms shows that the projections for world imports and exports are moving further out of balance and may be interpreted as indicating a tension in the forecast, which could be resolved by either a larger-than-projected external adjustment in the crisis-afflicted countries or a smaller-than-projected deterioration in the current account balances of the industrial countries, or a combination of the two.

Alternative Scenario

Chapter I lists a number of uncertainties about the world economy that have not been taken into account in the baseline scenario, but that nevertheless warrant some consideration. Consequently, an alternative scenario was constructed to examine the possible implications if three of these risks were to materialize—namely, a failure of capital flows to emerging economies to recover, a correction in equity prices in the industrial countries, and a shift in the pattern of exchange rates among the major advanced economies as investors become concerned about the sustainability of the large current account deficits of the United States.[4]

As discussed in the preceding chapters, there is some risk that the recent loss of appetite for investments in emerging markets would continue into 1999, either as a result of high risk aversion or perceptions, or in response to continued contagion or new crises. To illustrate this risk, capital flows to emerging market countries are assumed to decline further in 1999 by $25 billion to a level of some $75 billion lower than assumed in the baseline for 1999. A similar shortfall is assumed for 2000, with adjustment toward baseline levels thereafter.

---

[4]The scenario was estimated using the IMF's international macroeconomic model, MULTIMOD. See Douglas Laxton, Peter Isard, Hamid Faruqee, Eswar Prasad, and Bart Turtelboom, *MULTIMOD Mark III: The Core Dynamic and Steady-State Models,* Occasional Paper 164 (Washington: IMF, May 1998).

Table 4.9. Developing Countries, Countries in Transition, and Selected Newly Industrialized Asian Economies: Net Capital Flows[1]

(Billions of U.S. dollars)

	1984–89[2]	1990–96[2]	1994	1995	1996	1997	1998	1999
Total								
Net private capital flows[3]	12.5	141.7	156.3	194.0	214.8	117.8	69.5	89.7
Net direct investment	13.1	64.6	83.5	99.3	121.1	145.0	127.3	119.2
Net portfolio investment	4.4	64.0	106.6	39.3	79.9	66.6	42.0	25.1
Other net investment	–4.9	13.0	–33.8	55.4	13.9	–93.8	–99.8	–54.5
Net official flows	26.5	17.4	–2.4	22.9	2.4	22.5	36.8	7.2
Change in reserves[4]	–11.2	–71.3	–65.3	–120.0	–105.5	–44.2	–29.2	–32.7
Developing countries								
Net private capital flows[3]	17.5	128.8	133.6	147.3	190.9	131.8	87.6	104.1
Net direct investment	12.2	57.9	76.3	86.3	108.6	126.7	106.2	96.2
Net portfolio investment	4.9	51.1	85.8	22.2	52.5	51.8	38.0	18.9
Other net investment	0.4	19.8	–28.6	38.8	29.7	–46.6	–56.6	–11.0
Net official flows	27.4	16.8	9.9	31.9	2.6	–3.0	15.6	12.6
Change in reserves[4]	5.1	–55.8	–43.6	–72.2	–95.5	–50.9	13.0	–12.7
Africa								
Net private capital flows[3]	2.3	3.7	8.8	10.4	5.1	14.1	7.3	14.2
Net direct investment	1.2	2.9	3.5	4.2	5.1	7.3	6.2	7.1
Net portfolio investment	–0.8	–0.2	0.5	1.5	–0.3	2.9	2.8	–0.1
Other net investment	1.8	0.9	4.8	4.7	0.3	3.9	–1.7	7.3
Net official flows	6.7	7.6	9.2	7.4	6.6	–2.7	2.9	0.2
Change in reserves[4]	0.1	–2.2	–5.0	–1.9	–6.7	–13.5	0.3	1.2
Asia								
Net private capital flows[3]	13.1	56.0	64.8	91.7	100.2	21.5	–18.3	–7.3
Net direct investment	4.5	32.9	44.4	51.0	60.2	60.2	45.1	35.0
Net portfolio investment	1.5	6.7	11.5	10.0	10.1	7.5	–6.5	–3.0
Other net investment	7.0	16.4	9.0	30.8	29.9	–46.3	–56.9	–39.3
Net official flows	7.8	8.5	5.6	5.1	10.3	7.9	12.7	12.2
Change in reserves[4]	–2.1	–29.7	–39.8	–33.0	–49.1	–12.1	–7.3	–8.9
Middle East and Europe								
Net private capital flows[3]	2.3	22.9	13.0	7.0	3.9	7.9	24.9	21.9
Net direct investment	1.1	2.9	3.7	5.1	4.1	5.0	3.9	5.6
Net portfolio investment	5.1	12.3	13.0	9.1	2.8	3.0	7.5	7.0
Other net investment	–3.9	7.7	–3.6	–7.1	–3.0	–0.2	13.4	9.3
Net official flows	4.8	–0.4	–1.0	–1.1	–0.6	–0.6	–0.9	–1.2
Change in reserves[4]	6.6	–5.6	–3.1	–11.6	–11.3	–10.3	—	–1.2
Western Hemisphere								
Net private capital flows[3]	–0.2	46.1	46.9	38.1	81.7	88.3	73.6	75.3
Net direct investment	5.3	19.1	24.8	26.0	39.2	54.2	51.0	48.6
Net portfolio investment	–0.9	32.3	60.9	1.7	40.0	38.3	34.2	15.1
Other net investment	–4.6	–5.3	–38.7	10.4	2.5	–4.1	–11.5	11.6
Net official flows	8.2	1.2	–3.9	20.5	–13.7	–7.7	0.8	1.5
Change in reserves[4]	0.5	–18.4	4.2	–25.7	–28.3	–15.0	20.0	–3.8
Countries in transition								
Net private capital flows[3]	–1.7	10.6	18.9	42.6	16.0	22.6	13.2	16.4
Net direct investment	–0.2	6.4	5.4	13.4	13.4	18.2	17.1	18.2
Net portfolio investment	—	10.4	20.5	18.8	24.3	20.8	7.0	8.2
Other net investment	–1.6	–6.2	–7.0	10.4	–21.7	–16.4	–10.9	–10.0
Net official flows	0.2	1.1	–12.1	–8.4	–0.2	9.7	11.4	0.9
Change in reserves[4]	–2.7	–5.0	–6.9	–36.2	–0.2	–6.3	–3.4	–6.5
Selected newly industrialized Asian economies[5]								
Net private capital flows[3]	–3.2	2.3	3.9	4.1	7.9	–36.6	–31.2	–30.8
Net direct investment	1.0	0.4	1.8	–0.4	–1.0	0.1	4.0	4.8
Net portfolio investment	–0.5	2.5	0.3	–1.7	3.1	–5.9	–3.0	–2.1
Other net investment	–3.7	–0.6	1.9	6.2	5.9	–30.7	–32.2	–33.5
Net official flows	–1.1	–0.5	–0.3	–0.6	—	15.8	9.8	–6.4
Change in reserves[4]	–13.6	–10.5	–14.8	–11.7	–9.9	13.0	–38.8	–13.5

[1]Net capital flows comprise net direct investment, net portfolio investment, and other long- and short-term net investment flows, including official and private borrowing.

[2]Annual averages.

[3]Because of data limitations, other net investment may include some official flows.

[4]A minus sign indicates an increase.

[5]Korea, Singapore, and Taiwan Province of China.

Events over the past few months have also underscored the risk of a renewed correction in equity markets (see Chapter III and Box 3.2). As noted above in the context of the projections for the United States, a stock market correction would be expected to have significant effects on consumer and business spending. To examine the effects of such a correction, the scenario assumes a (relatively modest) drop in stock market prices in all the major industrial countries of about 13 percent in the first year of the shock. Finally, the scenario assumes that the U.S. dollar depreciates by about 10 percent against other major currencies. This assumption carries implications for the distribution of the large trade imbalances that have emerged as a result of the Asian crisis.

Each of these risks might materialize independently. However, they are potentially interrelated, with the materialization of any one giving rise to a chain reaction and an increasing chance that the other risks might emerge. For example, a generalized increase in risk aversion might make investors in Japan and Europe less willing to finance the U.S. current account deficit, at the same time as they may attempt to reduce their exposure in emerging markets generally, as has been the case in Asia. The resulting negative impact of these events on global growth prospects and business profits might then lead to price declines in the major stock markets. Because these risks are potentially interrelated, they are assumed to occur simultaneously in the scenario.

The results of the alternative scenario are summarized in Table 4.11. In the first year of the shock, global output falls relative to the baseline by 1¼ percent, with slightly larger relative adjustment—an output fall of 1½ percent—occurring in the emerging market economies owing to the compression of imports required by the reduction in external financing. This import compression, taken alone, results in lower exports from the industrial economies and accounts for about one-fourth of the initial fall in output in those economies. In the developing countries, domestic demand falls more sharply than total output, with declines in domestic spending generating most of the fall in imports.

Within the industrial country group, the assumed depreciation of the U.S. dollar relative to other major currencies tends to amplify the decline in output in the euro area relative to the United States as the latter becomes more competitive. This improvement in competitiveness contributes to the reduction in the U.S. current account deficit (by $25 billion after three years) and to smaller surpluses in Europe and Japan. The assumed decline in equity prices in mature markets contributes to reductions in domestic demand in the industrial countries and helps to reduce the private saving-investment deficit in the United States relative to the baseline projections and thus to reduce the U.S. current account deficit. Output in Europe and Japan is

Table 4.10. Selected Economies: Current Account Positions

(Percent of GDP)

	1995	1996	1997	1998	1999
Advanced economies					
United States	−1.6	−1.8	−1.9	−2.7	−3.3
Japan	2.2	1.4	2.2	3.4	3.3
Germany	−0.9	−0.6	−0.2	0.1	0.2
France	0.7	1.3	2.8	2.1	1.6
Italy	2.3	3.3	2.9	2.5	2.5
United Kingdom	−0.5	−0.2	0.6	−0.5	−0.7
Canada	−0.8	0.5	−1.5	−2.1	−1.7
Australia	−5.5	−4.0	−3.2	−5.2	−5.6
Austria	−2.0	−1.8	−1.3	−0.6	−0.6
Finland	4.1	4.0	5.5	4.6	4.3
Greece	−2.1	−2.6	−2.4	−2.3	−2.0
Hong Kong SAR[1]	−3.9	−1.1	−3.1	—	1.2
Ireland	2.7	2.7	2.8	3.0	2.9
Israel	−5.6	−5.4	−3.3	−2.8	−2.9
Korea	−1.9	−4.7	−1.8	13.2	8.7
New Zealand	−3.1	−3.9	−7.7	−6.9	−6.9
Norway	3.3	6.7	5.2	0.1	2.7
Singapore	16.9	15.9	15.4	19.2	18.4
Spain	0.2	0.3	0.5	0.2	−0.3
Sweden	2.1	2.4	2.7	2.8	2.5
Switzerland	7.0	7.4	8.9	9.1	9.1
Taiwan Province of China	2.1	4.0	2.7	2.0	2.2
Memorandum					
European Union	0.6	1.0	1.5	1.2	1.0
Developing countries					
Algeria	−5.3	2.7	7.4	−2.2	−2.1
Argentina	−1.5	−1.9	−3.5	−4.5	−4.2
Brazil	−2.6	−3.0	−4.1	−4.2	−3.6
Cameroon	−0.8	−2.3	−1.3	−2.4	−2.5
Chile	−2.1	−5.4	−5.3	−6.8	−5.2
China	0.2	0.9	3.3	2.4	1.8
Côte d'Ivoïre	−6.0	−4.8	−4.5	−3.8	−2.6
Egypt	0.7	−0.3	0.2	−3.4	−3.0
India	−1.6	−1.4	−1.6	−1.9	−2.0
Indonesia	−3.3	−3.3	−1.8	3.0	2.0
Malaysia	−10.0	−4.9	−4.2	11.0	9.2
Mexico	−0.6	−0.7	−1.9	−3.5	−2.2
Nigeria	−3.2	11.9	4.9	−11.6	−16.0
Pakistan	−3.4	−7.1	−5.8	−2.9	−2.8
Philippines	−4.4	−4.7	−5.2	1.2	0.6
Saudi Arabia	−4.3	0.2	0.2	−8.0	−6.8
South Africa	−2.0	−1.3	−1.5	−1.4	−0.9
Thailand	−7.9	−7.9	−2.0	11.4	8.4
Turkey	−0.5	−1.4	−1.4	−2.2	−2.6
Uganda	−2.4	−1.5	−1.4	−2.9	−3.2
Countries in transition					
Czech Republic	−2.7	−7.6	−6.1	−2.0	−2.0
Estonia	−5.1	−9.7	−12.9	−9.1	−6.9
Hungary	−5.7	−3.8	−2.2	−2.9	−3.3
Latvia	−3.4	−4.0	−5.0	−5.5	−6.9
Lithuania	−10.2	−9.1	−10.2	−13.5	−15.0
Poland[2]	3.3	−1.0	−3.2	−3.8	−4.9
Russia	1.6	0.6	−0.1	1.6	6.7
Slovak Republic	2	−11	−11	−10	−4
Ukraine	−4	−3	−3	−2	−2

[1]Data include only goods and nonfactor services.
[2]Based on data for the current balance, including a surplus on unrecorded trade transactions, as estimated by IMF staff.

Table 4.11. Alternative Scenario: Simulation Results[1]

(Deviations from baseline, in percent unless otherwise noted)

	First Year	Second Year	Third Year	Fourth Year
World				
Real GDP	−1.3	−0.7	0.2	0.2
Industrial countries[2]				
Real GDP	−1.3	−0.8	0.3	0.3
Real domestic demand	−1.0	−0.5	0.3	0.4
Short-term interest rate	−0.4	−0.7	−0.6	−0.5
Long-term interest rate	−0.3	−0.2	−0.1	−0.1
Consumer price index inflation	−0.2	−0.3	−0.1	0.0
Current account balance (billions of U.S. dollars)	−52.4	−72.9	−19.2	−28.3
Developing countries[3]				
Real GDP	−1.5	−0.4	0.0	0.1
Real domestic demand	−2.6	−1.3	−0.1	−0.2
Current account balance (billions of U.S. dollars)	52.4	72.3	19.3	28.3

[1]Baseline is based on current *World Economic Outlook* database, with shocks starting in 1999. The scenario models a reduction in financial flows to the emerging market economies of $70–75 billion in 1999 and 2000, a reduction in equity prices in the industrial countries, and a depreciation in the value of the U.S. dollar.

[2]Comprises Canada, France, Germany, Italy, Japan, the United Kingdom, the United States, and the following smaller industrial countries: Australia, Austria, Belgium, Denmark, Finland, Greece, Ireland, the Netherlands, New Zealand, Norway, Portugal, Spain, and Switzerland.

[3]Comprises all countries except the industrial countries.

more affected by the combined demand shocks than output in the United States, in part because of greater rigidities in the former economies. For the same reasons, the rise in unemployment is smaller in the United States.

* * *

This alternative scenario, it should be emphasized, deals with risks to a baseline projection that summarizes the most likely path for the world economy going forward—comparatively weak growth in 1999, but the avoidance of world recession. The baseline scenario, however, is contingent upon a set of assumptions that may not be realized. The turbulent events of August–October and the subsequent policy responses that have restored an important measure of calm testify both to the importance of taking risks seriously when they emerge and to the role and importance of timely and vigorous policy response.

Annex

Emerging Market Banking Systems

The turbulence in international capital markets in the period beginning in August 1998 had a differentiated impact on various emerging market banking systems that reflects both the relative soundness of the different systems and the magnitude of the spillovers across regions. This annex reviews developments in the major emerging markets' banking systems since midyear, with a focus on those systems where banking problems and vulnerabilities are considered to be significant by market participants and the major rating agencies.[1]

Although the recent financial turbulence has not had a major impact in Asia, most banking systems in the region have experienced further deteriorations in asset quality as their economies have continued to weaken. Moreover, the slow progress in corporate restructuring has threatened to delay the final resolution of problems in the banking systems. In addition, the reduction in market interest rates has not been fully reflected in lending rates, and banks have continued to be cautious about extending new loans. It is now evident that the restructuring of the banking systems will take time to complete, but it is important in the interim not to take actions that could increase the ultimate restructuring costs that already amount to a large share of GDP in most affected countries (see Table A1). In this regard, measures that put pressures on banks to expand their lending—such as those that have been taken in China and Malaysia—create the risk that banks could further add to their stock of bad loans. Meanwhile, the operating environment for Latin American banks has deteriorated in the aftermath of the Russian crisis, following the drying up of external financing, increases in interest rates, and the associated slowdown in economic activity. Most banks in the region have suffered losses associated with their securities portfolios and are expecting a deterioration in their loan portfolios, but systemic risks continue to be relatively low. The impact of financial turbulence on most of eastern Europe's banks has been relatively minor, since direct exposure to Russia and spillovers to the region have

been limited. The restructuring of Russia's banking system is a top priority of the government's anticrisis plan, but the restructuring process is likely to face severe financing constraints.

Asia

As *China* has attempted to fend off the effects on its economy of the regional slowdown, the need to accelerate financial sector reform and address the vulnerabilities of its banking system has become a critical issue. At the beginning of 1998, the system of quotas that used to guide state-owned banks' loan growth was abolished, in an attempt to strengthen the banks' efforts to manage their problem loans and to induce them to become more commercially oriented.[2] As a result, credit growth slowed in the first quarter of the year, prompting the government to declare that while banks were free to make their own decisions, they must bear in mind their duty to support the government's objective of achieving 8 percent GDP growth in 1998. So far, the government has adopted a policy of gradually writing off bad loans accumulated in the past so as to achieve a "soft landing" in solving the bad-loan problem in tandem with the restructuring of state-owned enterprises. However, analysts worry that faster loan growth may cause problem loans to grow faster than the banks can write them off, deepening the banks' problems of asset quality.

Meanwhile, the authorities have moved decisively to deal with the weaknesses of China's nonbank financial institutions. Spurred by the lessons from the Asian crisis, where nonbank financial institutions were often at the heart of the financial crises, in October the People's Bank of China ordered the closure of Guandong International Trust and Investment Company (GITIC) and 12 credit cooperatives in Beihai. Other international trust and investment corporations—the so-called ITICs—have, like GITIC, taken

---

[1]See the September 1998 *International Capital Markets* report for an analysis of the major Asian banking crises and a discussion of developments in the systemically important emerging markets' banking systems in the period from July 1997 to June 1998. The analysis draws on publicly available material published by national authorities, banks, and rating agencies.

[2]China's four state commercial banks account for two-thirds of total bank assets, and while their nonperforming loans are estimated at 20–25 percent on Chinese definitions, market participants believe them to be closer to 40 percent (see the September 1998 *International Capital Markets* report). The authorities have used a Y 270 billion (about 3 percent of GDP) bond issuance to recapitalize these banks.

Table A1. Asia: Estimated Costs of Bank Restructuring[1]

	Local Currency Cost	U.S. Dollar Equivalent[2] (billions of U.S. dollars)	Percent of GDP
Interest costs			
Indonesia	Rp 40 trillion	5.4	3.50
Korea	W 8 trillion	6.4	2.00
Thailand	B 143 billion	4.0	3.00
Malaysia	RM 3.5 billion	0.9	1.25
Philippines	P 11.9 billion	0.3[3]	0.25–0.50
Total		17.0	
Total cost (stock of debt issued)			
Indonesia	Rp 300 trillion	40	29.00
Korea[4]	W 74.7 trillion	60	17.50
Thailand	B 1,583 billion	43	32.00
Malaysia	RM 48.4 billion	13	18.00
Philippines	P 110 billion	3	4.00
Total		159	

[1]IMF staff estimates as of November 30, 1998. The estimates do not necessarily reflect the assessments of the authorities. The numbers are highly tentative and depend on many factors, including the evolution of real interest rates. They include both budgetary and extrabudgetary costs and are intended to measure the up-front financing costs (that is, they do not include receipts from any eventual sale of problem assets).
[2]Converted at exchange rates on November 30.
[3]Assumes 10 percent interest rate.
[4]Includes asset swaps of public enterprise stocks (W 8.9 trillion).

on short-term borrowings to finance long-term infrastructure and industrial projects and may face similar problems. GITIC's default on foreign obligations was interpreted by some market participants as a change in the rules of the game,[3] and this prompted a number of foreign banks to retreat from lending to the other ITICs as well as to the "window" companies controlled by Chinese provincial governments and listed in Hong Kong SAR. Although the ITICs account for only 2 percent of total financial system assets in China, market participants worry that their difficulties may cause a credit squeeze, with repercussions for the whole economy. However, the closure of nonbank financial institutions may consolidate the strength and strategic importance of China's banks—as depositors move their funds from the ITICs and credit cooperatives to the banking system—and would constitute a more desirable precedent than would comprehensive bailouts.

The banking systems of the financial centers of *Hong Kong SAR* and *Singapore* were affected differently by the financial turmoil, but most banks' strong capital positions and good profitability have given them enough cushion to absorb the expected increase in nonperforming loans. Problem loans of Hong Kong banks grew to above 3 percent of total assets in 1998.

While some analysts expect the ratio to increase significantly, Hong Kong banks are well capitalized and prepared to absorb such losses. Nonperforming loans have risen to just over 5 percent for Singapore's banks; although their regional exposures are high, their Basle risk-adjusted capital-to-asset ratios are between 15 and 20 percent.

In *Indonesia,* the authorities have begun to restructure the severely damaged banking system[4] through a mixture of bank closures, mergers, and takeovers. At the same time, efforts to recover liquidity credits extended to many banks earlier in the year have been stepped up. On August 21, 1998, the Indonesian authorities announced the resolution of the six large private banks taken over by the Indonesian Bank Restructuring Agency (IBRA) in April 1998. In addition, the authorities announced the merger of four of the seven state banks, with the new bank being placed under the management of a major international bank. Under threat of legal action, several former owners of failed banks pledged assets nominally worth around $16 billion to cover the obligations derived from the emergency assistance provided by the central bank. In an effort to avoid an asset "fire sale," the government will hold the assets as collateral as the bankers pay their debts over the next four years. Meanwhile, negative margins between loan and deposit rates are in-

[3]Some investors had interpreted previous statements of local government officials as implicit guarantees on debts that had been registered with the State Administration for Foreign Exchange Approval (SAFE). However, the "implicit guarantees" by local governments had not been authorized by the central government. Market participants expect further clarification of the authorities' repayment policies.

[4]The authorities have recognized that the level of nonperforming loans exceeds 50 percent of the loans of the system, while private estimates range between 60 and 75 percent. Analysts estimate that most sectors of the banking system, public and private, are experiencing widespread insolvency, and the negative net worth of the system is estimated at around 30 percent of GDP.

creasing insolvencies in the banking system, and only a few banks with low ratios of loans to deposits are expected to survive in the current environment.

Progress with corporate restructuring has been very slow, but a framework for the voluntary restructuring of corporate debt—the Jakarta Initiative—was announced on September 9, 1998, to complement the Indonesia Debt Restructuring Agency (INDRA) scheme and the newly amended bankruptcy law. The INDRA scheme provides exchange risk protection to private debtors who agree with their creditors to restructure their external debts while the Jakarta Initiative provides a set of principles to guide and streamline out-of-court corporate restructuring. The potential initiation of bankruptcy procedures provides an important incentive for the conclusion of restructuring agreements under the initiative. Although the government's role is limited to facilitating negotiations among private parties, in circumstances where a debtor is not cooperating within the framework the principles recognize the authority of the public prosecutor to initiate bankruptcy procedures against a public company for reasons of public interest.

Since mid-1998, with the asset quality of *Korean* banks continuing to deteriorate, the authorities accelerated the process of consolidation through a series of bank mergers. However, the lack of progress in corporate restructuring could delay any final resolution of the problems in the banking sector. The Financial Supervisory Commission (FSC) announced that problem loans—broadly defined to include loans classified as "precautionary"—amounted to about 22 percent of total loans in the financial sector as of end-June 1998. Of the eight major banks, four did not achieve the 8 percent minimum capital adequacy ratio at end-June, and other banks are also likely to face capital shortages following the tightening of regulations announced in the latest Letter of Intent to the IMF. Since June 1998, the FSC has ordered sound banks to take over five insolvent banks and forced a number of big banks to merge, all in return for the government's promise to buy nonperforming loans of merged banks and supply funds for recapitalization.[5] On September 3, the country's largest *chaebol* announced plans to merge some of their operations, but these so-called "big deals" fell short of what had been expected, and their implementation has faced several problems. The lack of progress has prompted the government to set a deadline of December 15 for the *chaebol* to devise proposals for the comprehensive restructuring of their activities or face the prospect of forced closure of fail-

ing affiliates, the cutting off of credit lines, or both. The government has also asked banks to gradually reduce their exposures to any single entity from the current ceiling of 45 percent of total capital to 25 percent by 2002. Finally, the privatization of Korea First Bank and Seoul Bank is scheduled for January 1999, but foreign interest remains uncertain.

The problems of the *Malaysian* banking system have intensified as economic conditions have deteriorated in 1998. Official estimates of nonperforming loans reached 17.8 percent of outstanding loans at end-September 1998, up from the 10.6 percent recorded at end-April. The authorities estimate that the financial system's recapitalization requirements for 1998–99 will amount to around 11.8 percent of GDP. The capital controls introduced in September have not had a major direct impact on Malaysian banks, other than the loss of some foreign exchange income and a higher cost of doing business, and the decline in domestic interest rates may have a positive impact on asset quality. Moreover, the forced repatriation of all ringgit held abroad, combined with the progressive lowering of statutory reserve requirements, has significantly expanded liquidity within the banking system. In addition, the relaxation of restrictions on lending to the property and equity sectors has been accompanied by increasing government pressure on the banks to increase their lending activities. If these policies result in a significant expansion of the banks' loan book on the basis of noncommercial criteria, especially in the midst of a severe recession, there is clearly a risk of a further deterioration in asset quality.[6]

The Malaysian authorities have taken several steps to shore up the banking system, but there are concerns among market participants that the decision to relax banks' disclosure and provisioning requirements may conceal, rather than address, the banking system's problems. In recent months, Danamodal Nasional, the government agency set up to recapitalize banks, has injected capital into several weak banks and finance companies, and the agency is well placed to encourage these institutions to merge and restructure. Danaharta, the agency set up in June 1998 to purchase nonperforming loans, also started operations in August 1998. Soon after the imposition of capital controls, the government reversed a recent central bank regulation requiring loans to be classified as nonperforming when three months in arrears—compared to six months previously—a move that constitutes a departure from international standards.[7]

[5]By mid-October, the Korea Asset Management Corporation had spent W 18 trillion purchasing nonperforming loans at an average discount of 45 percent. It is unclear whether realistic loan-recovery values are included in such discounts or whether these transactions will add to the increasing government support to the restructuring process.

[6]More recently, the authorities have recognized that the 8 percent minimum loan growth target would not be attainable and have estimated loan growth of 2–3 percent for 1998.

[7]The change in the three-month arrears standard has technically reduced the volume of the banks' nonperforming loans from 17.8 percent to 12.4 percent as of end-September 1998.

In *Thailand,* the banking system has continued to face severe difficulties. For the first half of the year, larger banks reported losses ranging from 10 to 30 percent of end-1997 equity, while most of the smaller banks reported losses exceeding 60 percent of equity. Nonperforming loans throughout the banking system have grown to an average of around 40 percent (for nonintervened banks). Market participants have expressed concern over the health of a number of medium-sized banks, accounting for roughly one-fourth of deposits. Responding to these difficulties, on August 14 the authorities announced a bank restructuring plan, which accelerated the consolidation of banks and finance companies, prepared for the privatization of intervened banks, and introduced bank capital support facilities for banks that either raise new private capital (the Tier-1 capital support scheme) or bring forward debt restructuring and new lending to the private sector (Tier-2 capital support).[8] However, while the fear of ownership dilution and the requirement to bring forward Year 2000 provisioning rules have made banks reluctant to make use of the Tier-1 scheme, there is growing interest in the use of the Tier-2 capital support facilities. At the same time, the Bank of Thailand will continue to review banks' capital adequacy and their adherence to best-practice provisioning requirements (which are being phased in); banks in need of additional capital will be required to sign detailed Memoranda of Understanding with the Bank of Thailand. Finally, the process of auctioning the assets of the closed 56 finance companies has proceeded according to plan, and is now entering its final stage, with the next major auction of $11 billion of assets scheduled for mid-December. This auction of business loans is crucial, not only for its size, but also for bringing back liquidity to the commercial real estate market and for helping to set new benchmark prices.

Latin America

Argentina's banking system is well capitalized and is regarded by bank analysts as one of the strongest in the region, and it has been only modestly affected by the relatively small increase in interest rates that Argentina experienced during the recent financial turmoil. Nevertheless, banks have been affected by some losses in their fixed-income portfolios and slower loan growth. As a result, some asset quality deterioration is likely to have lowered the banks' performance in the second half of 1998.[9] Although two medium-sized banks experienced liquidity problems in October, and one of them was suspended, deposits in the banking system continued to grow. Moreover, the liquidity problems were limited and had no systemic implications. Some banks in *Chile* have experienced declines in profits in the third quarter of this year, but most Chilean banks are well reserved and continue to be viewed as having the best asset quality in the region: past-due loans increased from 0.97 percent of total loans in December 1997 to 1.19 percent in July 1998. *Venezuelan* banks have already shown the initial signs of a deterioration in asset quality as a result of lower oil prices, political uncertainty, and high interest rates; as a result, some banks have been downgraded by the major rating agencies. The ratio of nonperforming loans (including interest in arrears) to total loans rose from 3.7 percent in December 1997 to 7.7 percent in September 1998.

Although the banking system in *Brazil* is highly capitalized, it has suffered from the extreme financial volatility of the past few months and will come under pressure as the government strives to fully regain the confidence of international investors. Rating agencies have expressed concerns that an extended period of low access to international capital markets could affect those large Brazilian banks that are more dependent on foreign funding. Also, while banks are unlikely to experience major losses on their securities portfolios—as domestic securities are now mostly floating-rate instruments, contrary to the October 1997 episode—credit risk has clearly increased. Although lending is a relatively small fraction of the banks' assets,[10] high real interest rates and a slowdown in economic activity have reduced loan growth and will likely reduce the credit quality of loan portfolios—especially in some of the less well-capitalized medium-sized and small banks—but systemic risk remains low.

Mexican banks continue to struggle with asset quality problems, and market participants expect the operating environment to remain weak for at least one more year. Almost one-third of the assets of those banks participating in the loan purchase and capitalization scheme are in illiquid FOBAPROA securities that do not produce any cash flow or are linked to money market interest rates. Earnings in the second quarter were weak, in large part due to losses in securities portfolios, and analysts expect the weakness to continue in the second half of the year. Asset quality improved marginally in the second quarter, but market analysts expect a deterioration going into 1999.

---

[8]This plan has been complemented by additional efforts to speed restructuring of corporate debt, including improvements to the bankruptcy and foreclosure laws to encourage debtors to enter negotiations, development of a framework to guide restructuring (the Bangkok Approach), and removal of numerous tax impediments to corporate debt restructuring.

[9]Nonperforming loans in the overall banking system continued to fall in the first half of the year and were 9.7 percent of total loans at end-June. For the private banks, the nonperforming loan ratio—net of provisions—was 2.4 percent.

[10]The ratio of loans to total assets of the five largest banks was 28.8 percent at end-June 1998, even lower than the ratio evident before the *Real Plan.*

Eastern Europe and Russia

Events in Russia have had a minor impact on most of eastern Europe's banking systems—with an exception perhaps in the *Czech Republic*—as direct exposures are relatively small. Russian assets of regional banking systems are generally less than 2 percent of total assets, and are mostly trade-related rather than financial assets. Asset quality and capitalization have continued to improve in *Poland* and *Hungary,* despite the fact that loan growth has been rapid and the share of government loans in total assets has declined. In contrast, Czech banks have experienced a deterioration in credit quality during the recent economic recession. The three major Czech banks have recently been downgraded by a major rating agency on grounds of large exposures to a weak corporate sector and a deteriorating external environment. Market participants remain concerned that the banking sector may deteriorate further if an economic recovery does not occur.

The banking system has been one of the main intermediaries of capital inflows in *Turkey,* and the recent financial turbulence is likely to increase the system's vulnerability to market and credit risk. Private sector commercial banks[11] have large net foreign exchange positions (amounting to $2.5 billion at mid-September 1998) and have relied on international funding to finance large holdings of high-yielding government securities.[12] The banks have also financed their large operations in government securities mainly through repurchase agreements (repos), in part because of regulatory and tax incentives. The growing use of repos in 1997 and 1998 has increased the banks' maturity mismatch as well as their off-balance-sheet exposure. Many of the private banks are owned by large corporate groups, and rating agencies worry that lending limits may be easily breached, increasing the credit risks suggested by a relatively low level of nonperforming loans (2.2 percent of total loans at end-June 1998).

The developments of August 17, 1998 delivered a double blow to the *Russian* banking system, because the largest banks hold a large proportion of their total assets as government securities and because of the scale of their foreign currency liabilities—including those derived from forward foreign exchange contracts. In addition to the highly speculative activities in securities and foreign exchange markets, most Russian banks have close links with their business clients and the government. In particular, a large number of banks belong to the so-called financial and industrial groups (FIGs), which have large shareholdings and exposures to the industrial sector, high levels of connected lending, and rely on a few large corporate accounts for funding. Poor accounting rules, prudential regulation, and supervision further contributed to the weak financial condition of most banks, which brought about the collapse of the system in the aftermath of the ruble's devaluation. Over the past three months, the Central Bank of Russia has granted liquidity support to many banks and more recently has submitted a bank restructuring program to the State Duma. The program recognizes that the recapitalization of the banking system is a top priority of the government anticrisis plan and would divide the banks into four groups: (1) financially sound banks (some 500 small and medium-sized banks with little exposure to GKOs—ruble-denominated discount instruments—and foreign exchange); (2) banks having positive equity capital but facing liquidity problems (some 400 regional banks with large branch networks); (3) large banks that are bankrupt but whose closure would have grave social and economic consequences; and (4) insolvent banks that are considered nonessential. The last group of banks will be liquidated, while the first will receive only temporary liquidity assistance. Banks in the second and third groups will receive central bank funds against controlling stakes in their equity and will be managed by external management teams that would have an option to buy a controlling stake. A key issue will be which banks will be listed in the third—rather than the fourth—category. Market participants consider that most of the large Moscow-based banks are likely to be included in the third group, although this strategy would face severe financing constraints as external financing for the banking system is unlikely to be forthcoming. Moreover, this strategy would make it difficult to address the severe governance problems currently embedded in the system.

---

[11]State banks account for more than one-third of the system's total assets and do a fair amount of subsidized lending to favored sectors.

[12]The foreign liabilities of private commercial banks were $12.5 billion at end-June 1998. International banks have long had an appetite for Turkish bank risk, in part because the country's OECD membership implies lower risk weightings for such facilities.

Statistical Appendix

Eight statistical tables are included in this appendix. They focus on global developments and represent a subset of the traditional 46 Statistical Appendix tables in the *World Economic Outlook*. Data in these tables have been compiled on the basis of information available in mid-December 1998.

Assumptions

Key assumptions underlying the estimates for 1999 and beyond are:

• Real effective *exchange rates* for the advanced economies are assumed to remain constant at their average levels during the period October 19–November 4, 1998, except that the bilateral exchange rates among the ERM currencies are assumed to re-

main constant in nominal terms. For 1999, these assumptions imply an average U.S. dollar/SDR conversion rate of 1.407.

• Established *policies* of national authorities are assumed to be maintained.

• It is assumed that the *price of oil* will average $14.51 a barrel in 1999 and remain unchanged in real terms thereafter.

• With regard to *interest rates,* it is assumed that the London interbank offered rate (LIBOR) on six-month U.S. dollar deposits will average 5 percent from 1999 onward.

For a full description of *World Economic Outlook* data and conventions, as well as the classification of countries in the various groups presented in the following tables, see the October 1998 *World Economic Outlook,* pp. 158–68.

List of Tables

Table 1. World Output[1]

(Annual percent change)

	Average 1980–89	1990	1991	1992	1993	1994	1995	1996	1997	1998	1999
World	**3.4**	**2.7**	**1.8**	**2.5**	**2.6**	**4.0**	**3.7**	**4.3**	**4.2**	**2.2**	**2.2**
Advanced economies	**2.9**	**2.8**	**1.2**	**1.9**	**1.2**	**3.2**	**2.6**	**3.2**	**3.2**	**2.0**	**1.6**
Major industrial countries	2.7	2.5	0.8	1.8	1.1	2.9	2.1	3.0	3.0	2.1	1.5
United States	2.7	1.2	–0.9	2.7	2.3	3.5	2.3	3.4	3.9	3.6	1.8
Japan	3.8	5.1	3.8	1.0	0.3	0.6	1.5	5.0	1.4	–2.8	–0.5
Germany[2]	1.8	5.7	5.0	2.2	–1.2	2.7	1.2	1.3	2.2	2.7	2.0
France	2.3	2.5	0.8	1.2	–1.3	2.8	2.1	1.6	2.3	3.0	2.6
Italy	2.4	2.2	1.1	0.6	–1.2	2.2	2.9	0.7	1.5	1.3	1.9
United Kingdom	2.4	0.6	–1.5	0.1	2.3	4.4	2.8	2.6	3.5	2.6	0.9
Canada	2.9	0.3	–1.9	0.9	2.3	4.7	2.6	1.2	3.8	2.8	2.2
Other advanced economies	3.7	4.0	2.9	2.5	2.0	4.6	4.4	3.8	4.2	1.5	2.0
Memorandum											
Industrial countries	2.7	2.5	0.8	1.7	0.9	2.9	2.2	3.0	3.0	2.3	1.7
European Union	2.3	3.1	1.7	1.1	–0.5	3.0	2.4	1.8	2.7	2.8	2.2
Euro area	2.3	3.7	2.4	1.3	–1.0	2.7	2.3	1.6	2.5	2.8	2.4
Newly industrialized Asian economies	7.8	7.3	7.9	5.8	6.3	7.6	7.3	6.3	6.0	–2.6	0.5
Developing countries	**4.3**	**4.0**	**5.0**	**6.6**	**6.5**	**6.8**	**6.0**	**6.5**	**5.7**	**2.8**	**3.5**
Regional groups											
Africa	2.5	2.3	1.8	0.3	0.7	2.1	3.0	5.8	3.2	3.6	3.8
Asia	7.0	5.6	6.6	9.5	9.3	9.6	9.0	8.2	6.6	2.6	4.3
Middle East and Europe	2.2	5.6	3.5	6.5	3.9	0.7	3.8	4.7	4.5	3.3	2.9
Western Hemisphere	2.2	1.0	3.8	3.3	3.9	5.2	1.2	3.5	5.1	2.5	1.5
Analytical groups											
By source of export earnings											
Fuel	0.8	4.9	4.8	6.3	1.5	0.2	2.6	3.5	3.2	1.7	1.7
Nonfuel	5.0	3.9	5.0	6.7	7.1	7.6	6.4	6.9	6.0	2.9	3.7
By external financing source											
Net creditor countries	0.4	7.2	5.0	8.4	4.0	1.7	1.2	3.0	2.6	1.6	1.3
Net debtor countries	4.5	3.9	5.0	6.6	6.6	7.0	6.2	6.6	5.8	2.8	3.6
Official financing	3.5	3.8	3.9	3.0	2.5	3.3	3.8	5.7	3.0	4.4	3.7
Private financing	4.6	3.6	6.0	7.8	7.9	7.8	6.3	6.7	6.4	3.9	3.9
Diversified financing	4.5	4.7	2.9	4.9	4.7	6.4	6.8	6.9	5.3	–0.8	2.6
Net debtor countries by debt-servicing experience											
Countries with arrears and/or rescheduling during 1993–97	2.3	0.7	2.3	2.1	2.6	3.2	4.1	3.8	4.0	2.1	2.1
Other net debtor countries	5.6	5.3	6.1	8.3	8.0	8.3	6.9	7.6	6.4	3.0	4.0
Countries in transition	**2.8**	**–3.5**	**–7.6**	**–14.0**	**–7.3**	**–7.1**	**–1.5**	**–1.0**	**1.9**	**–0.8**	**–1.9**
Central and eastern Europe	. . .	. . .	–10.0	–8.7	–3.8	–2.8	1.6	1.6	2.8	2.5	2.2
Excluding Belarus and Ukraine	. . .	. . .	–10.7	–5.2	0.2	3.3	5.5	3.7	3.2	2.9	3.2
Russia	. . .	. . .	–5.4	–19.4	–10.4	–11.6	–4.8	–5.0	0.7	–5.7	–8.3
Transcaucasus and central Asia	. . .	. . .	–5.7	–18.5	–10.4	–11.4	–4.7	–3.7	1.0	–4.2	–6.1
Memorandum											
Median growth rate											
Advanced economies	3.0	3.2	2.2	1.4	1.3	3.6	2.9	3.5	3.5	2.9	2.2
Developing countries	3.2	3.1	2.9	3.6	2.9	3.5	4.4	4.5	4.4	4.1	4.4
Countries in transition	3.5	–2.9	–10.8	–11.4	–8.1	–1.8	1.8	3.0	3.4	4.2	3.7
Output per capita											
Advanced economies	2.2	1.9	0.4	1.2	0.6	2.5	1.9	2.5	2.6	1.4	1.1
Developing countries	1.9	2.1	3.0	4.0	4.5	4.9	4.3	4.8	4.2	1.1	1.9
Countries in transition	2.1	–4.1	–7.8	–14.1	–7.4	–7.1	–1.5	–0.8	1.9	–0.8	–2.0
World growth based on market exchange rates	**3.0**	**2.2**	**0.5**	**0.6**	**0.9**	**2.8**	**2.6**	**3.5**	**3.3**	**1.8**	**1.6**
Value of world output in billions of U.S. dollars											
At market exchange rates	. . .	22,492	23,643	23,576	24,182	25,960	28,760	29,545	29,437	29,249	31,030
At purchasing power parities	. . .	25,524	26,986	28,435	29,880	31,713	33,639	35,759	38,047	40,685	43,606

[1]Real GDP. For classification of countries in groups shown in this table, and conventions used to calculate the group composites and multiyear averages, see the introduction to *World Economic Outlook—Statistical Appendix*.

[2]Data through 1991 apply to west Germany only.

Table 2. Advanced Economies: Employment and Unemployment[1]
(Percent)

	Average[2] 1980–89	1990	1991	1992	1993	1994	1995	1996	1997	1998	1999
Growth in employment											
Advanced economies	**1.2**	**1.6**	**0.1**	**–0.1**	**–0.1**	**1.1**	**1.1**	**1.0**	**1.3**	**0.9**	**0.6**
Major industrial countries	1.1	1.5	—	–0.1	—	1.0	0.8	0.7	1.3	0.8	0.4
United States	1.7	1.3	–0.9	0.7	1.5	2.3	1.5	1.4	2.2	1.4	0.8
Japan	1.1	2.0	1.9	1.1	0.2	0.1	0.1	0.5	1.1	–0.7	–0.5
Germany[3]	0.4	3.0	1.7	–1.9	–1.8	–0.7	–0.4	–1.3	–1.3	0.2	0.1
France	0.1	1.1	0.2	–0.6	–1.2	–0.1	1.1	—	0.6	2.1	1.3
Italy	0.4	1.4	1.4	–1.1	–4.1	–1.7	–0.5	0.4	—	0.2	0.4
United Kingdom	0.6	0.4	–3.1	–2.4	–0.8	1.8	0.9	1.2	1.6	0.9	–0.2
Canada	2.0	0.6	–1.9	–0.6	1.4	2.1	1.6	1.3	1.9	2.5	1.3
Other advanced economies	1.3	2.0	0.7	–0.2	–0.5	1.3	2.1	1.8	1.6	1.1	1.3
Memorandum											
Industrial countries	1.1	1.6	–0.1	–0.3	–0.3	0.9	1.0	0.9	1.3	1.0	0.6
European Union	0.4	1.7	0.1	–1.6	–2.0	–0.2	0.6	0.5	0.6	1.3	0.7
Euro area	0.4	2.1	1.0	–1.4	–2.3	–0.7	0.5	0.3	0.4	1.3	0.9
Newly industrialized Asian economies	2.5	2.3	2.3	1.9	1.5	2.8	2.2	2.0	1.9	–0.8	1.3
Unemployment rate											
Advanced economies	**6.9**	**5.9**	**6.5**	**7.3**	**7.7**	**7.6**	**7.2**	**7.3**	**7.0**	**6.9**	**7.0**
Major industrial countries	6.9	5.8	6.5	7.2	7.3	7.2	6.8	6.9	6.7	6.5	6.7
United States[4]	7.3	5.6	6.8	7.5	6.9	6.1	5.6	5.4	4.9	4.5	4.8
Japan	2.5	2.1	2.1	2.2	2.5	2.9	3.1	3.3	3.4	4.2	4.9
Germany[3]	7.0	6.2	5.5	7.7	8.8	9.6	9.4	10.4	11.5	10.9	10.5
France	9.0	8.9	9.4	10.3	11.6	12.3	11.6	12.4	12.7	11.7	11.3
Italy[5]	9.8	11.0	10.9	10.7	10.2	11.3	12.0	12.1	12.3	12.2	12.0
United Kingdom	9.0	5.8	8.0	9.7	10.3	9.3	8.0	7.3	5.5	4.7	5.1
Canada	9.3	8.1	10.4	11.3	11.2	10.4	9.5	9.7	9.2	8.4	8.4
Other advanced economies	7.1	6.2	6.6	7.5	8.8	8.9	8.4	8.3	8.0	8.3	8.2
Memorandum											
Industrial countries	7.2	6.1	6.9	7.7	8.1	8.0	7.7	7.7	7.4	7.0	7.1
European Union	9.0	8.0	8.5	9.8	11.0	11.5	11.1	11.2	11.0	10.2	9.9
Euro area	9.3	8.8	8.7	10.0	11.3	12.2	11.9	12.3	12.4	11.6	11.2
Newly industrialized Asian economies	3.2	2.1	2.0	2.1	2.3	2.1	2.1	2.2	2.6	5.5	6.2

[1]For classification of industrial countries in groups shown in this table, and conventions used to calculate the composites, see the introduction to *World Economic Outlook—Statistical Appendix.*

[2]For employment, compound annual rate of change; for unemployment rate, arithmetic average.

[3]Data through 1991 apply to west Germany only.

[4]The projections for unemployment have been adjusted to reflect the new survey techniques adopted by the U.S. Bureau of Labor Statistics in January 1994.

[5]New series starting in 1993, reflecting revisions in the labor force surveys and the definition of unemployment to bring data in line with those of other industrial countries.

Table 3. Inflation[1]

(Percent)

	Average 1980–89	1990	1991	1992	1993	1994	1995	1996	1997	1998	1999
GDP deflator											
Advanced economies	**6.1**	**4.6**	**5.2**	**3.3**	**2.8**	**2.2**	**2.2**	**1.7**	**1.6**	**1.4**	**1.4**
Major industrial countries	5.3	4.2	5.0	3.0	2.5	1.9	1.9	1.5	1.4	1.0	1.2
United States	5.0	4.3	4.0	2.8	2.6	2.4	2.3	1.9	1.9	1.1	1.8
Japan	2.2	2.3	2.7	1.7	0.6	0.2	–0.6	–1.4	0.1	0.3	–0.9
Germany[2]	3.0	3.1	12.0	5.6	4.0	2.4	2.2	1.0	0.6	1.0	1.3
France	7.1	3.1	3.3	2.1	2.5	1.5	1.6	1.2	0.9	0.9	1.3
Italy	11.7	7.6	7.7	4.7	4.4	3.5	5.1	5.0	2.6	2.6	2.1
United Kingdom	7.5	7.6	6.7	4.0	2.8	1.5	2.5	3.3	2.7	2.1	2.2
Canada	5.8	3.1	2.7	1.3	1.5	1.1	2.4	1.5	0.7	–0.4	0.5
Other advanced economies	10.2	6.5	6.3	4.7	4.1	3.5	3.5	2.9	2.4	3.0	2.1
Memorandum											
Industrial countries	5.6	4.4	5.0	3.1	2.6	2.0	2.1	1.6	1.5	1.1	1.3
European Union	7.2	5.5	7.3	4.4	3.6	2.6	2.9	2.4	1.8	1.7	1.8
Euro area	7.0	4.7	7.3	4.4	3.7	2.7	2.9	2.2	1.5	1.6	1.7
Newly industrialized Asian economies	6.8	7.3	7.6	5.6	5.1	4.4	3.9	3.4	2.7	5.3	1.7
Consumer prices											
Advanced economies	**6.3**	**5.2**	**4.7**	**3.5**	**3.1**	**2.6**	**2.5**	**2.4**	**2.1**	**1.6**	**1.6**
Major industrial countries	5.5	4.8	4.3	3.2	2.8	2.2	2.3	2.2	2.0	1.3	1.5
United States	5.5	5.4	4.2	3.0	3.0	2.6	2.8	2.9	2.3	1.6	2.2
Japan	2.5	3.1	3.3	1.7	1.2	0.7	–0.1	0.1	1.7	0.4	–0.7
Germany[2]	2.9	2.7	3.5	4.7	4.4	2.7	1.8	1.5	1.8	1.0	1.2
France	7.3	3.4	3.2	2.4	2.1	1.7	1.8	2.0	1.2	0.7	0.9
Italy	11.2	6.5	6.3	5.3	4.6	4.1	5.2	3.9	1.7	1.7	1.6
United Kingdom[3]	7.0	8.1	6.8	4.7	3.0	2.4	2.8	2.9	2.8	2.6	2.5
Canada	6.5	4.8	5.6	1.5	1.8	0.2	2.2	1.6	1.4	1.2	1.8
Other advanced economies	10.1	6.7	6.3	4.9	4.1	4.1	3.7	3.2	2.5	2.7	2.2
Memorandum											
Industrial countries	5.8	5.0	4.5	3.3	2.9	2.3	2.4	2.3	2.0	1.4	1.5
European Union	7.0	5.4	5.1	4.4	3.8	3.0	2.9	2.5	1.9	1.5	1.6
Euro area	6.9	4.4	4.4	4.3	3.8	3.0	2.9	2.4	1.7	1.3	1.4
Newly industrialized Asian economies	6.7	7.0	7.5	5.9	4.6	5.6	4.6	4.3	3.4	4.7	2.3
Developing countries	**35.9**	**68.2**	**36.4**	**38.7**	**47.3**	**51.6**	**22.3**	**14.1**	**9.2**	**10.2**	**8.4**
Regional groups											
Africa	15.0	16.0	24.4	32.4	30.8	37.5	34.1	26.7	11.0	8.5	7.8
Asia	8.8	7.0	8.2	7.2	11.1	15.9	12.8	7.9	4.7	7.9	6.4
Middle East and Europe	19.5	22.4	27.5	25.6	24.6	31.9	35.9	24.6	22.8	23.6	20.5
Western Hemisphere	116.7	438.4	129.0	151.4	208.5	208.3	35.9	20.8	13.9	10.3	8.3
Analytical groups											
By source of export earnings											
Fuel	13.3	14.3	21.3	22.8	26.1	32.4	42.7	30.7	15.1	14.9	11.8
Nonfuel	40.3	77.7	38.7	41.0	50.2	54.1	20.1	12.4	8.5	9.7	8.0
By external financing source											
Net creditor countries	2.6	3.9	6.1	3.2	4.2	3.4	5.0	2.4	1.3	1.3	1.7
Net debtor countries	37.4	71.2	37.7	40.1	49.1	53.5	22.9	14.5	9.4	10.4	8.6
Net debtor countries by debt-servicing experience											
Countries with arrears and/or rescheduling during 1993–97	69.4	273.9	111.6	152.7	216.2	233.2	43.0	22.2	12.6	10.4	8.0
Other net debtor countries	23.7	22.4	15.5	11.6	13.2	17.1	16.7	12.1	8.4	10.4	8.8
Countries in transition	**8.6**	**38.6**	**95.8**	**656.6**	**609.3**	**268.4**	**124.1**	**41.4**	**27.9**	**21.0**	**30.2**
Central and eastern Europe	...	...	95.4	283.1	357.7	153.3	75.3	32.4	38.4	17.6	16.4
Excluding Belarus and Ukraine	...	...	98.9	103.8	79.9	45.1	25.1	23.4	40.9	16.4	10.4
Russia	...	...	92.7	1,353.0	895.9	302.0	190.1	47.8	14.7	26.0	56.3
Transcaucasus and central Asia	...	...	110.9	945.3	1,224.2	1,667.7	183.6	68.7	30.8	19.8	11.8
Memorandum											
Median inflation rate											
Advanced economies	6.9	5.4	4.0	3.2	3.0	2.4	2.4	2.1	1.8	1.7	1.7
Developing countries	9.8	10.4	11.8	9.8	9.5	10.6	10.0	7.3	6.2	5.0	4.7
Countries in transition	1.2	7.8	101.4	839.6	472.2	131.6	46.0	24.1	14.9	11.1	8.3

[1]For classification of countries in groups shown in this table, and conventions used to calculate the group composites and multiyear averages, see the introduction to *World Economic Outlook—Statistical Appendix.*

[2]Data through 1991 apply to west Germany only.

[3]Retail price index excluding mortgage interest.

Table 4. Fiscal Indicators[1,2]

(Percent of GDP)

	1990	1991	1992	1993	1994	1995	1996	1997	1998	1999
Advanced economies										
Central government fiscal balance										
Advanced economies	−2.6	−3.0	−4.0	−4.2	−3.6	−3.2	−2.6	−1.3	−1.3	−1.4
United States	−3.0	−3.5	−4.7	−3.9	−2.7	−2.3	−1.4	−0.3	0.6	0.6
Japan	−0.5	−0.2	−1.7	−2.7	−3.5	−4.0	−4.3	−4.1	−5.5	−6.3
Germany[3]	−2.0	−1.9	−1.3	−2.1	−1.5	−1.5	−2.2	−1.7	−1.5	−1.4
France	−1.7	−1.7	−2.9	−4.3	−4.7	−4.0	−3.6	−2.6	−2.8	−2.6
Italy	−10.2	−10.3	−10.4	−10.0	−9.2	−7.1	−6.9	−2.7	−2.7	−2.5
United Kingdom	−1.1	−2.2	−6.9	−7.9	−6.7	−5.3	−4.7	−2.0	−0.2	−0.8
Canada	−3.7	−4.3	−4.0	−4.7	−3.4	−3.0	−1.4	0.8	1.3	0.9
General government fiscal balance										
Advanced economies	−2.1	−2.7	−3.6	−4.1	−3.4	−3.2	−2.5	−1.1	−1.2	−1.5
United States	−2.7	−3.3	−4.4	−3.6	−2.3	−1.9	−0.9	0.2	1.1	1.1
Japan	2.9	2.9	1.5	−1.6	−2.3	−3.6	−4.2	−3.5	−6.2	−8.5
Germany[3]	−2.0	−3.3	−2.8	−3.2	−2.4	−3.3	−3.4	−2.7	−2.4	−2.3
France	−1.7	−2.2	−3.8	−5.8	−5.7	−4.9	−4.2	−3.0	−2.9	−2.3
Italy	−11.1	−10.1	−9.6	−9.5	−9.2	−7.7	−6.7	−2.7	−2.8	−2.4
United Kingdom	−1.2	−2.5	−6.2	−7.8	−6.8	−5.5	−4.5	−1.9	0.1	−0.7
Canada	−4.5	−7.2	−8.0	−7.6	−5.6	−4.5	−2.2	0.9	1.5	1.4
General government structural balance[4]										
Advanced economies	−3.0	−2.8	−3.2	−3.0	−2.5	−2.5	−1.9	−0.7	−0.6	−0.8
United States	−2.7	−2.1	−3.1	−2.3	−1.4	−1.1	−0.5	0.2	0.6	0.7
Japan	1.9	2.0	1.2	−1.2	−1.4	−2.6	−4.2	−3.2	−4.2	−5.8
Excluding social security	−1.3	−1.4	−2.2	−4.5	−4.5	−5.8	−6.8	−5.4	−6.6	−8.4
Germany	−3.2	−5.4	−4.0	−2.2	−1.2	−2.0	−1.5	−0.7	−0.9	−0.8
France	−2.9	−2.5	−3.4	−3.2	−3.6	−3.0	−1.9	−0.8	−1.3	−0.9
Italy	−12.2	−10.7	−9.5	−8.2	−7.9	−7.1	−5.7	−1.6	−1.5	−1.2
United Kingdom	−3.8	−2.7	−3.7	−4.5	−4.5	−4.3	−3.9	−1.9	−0.6	−0.8
Canada	−5.0	−4.7	−4.4	−4.6	−4.2	−3.4	−0.6	1.8	2.1	2.1
Developing countries										
Central government fiscal balance										
Weighted average	−3.1	−3.4	−2.9	−3.2	−2.7	−2.5	−2.3	−2.3	−3.6	−3.3
Median	−4.1	−3.9	−3.8	−4.1	−3.7	−3.5	−2.7	−2.6	−3.0	−2.5
General government fiscal balance										
Weighted average	−3.8	−3.8	−3.4	−3.6	−3.3	−3.1	−2.9	−2.9	−3.8	−3.4
Median	−4.0	−3.8	−3.9	−4.1	−3.7	−3.5	−2.8	−2.6	−2.7	−2.3
Countries in transition										
Central government fiscal balance	−4.2	−9.4	−10.8	−5.9	−7.4	−4.0	−4.9	−4.5	−4.4	−3.4
General government fiscal balance	−4.3	−9.6	−15.5	−6.8	−7.2	−4.5	−5.6	−5.0	−5.1	−4.1

[1]For classification of countries in groups shown in this table, and conventions used to calculate the group composites, see the introduction to *World Economic Outlook—Statistical Appendix*.

[2]See *World Economic Outlook—Statistical Appendix*, Tables 15–16, for definitions.

[3]Data through 1990 apply to west Germany only.

[4]Percent of potential GDP.

Table 5. World Trade Volumes and Prices[1]

(Annual percent change)

	Average 1980–89	1990	1991	1992	1993	1994	1995	1996	1997	1998	1999
Trade in goods and services											
World trade[2]											
Volume	4.4	5.6	4.6	4.7	3.6	9.2	9.5	7.0	9.9	3.3	4.4
Price deflator											
In U.S. dollars	2.5	8.8	−2.1	2.6	−3.8	2.4	8.4	−1.4	−5.8	−4.1	2.7
In SDRs	2.6	2.8	−2.9	−0.3	−3.0	−0.1	2.3	3.0	−0.6	−3.1	−0.6
Volume of trade											
Exports											
Advanced economies	5.3	6.7	5.8	5.2	3.4	8.9	9.0	6.3	10.4	3.3	3.7
Developing countries	2.1	7.5	6.7	10.4	7.5	13.1	10.5	8.7	11.3	2.9	5.4
Imports											
Advanced economies	5.2	5.7	3.3	4.7	1.7	9.7	9.0	6.5	9.2	4.6	4.6
Developing countries	2.1	6.0	9.1	9.8	8.7	7.1	11.5	9.5	10.4	−0.7	5.7
Terms of trade											
Advanced economies	0.3	−0.4	−1.7	0.6	0.9	—	0.1	−0.3	−0.6	1.1	—
Developing countries	−0.8	1.5	−5.4	−3.4	−2.8	−0.1	2.6	2.3	0.1	−5.0	1.3
Trade in goods											
World trade[2]											
Volume	4.4	5.1	4.8	5.1	3.8	10.1	10.2	6.7	10.4	3.3	4.3
Price deflator											
In U.S. dollars	2.3	8.1	−2.4	1.9	−4.5	2.6	8.7	−1.5	−6.3	−4.4	2.8
In SDRs	2.4	2.1	−3.2	−1.0	−3.7	—	2.6	3.0	−1.1	−3.5	−0.5
Volume of trade											
Exports											
Advanced economies	5.3	6.2	5.7	4.9	3.0	9.6	9.3	6.1	11.2	3.6	3.4
Developing countries	1.7	8.5	5.5	10.6	7.5	14.0	12.0	8.6	11.3	2.4	5.4
Fuel exporters	−2.1	9.0	1.8	12.0	2.5	8.1	3.8	6.9	7.4	−2.5	3.9
Nonfuel exporters	5.7	8.3	7.5	10.0	9.6	16.1	14.5	9.1	12.5	3.8	5.8
Imports											
Advanced economies	5.2	5.1	4.1	4.8	2.3	11.1	9.4	6.0	9.8	4.7	4.8
Developing countries	2.9	6.0	6.9	15.5	10.4	7.9	12.3	9.1	9.6	−1.0	5.5
Fuel exporters	−1.1	2.8	3.2	26.8	−5.7	−12.2	3.6	1.7	12.8	3.6	4.8
Nonfuel exporters	4.3	7.0	8.0	12.2	14.9	12.5	13.8	10.3	9.1	−1.8	5.6
World trade prices in U.S. dollars[3]											
Manufactures	3.2	9.9	−0.3	3.5	−5.7	3.1	10.1	−3.0	−8.1	−2.5	4.0
Oil	...	28.4	−15.7	−1.7	−11.8	−5.0	7.9	18.4	−5.4	−30.5	8.4
Nonfuel primary commodities	0.6	−6.4	−5.7	0.1	1.8	13.4	8.4	−1.2	−3.3	−15.6	−0.6
World trade prices in SDRs[2]											
Manufactures	3.3	3.8	−1.1	0.6	−4.9	0.5	3.9	1.3	−3.1	−1.5	0.6
Oil	...	21.3	−16.4	−4.5	−11.1	−7.3	1.8	23.7	−0.2	−29.8	4.9
Nonfuel primary commodities	0.6	−11.6	−6.5	−2.8	2.7	10.6	2.3	3.3	2.0	−14.7	−3.8
Terms of trade											
Advanced economies	0.4	−0.7	−1.0	1.3	2.0	0.5	0.2	−0.8	−1.1	0.9	—
Developing countries	−0.5	1.1	−5.7	0.1	−3.4	−0.3	1.6	2.1	0.2	−4.8	1.1
Fuel exporters	−2.7	11.6	−17.4	5.8	−10.7	−6.1	−0.5	9.3	−0.2	−14.9	3.6
Nonfuel exporters	−0.2	−3.6	−0.4	−1.1	−0.5	1.8	2.0	0.3	0.3	−2.1	0.4
Memorandum											
World exports in billions of U.S. dollars											
Goods and services	2,146	4,273	4,403	4,705	4,709	5,262	6,239	6,560	6,801	6,731	7,218
Goods	1,725	3,403	3,494	3,720	3,706	4,184	5,008	5,246	5,433	5,364	5,744

[1]For classification of countries in groups shown in this table, and conventions used to calculate the group composites and multiyear averages, see the introduction to *World Economic Outlook—Statistical Appendix.*

[2]Average of annual percent change for world exports and imports. The estimates of world trade comprise, in addition to trade of advanced economies and developing countries (which is summarized in the table), trade of countries in transition.

[3]As represented, respectively, by the export unit value index for the manufactures of the advanced economies; the average of U.K. Brent, Dubai, and West Texas Intermediate crude oil spot prices; and the average of world market prices for nonfuel primary commodities weighted by their 1987–89 shares in world commodity exports.

Table 6. Payments Balances on Current Account[1]
(Billions of U.S. dollars)

	1990	1991	1992	1993	1994	1995	1996	1997	1998	1999
Advanced economies	**−87**	**−24**	**−17**	**62**	**33**	**51**	**35**	**72**	**44**	**−6**
Major industrial countries	−79	−21	−23	12	−9	−1	−21	6	−60	−107
United States	−92	−4	−51	−86	−124	−115	−135	−155	−231	−288
Japan	44	68	112	132	131	111	66	94	128	139
Germany[2]	49	−18	−19	−14	−20	−23	−14	−4	3	4
France	−10	−6	4	9	7	11	21	39	31	25
Italy	−17	−25	−30	8	13	25	41	34	29	32
United Kingdom	−33	−14	−18	−15	−3	−6	−3	7	−7	−10
Canada	−2()	−22	−21	−22	−13	−5	3	−9	−13	−10
Other advanced economies	−8	−3	6	50	42	52	56	66	104	101
Memorandum										
Industrial countries	−106	−39	−34	43	19	50	39	66	−15	−57
European Union	−33	−83	−81	6	22	53	90	123	100	95
Euro area	10	−63	−57	23	22	55	87	112	103	102
Newly industrialized Asian economies	19	16	16	21	16	6	1	9	62	54
Developing countries	**−25**	**−98**	**−79**	**−121**	**−89**	**−94**	**−74**	**−66**	**−95**	**−84**
Regional groups										
Africa	−8	−7	−10	−11	−12	−16	−5	−5	−16	−17
Asia	−16	−11	−13	−34	−20	−42	−39	—	33	24
Middle East and Europe	1	−63	−21	−30	−6	−1	8	4	−25	−21
Western Hemisphere	−1	−17	−35	−46	−51	−36	−38	−65	−87	−70
Analytical groups										
By source of export earnings										
Fuel	18	−60	−25	−25	−6	3	29	22	−20	−14
Nonfuel	−43	−38	−54	−96	−83	−97	−102	−88	−76	−70
By external financing source										
Net creditor countries	11	−49	−10	−15	−8	3	11	10	−8	−4
Net debtor countries	−36	−49	−69	−107	−81	−97	−84	−76	−87	−80
Official financing	−14	−13	−14	−18	−15	−16	−14	−13	−18	−19
Private financing	3	−22	−42	−74	−49	−57	−47	−41	−53	−43
Diversified financing	−25	−14	−12	−15	−17	−24	−24	−22	−16	−18
Net debtor countries by debt-servicing experience										
Countries with arrears and/or rescheduling during 1993–97	−19	−25	−20	−29	−16	−38	−25	−40	−64	−56
Other net debtor countries	−17	−24	−49	−78	−65	−60	−59	−36	−23	−24
Countries in transition	**−20**	**5**	**—**	**−7**	**4**	**−2**	**−18**	**−25**	**−21**	**−12**
Central and eastern Europe	...	−5	3	−9	−4	−6	−17	−20	−20	−21
Excluding Belarus and Ukraine	...	3	3	−7	−2	−4	−15	−18	−18	−19
Russia	...	4	−1	3	9	6	3	−1	5	14
Transcaucasus and central Asia	...	6	−2	−1	−1	−2	−4	−4	−6	−5
Total[3]	**−132**	**−117**	**−96**	**−66**	**−52**	**−45**	**−57**	**−19**	**−72**	**−101**

[1]For classification of countries in groups in this table, and conventions used to calculate the group composites and multiyear averages, see the introduction to the *World Economic Outlook—Statistical Appendix.*

[2]Data through June 1990 apply to west Germany only.

[3]Reflects errors, omissions, and asymmetries in balance of payments statistics on current account, as well as the exclusion of data for international organizations and a limited number of countries.

Table 7. External Debt and Debt Service

	1990	1991	1992	1993	1994	1995	1996	1997	1998	1999
	Percent of exports of goods and services									
External debt[3]										
Developing countries	**177.6**	**184.0**	**180.7**	**191.9**	**179.3**	**163.3**	**152.1**	**143.1**	**160.2**	**157.0**
Regional groups										
Africa	217.7	234.5	232.2	264.4	273.6	248.1	226.4	210.5	233.5	221.1
Asia	163.2	159.4	153.2	151.9	139.3	124.0	119.7	115.7	124.0	121.8
Middle East and Europe	92.3	97.9	100.9	115.0	111.1	100.3	89.1	84.8	103.6	100.8
Western Hemisphere	266.7	277.3	276.5	293.3	264.6	248.8	231.3	213.6	240.5	235.7
Analytical groups										
By external financing source										
Net creditor countries	12.3	13.1	18.1	21.0	21.2	16.5	14.3	14.9	22.9	24.6
Net debtor countries	210.9	216.3	210.2	219.4	201.8	182.9	170.4	159.8	176.1	172.3
Official financing	331.9	350.7	351.7	370.8	368.3	324.1	295.3	280.5	299.5	284.7
Private financing	169.5	172.4	168.6	181.9	161.2	150.2	140.8	132.5	150.0	149.5
Diversified financing	271.9	288.4	275.7	270.8	268.9	234.1	217.7	203.7	211.8	200.3
Net debtor countries by debt-servicing experience										
Countries with arrears and/or rescheduling during 1993–97	284.9	314.1	313.8	332.0	323.4	290.1	262.7	242.9	277.4	265.7
Other net debtor countries	172.0	172.1	166.0	174.8	158.7	146.6	138.4	131.3	143.0	140.2
Countries in transition	**100.0**	**106.7**	**128.3**	**126.1**	**120.1**	**100.1**	**95.4**	**94.8**	**106.6**	**103.8**
Central and eastern Europe	. . .	115.7	107.9	109.8	103.0	87.9	83.0	82.3	87.9	87.6
Excluding Belarus and Russia	. . .	157.4	123.0	127.0	111.4	93.7	90.9	88.3	93.7	92.7
Russia	. . .	154.8	183.4	171.1	156.1	126.6	121.7	121.3	150.7	145.6
Transcaucasus and central Asia	. . .	2.5	17.1	35.9	60.1	60.8	63.7	73.3	85.8	82.6
Debt-service payments										
Developing countries	**21.9**	**22.4**	**23.5**	**24.0**	**23.5**	**21.9**	**22.0**	**21.5**	**24.6**	**23.2**
Regional groups										
Africa	24.6	27.7	26.9	26.3	26.8	26.0	24.8	21.0	25.7	24.3
Asia	18.4	17.1	18.4	18.0	16.9	16.2	15.9	13.9	17.9	17.4
Middle East and Europe	10.3	10.3	11.7	13.2	12.4	10.9	10.6	9.0	14.4	12.7
Western Hemisphere	37.7	39.3	41.9	43.2	43.3	39.7	41.7	46.5	44.5	41.0
Analytical groups										
By external financing source										
Net creditor countries	1.2	0.8	0.9	1.5	4.3	5.3	4.4	2.4	2.5	2.7
Net debtor countries	26.0	26.5	27.6	27.6	26.2	24.1	24.3	24.0	27.1	25.5
Official financing	23.3	26.9	26.2	25.4	27.8	27.4	21.2	21.5	25.0	24.8
Private financing	25.9	25.9	26.6	27.0	25.5	23.4	24.1	24.6	26.6	25.2
Diversified financing	28.0	28.4	31.9	31.0	28.2	24.8	26.6	22.7	29.9	27.1
Net debtor countries by debt-servicing experience										
Countries with arrears and/or rescheduling during 1993–97	30.5	33.4	32.6	35.3	30.8	29.6	29.4	32.8	39.5	35.2
Other net debtor countries	23.7	23.4	25.5	24.6	24.6	22.2	22.6	21.0	23.1	22.2
Countries in transition	**18.1**	**18.7**	**14.5**	**10.1**	**13.6**	**11.0**	**9.8**	**9.7**	**15.2**	**14.4**
Central and eastern Europe	. . .	20.9	11.6	11.5	19.7	13.8	11.9	12.3	14.9	13.9
Excluding Belarus and Ukraine	. . .	28.5	13.7	13.8	21.2	14.8	13.2	13.5	15.5	15.0
Russia	. . .	26.4	21.9	9.4	5.6	6.7	6.7	5.8	15.6	17.7
Transcaucasus and central Asia	. . .	—	1.0	2.3	5.1	8.7	7.2	6.8	15.9	6.4
	Billions of U.S. dollars									
Memorandum										
External debt										
Developing countries	1,180.9	1,233.8	1,312.9	1,459.0	1,552.0	1,683.7	1,748.4	1,791.2	1,925.0	2,000.1
Countries in transition	. . .	210.5	212.4	234.3	248.9	266.9	277.8	286.1	322.7	335.8
Debt-service payments										
Developing countries	145.5	150.3	170.8	182.6	203.3	225.5	252.6	268.8	295.5	295.2
Countries in transition	. . .	37.0	24.0	18.7	28.2	29.3	28.5	29.3	46.0	46.6

[1]For classification of countries in groups shown in this table, and conventions used to calculate the group composites and multiyear averages, see the introduction to *World Economic Outlook—Statistical Appendix*.

[2]Debt-service payments refer to actual payments of interest on total debt plus actual amortization payments on long-term debt. The projections incorporate the impact of exceptional financing items.

[3]Total debt at year-end in percent of exports of goods and services in year indicated.

Table 8. External Financing[1]
(Billions of U.S. dollars)

	1990	1991	1992	1993	1994	1995	1996	1997	1998	1999
Developing countries and countries in transition										
Balance of payments										
Balance on current account	−45.1	−93.0	−78.9	−128.3	−85.1	−96.0	−91.5	−90.6	−116.5	−95.6
Balance on capital and financial account	45.1	93.0	78.9	128.3	85.1	96.0	91.5	90.6	116.5	95.6
By balance of payments component										
Capital transfers[2]	24.9	9.2	3.8	5.2	12.5	2.9	9.2	7.6	11.0	6.3
Net financial flows	65.8	138.7	132.4	191.1	150.2	213.3	209.3	161.1	127.7	134.1
Errors and omissions, net	−17.7	−15.3	−13.8	−7.8	−27.1	−11.8	−31.4	−20.9	−31.9	−25.6
Change in reserves (− = increase)	−28.0	−39.6	−43.6	−60.2	−50.5	−108.3	−95.7	−57.2	9.6	−19.2
By type of financing flow										
Nonexceptional financing flows	12.5	92.6	70.6	131.6	81.3	166.9	164.1	141.4	104.4	96.4
Exceptional financing flows	60.5	40.0	51.8	56.8	54.4	37.4	23.0	6.4	2.5	18.3
Arrears on debt service	27.4	23.1	16.1	17.1	−1.0	−14.6	−12.3	−6.1	...	...
Debt forgiveness	22.8	5.4	0.5	1.3	9.1	2.8	6.5	3.3	...	...
Rescheduling of debt service	21.5	20.9	26.5	38.5	40.6	45.4	26.5	18.3	...	...
Change in reserves (− = increase)	−28.0	−39.6	−43.6	−60.2	−50.5	−108.3	−95.7	−57.2	9.6	−19.2
External financing										
Balance on current account	−45.1	−93.0	−78.9	−128.3	−85.1	−96.0	−91.5	−90.6	−116.5	−95.6
Change in reserves (− = increase)[3]	−28.0	−39.6	−43.6	−60.2	−50.5	−108.3	−95.7	−57.2	9.6	−19.2
Asset transactions, including net errors and omissions[4]	−42.2	27.2	−22.7	−2.5	−31.8	−14.8	−70.7	−113.3	−117.8	−91.4
Total, net external financing[5]	**115.2**	**105.4**	**145.1**	**190.9**	**167.5**	**219.2**	**257.8**	**261.1**	**224.7**	**206.1**
Non-debt-creating flows, net	44.1	44.1	49.1	87.9	112.7	114.6	149.2	174.3	137.8	128.5
Capital transfers[2]	24.9	9.2	3.8	5.2	12.5	2.9	9.2	7.6	11.0	6.3
Direct investment and portfolio investment equity flows	19.2	34.9	45.2	82.8	100.3	111.7	140.0	166.7	126.8	122.2
Net credit and loans from IMF[6]	−1.6	3.5	1.1	3.6	1.6	17.3	0.7	3.2	...	...
Net external borrowing[7]	72.7	57.8	94.9	99.4	53.2	87.2	107.9	83.6	81.0	96.3
Borrowing from official creditors[8]	24.5	36.7	20.8	19.4	−2.2	23.4	2.4	6.7	27.0	13.6
Borrowing from banks[9]	7.4	12.3	12.3	−2.6	−29.9	13.9	14.1	4.3	17.8	8.5
Other borrowing[10]	40.8	8.8	61.8	82.6	85.3	49.9	91.3	72.5	36.3	74.2
Memorandum										
Balance on goods and services in percent of GDP[11]	0.2	−0.4	−1.5	−2.3	−1.1	−1.0	−0.9	−0.8	−1.0	−0.5
Scheduled amortization of external debt	119.0	122.1	142.9	154.0	159.8	169.8	185.6	201.4	219.0	209.7
Gross external financing[12]	234.2	227.5	288.0	344.9	327.3	389.0	443.4	462.5	443.7	415.8
Gross external borrowing[12]	191.7	179.9	237.8	253.4	213.0	257.1	293.4	285.0	300.1	305.9
Net credit and loans from IMF[6]										
Advanced economies	—	—	0.3	—	—	−0.1	−0.1	11.3	...	...
Newly industrialized Asian economies	—	—	—	—	—	—	—	11.3	...	...
Developing countries	−1.9	1.1	−0.4	−0.1	−0.8	12.6	−2.9	0.8	...	...
Countries in transition	0.3	2.4	1.6	3.7	2.4	4.7	3.7	2.4	...	...

[1]For classification of countries in groups shown in this table, and conventions used to calculate the group composites and multiyear averages, see the introduction to *World Economic Outlook—Statistical Appendix*.

[2]Comprise debt forgiveness as well as all other identified transactions on capital account as defined in the fifth edition of the IMF's *Balance of Payments Manual*.

[3]Positioned here to reflect the discretionary nature of many countries' transactions in reserves.

[4]Include changes in recorded private external assets (mainly portfolio investment), export credit, the collateral for debt-reduction operations, and the net change in unrecorded balance of payments flows (net errors and omissions).

[5]Equals, with opposite sign, the sum of transactions listed above. It is the amount required to finance the deficit on goods and services, factor income, and current transfers; the increase in the official reserve level; the net asset transactions; and the transactions underlying net errors and omissions.

[6]Comprise use of IMF resources under the General Resources Account, Trust Fund, Structural Adjustment Facility (SAF), and Enhanced Structural Adjustment Facility (ESAF). For further detail, see Table 37 of *World Economic Outlook—Statistical Appendix*.

[7]Net disbursement of long- and short-term credits (including exceptional financing) by both official and private creditors.

[8]Net disbursements by official creditors (other than monetary authorities) based on directly reported flows, and flows derived from statistics on debt stocks. The estimates include the increase in official claims caused by the transfer of officially guaranteed claims to the guarantor agency in the creditor country, usually in the context of debt rescheduling.

[9]Net disbursements by commercial banks based on directly reported flows and on cross-border claims and liabilities reported in the International Banking section of the IMF's *International Financial Statistics*.

[10]Includes primary bond issues and loans on the international capital markets. Since the estimates are residually derived, they also reflect any underrecording or misclassification of official and commercial bank credits above.

[11]This is often referred to as the "resource balance" and, with opposite sign, the "net resource transfer."

[12]Net external financing or borrowing (see footnotes 5 and 7, respectively) plus amortization due on external debt.

World Economic Outlook and *Staff Studies for the World Economic Outlook,* Selected Topics, 1992–98

IV. Inflation and Deflation; Commodity Markets

V. Fiscal Policy

VI. Monetary Policy; Financial Markets; Flow of Funds

VII. Labor Market Issues

VIII. Exchange Rate Issues

IX. External Payments, Trade, Capital Movements, and Foreign Debt

X. Regional Issues

XI. Country-Specific Analyses

***Staff Studies for the
World Economic Outlook***

World Economic and Financial Surveys

This series (ISSN 0258-7440) contains biannual, annual, and periodic studies covering monetary and financial issues of importance to the global economy. The core elements of the series are the *World Economic Outlook* report, usually published in May and October, and the annual report on *International Capital Markets*. Other studies assess international trade policy, private market and official financing for developing countries, exchange and payments systems, export credit policies, and issues discussed in the *World Economic Outlook*. Please consult the IMF *Publications Catalog* for a complete listing of currently available World Economic and Financial Surveys.

World Economic Outlook: A Survey by the Staff of the International Monetary Fund

The *World Economic Outlook*, published twice a year in English, French, Spanish, and Arabic, presents IMF staff economists' analyses of global economic developments during the near and medium term. Chapters give an overview of the world economy; consider issues affecting industrial countries, developing countries, and economies in transition to the market; and address topics of pressing current interest.

ISSN 0256-6877.
$36.00 (academic rate: $25.00); paper.
1998 (Dec.). ISBN 1-55775-793-3. **Stock #WEO-1799.**
1998 (Oct.). ISBN 1-55775-773-9. **Stock #WEO-298.**
1998 (May). ISBN 1-55775-740-2. **Stock #WEO-198.**

Official Financing for Developing Countries
by a staff team in the IMF's Policy Development and Review Department led by Anthony R. Boote and Doris C. Ross

This study provides information on official financing for developing countries, with the focus on low-income countries. It updates the 1995 edition and reviews developments in direct financing by official and multilateral sources.

$25.00 (academic rate: $20.00); paper.
1998. ISBN 1-55775-702-X. **Stock #WEO-1397.**
1995. ISBN 1-55775-527-2. **Stock #WEO-1395.**

Issues in International Exchange and Payments Systems
by a staff team from the IMF's Monetary and Exchange Affairs Department

The global trend toward liberalization in countries' international exchange and payments systems has been widespread in both industrial and developing countries and most dramatic in central and eastern Europe. Countries in general have brought their exchange systems more in line with market principles and moved toward more flexible exchange rate arrangements in recent years.

$20.00 (academic rate: $12.00); paper.
1995. ISBN 1-55775-480-2. **Stock #WEO-895.**

Staff Studies for the World Economic Outlook
by the IMF's Research Department

These studies, supporting analyses and scenarios of the *World Economic Outlook*, provide a detailed examination of theory and evidence on major issues currently affecting the global economy.

$25.00 (academic rate: $20.00); paper.
1997. ISBN 1-55775-701-1. **Stock #WEO-397.**

International Capital Markets: Developments, Prospects, and Key Policy Issues
by a staff team led by Charles Adams, Donald J. Mathieson, Garry Schinasi, and Bankim Chadha

The 1998 report provides a comprehensive survey of recent developments and trends in the advanced and emerging capital markets, focusing on financial market behavior during the Asian crisis, policy lessons for dealing with volatility in capital flows, banking sector developments in the advanced and emerging markets, initiatives in banking system supervision and regulation, and the financial infrastructure for managing systemic risk in EMU.

$25.00 (academic rate: $20.00); paper.
1998 (Dec.). ISBN 1-55775-793-3. **Stock #WEO-1799.**
1998. ISBN 1-55775-770-4. **Stock #WEO-698**
1997. ISBN 1-55775-686-4. **Stock #WEO-697**

Private Market Financing for Developing Countries
by a staff team from the IMF's Policy Development and Review Department led by Steven Dunaway

The latest study surveys recent trends in flows to developing countries through banking and securities markets. It also analyzes the institutional and regulatory framework for developing country finance; institutional investor behavior and pricing of developing country stocks; and progress in commercial bank debt restructuring in low-income countries.

$20.00 (academic rate: $12.00); paper.
1995. ISBN 1-55775-526-4. **Stock #WEO-1595.**

Toward a Framework for Financial Stability
by a staff team led by David Folkerts-Landau and Carl-Johan Lindgren

This study outlines the broad principles and characteristics of stable and sound financial systems, to facilitate IMF surveillance over banking sector issues of macroeconomic significance and to contribute to the general international effort to reduce the likelihood and diminish the intensity of future financial sector crises.

$25.00 (academic rate: $20.00); paper.
1998. ISBN 1-55775-706-2. **Stock #WEO-016.**

Trade Liberalization in IMF-Supported Programs
by a staff team led by Robert Sharer

This study assesses trade liberalization in programs supported by the IMF by reviewing multiyear arrangements in the 1990s and six detailed case studies. It also discusses the main economic factors affecting trade policy targets.

$25.00 (academic rate: $20.00); paper.
1998. ISBN 1-55775-707-0. **Stock #WEO-1897.**

Available by series subscription or single title (including back issues); academic rate available only to full-time university faculty and students. For earlier editions please inquire about prices.

The IMF *Catalog of Publications* is available on-line at the Internet address listed below.

Please send orders and inquiries to:
International Monetary Fund, Publication Services, 700 19th Street, N.W.
Washington, D.C. 20431, U.S.A.
Tel.: (202) 623-7430   Telefax: (202) 623-7201
E-mail: publications@imf.org
Internet: http://www.imf.org